PAUL
AND HIS INTERPRETERS

PAUL

AND

HIS INTERPRETERS

A CRITICAL HISTORY

BY

ALBERT SCHWEITZER

SCHOCKEN BOOKS · NEW YORK

First published in 1912, this work was translated by W. Montgomery from *Geschichte der Paulinischen Forschung*, 1911.

First SCHOCKEN PAPERBACK edition 1964

This edition is reprinted by arrangement with The Macmillan Company, New York

Library of Congress Catalog Card No. 64-16461. Manufactured in the United States of America.

PREFACE

THE present work forms the continuation of my History of the Critical Study of the Life of Jesus, which appeared in 1906 under the title " Von Reimarus zu Wrede." [1]

Any one who deals with the teaching and the life and work of Jesus, and offers any kind of new reading of it, ought not to stop there, but must be held under obligation to trace, from the stand-point at which he has arrived, the pathway leading to the history of dogma. Only in this way can it be clearly shown what his discovery is worth.

The great and still undischarged task which confronts those engaged in the historical study of primitive Christianity is to explain how the teaching of Jesus developed into the early Greek theology, in the form in which it appears in the works of Ignatius, Justin, Tertullian and Irenaeus. How could the doctrinal system of Paul arise on the basis of the life and work of Jesus and the beliefs of the primitive community ; and how did the early Greek theology arise out of Paulinism ?

Strauss and Renan recognised the obligation, and each endeavoured in a series of works to trace the path leading from Jesus to the history of dogma. Since their time no one who has dealt with the life of Jesus has attempted to follow this course.

Meanwhile the history of dogma, on its part, has come to place the teaching of Jesus, as well as that of Paul, outside the scope of its investigations and to regard its own task as

---

[1] Sub-title : " Eine Geschichte der Leben-Jesu-Forschung." English translation " The Quest of the Historical Jesus." London, A. & C. Black, 1910, 2nd ed. 1911.

beginning at the point where the undisputed and general Hellenisation of Christianity sets in. It describes therefore the growth of Greek theology, but not of Christian theology as a whole. And because it leaves the transition from Jesus to Paul, and from Paul to Justin and Ignatius, unexplained, and therefore fails to arrive at any intelligible and consistent conception of Christian dogma as a whole, the edifice which it erects has no secure basis. Any one who knows and admires Harnack's " History of Dogma " is aware that the solid mason-work only begins in the Greek period ; what precedes is not placed on firm foundations but only supported on piles.

Paulinism is an integral part of the history of dogma ; for the history of dogma begins immediately upon the death of Jesus.

Critical theology, in dividing up the history of the development of thought in primitive Christianity into the separate departments, Life of Jesus, Apostolic Age, History of Dogma, and clinging to this division as if it were something more than a mere convention of the academic syllabus, makes a confession of incompetence and resigns all hope of putting the history of dogma on a secure basis. Moreover, the separate departments thus left isolated are liable to fall into all kinds of confusions and errors, and it becomes a necessity of existence to them not to be compelled to follow their theories beyond the cunningly placed boundaries, or to be prepared to show at any moment how their view accords with the preceding and following stages in the development of thought.

This independence and autonomy of the different departments of study begins with the downfall of the edifice constructed by Baur. He was the last who dared to conceive, and to deal with, the history of dogma in the large and general sense as the scientific study of the development of the teaching of Jesus into the early Greek theology. After him begins, with Ritschl, the narrower and more convenient conception of the subject, which resigns its imperial authority over the departments of study dealing with the Life of Jesus,

*Primitive Christianity and Paulinism, and allows these to be-
come independent.   In the works of Ritschl himself this new
departure is not clearly apparent, because he still formally
includes the teaching of Jesus, of Paul, and of primitive
Christianity within the sphere of the history of dogma.
But instead of explaining the differences between the various
types of belief and doctrine, he glosses them over in such a
way that he practically denies the development of the thoughts,
and makes it impossible for a really scientific study of the
teaching of Jesus and of Paulinism to fit into the ready-
made frame which he provides.*

*Ritschl shares with Baur the presupposition that primitive
dogma arose out of the teaching of Jesus by an organic
and logical process.   The separate disciplines which began
after them have shown that this assumption is false.   Of a
"development" in the ordinary sense there can be no
question, because closer investigation has not confirmed the
existence of the natural lines of connexion which might
à priori have been supposed to be self-evident, but reveals
instead unintelligible gaps.   This is the real reason why the
different departments of study maintain their independence.*

*The system of the Apostle of the Gentiles stands over
against the teaching of Jesus as something of an entirely
different character, and does not create the impression of
having arisen out of it.   But how is such a new creation of
Christian ideas—and that within a bare two or three decades
after the death of Jesus—at all conceivable ?*

*From Paulinism, again, there are no visible lines of
connexion leading to early Greek theology.   Ignatius and
Justin do not take over his ideas, but create, in their turn,
something new.*

*According to the assumption which in itself appears
most natural, one would be prepared to see in the teaching
of Jesus a mountain-mass, continued by the lofty summits
of the Pauline range, and from these gradually falling away
to the lower levels of the early Catholic theology.   In reality
the teaching of Jesus and that of the great Apostle are like
two separate ranges of hills, lying irregularly disposed in*

front of the later " Gospel." Even the relation which each severally bears to primitive Christianity remains uncertain.

This want of connexion must have some explanation. The task of historical science is to understand why these two systems of teaching are necessarily independent, and at the same time to point out the geological fault and dislocation of the strata, and enable us to recognise the essential continuity of these formations and the process by which they have taken their present shape.

The edifice constructed by Baur has fallen ; but his large and comprehensive conception of the history of dogma ought not to be given up. It is wholly wrong to ignore the problem at which he laboured and so create the false impression that it has been solved. Present day criticism is far from having explained how Paulinism and Greek theology have arisen out of the teaching of Jesus. All it has really done is to have gained some insight into the difficulties, and to have made it increasingly evident that the question of the Hellenisation of Christianity is the fundamental problem of the history of dogma.

It could not really hope to find a solution, because it is still working away with the presuppositions of Baur, Ritschl, and Renan, and has already tried three or four times over all the experiments which are possible on this basis, without ever attaining to a real insight into the course of the development. It has approached this or that problem differently, has given a new version—not to say in some cases a perversion—of it ; but it has not succeeded in giving a satisfactory answer to the question when and how the Gospel was Hellenised.

It has not even attained to clearness in regard to the condition in which the Gospel existed prior to its Hellenisation. It has not ventured to mark off with perfect distinctness the two worlds of thought with which the process is concerned, and to formulate the problem as being that of explaining how the Gospel, which was originally purely Jewish and eschatological, became Greek in form and content. That this could really have come about, it takes to be à priori impossible. It therefore seeks to soften down the antitheses as much as possible, to find in the teaching of Jesus thoughts which force their way out of the frame of the Jewish eschatological conceptions and have the character of universal religion, and in the teaching of Paul to discover a " genuinely Christian," and also a Hellenic element, alongside of the Rabbinic material.

Theological science has in fact been dominated by the desire to minimise as much as possible the element of Jewish Apocalyptic in Jesus and Paul, and so far as possible to represent the Hellenisation of the Gospel as having been prepared for by them. It thinks it has gained something when in formulating the problem it has done its best to soften down the antitheses to the utmost with a view to providing every facility for conceiving the transition of the Gospel from one world of thought to the other.

In following this method Baur and Renan proceed with a simple confidence which is no longer possible to present day theology. But in spite of that it must still continue to follow the same lines, because it has still to work with the old presuppositions and the weakening down of the problem which they imply. The result is in every respect unsatisfactory. The solution remains as impossible as it was before, and the simplifications which were supposed to be provided in the statement of the problem have only created new difficulties.

The thoroughgoing application of Jewish eschatology to the interpretation of the teaching and work of Jesus has created a new fact upon which to base the history of dogma. If the view developed at the close of my " Quest of the Historical Jesus " is sound, the teaching of Jesus does not in any of its aspects go outside the Jewish world of thought and project itself into a non-Jewish world, but represents a deeply ethical and perfected version of the contemporary Apocalyptic.

Therefore the Gospel is at its starting-point exclusively Jewish-eschatological. The sharply antithetic formulation of the problem of the Hellenisation of Christianity, which it was always hoped to avoid, is proved by the facts recorded in the Synoptists to be the only admissible one. Accordingly, the history of dogma has to show how what was originally purely Jewish-eschatological has developed into something that is Greek.   The expedients and evasions hitherto current have been dismissed from circulation.

The primary task is to define the position of Paul.   Is he the first stage of the Hellenising process, or is his system of thought, like that of primitive Christianity, to be conceived as purely Jewish-eschatological ?   Usually the former is taken for granted, because he detached Christianity from Judaism, and because otherwise his thoughts do not seem to be easily explicable.   Besides, it was feared that if the teaching of the Apostle of the Gentiles, as well as primitive Christianity, were regarded as purely Jewish-eschatological, the problem of the Hellenisation of the Gospel would become so acute as to make the possibility of solving it more remote than ever.

Moreover, the theological study of history is apt, even though unconsciously, to give ear to practical considerations. At bottom, it is guided by the instinct that whatever in the primitive Gospel is capable of being Hellenised may also be considered capable of being modernised.   It therefore seeks to discern in Paul's teaching—as also in that of Jesus—as much as possible that " transcends Judaism," that has the character of " universal religion " and " essential Christianity."   It is haunted by the apprehension that the significance of Christianity, and its adaptation to our times, is dependent on justifying the modernisation of it on the lines hitherto followed and in accordance with the historical views hitherto current.

Those who have faced the recognition that the teaching of Jesus is eschatologically conditioned cannot be brought by considerations of this kind, scientific or unscientific, to entertain any doubt as to the task which awaits them. That is, to apply this new view to the explanation of the transition to the history of dogma, and as the first step in that direction, to undertake a new formulation of the problem of Paulinism.   They will naturally endeavour to find out how far the exclusively eschatological conception of the

Gospel manifests its influence in the thoughts of the Apostle of the Gentiles, and will take into account the possibility that his system, strange as this may at first sight appear, may have developed wholly and solely out of that conception.

As in the case of the study of the life of Jesus, the problem and the way to its solution will be developed by means of a survey of what has hitherto been done. At the same time this method of presentation will serve to promote the knowledge of the past periods of the science. Since it is impossible for students, and indeed for the younger teachers, to read for themselves all the works of earlier times, the danger arises that on the one hand the names will remain mere empty names, and on the other that, from ignorance, solutions will be tried over again which have already been advanced and have proved untenable. An attempt has therefore been made in this book to give a sufficient insight into what has been done so far, and to provide a substitute for the reading of such works as are not either of classical importance or still generally accessible.

For practical reasons the method adopted in my former book, of attaching the statement of the new view to the history of earlier views, has not been followed here. This view will be developed and defended in a separate work bearing the title " The Pauline Mysticism " (" Die Mystik des Apostels Paulus "), which will appear at an early date.

The English and American literature of the subject has not been included in this study, since the works in question were not in all cases accessible to me, and an insufficient acquaintance with the language raised a barrier.

Nor have I aimed at giving, even with this limitation, a complete enumeration of all the studies of Paul's teaching. I have only desired to cite works which either played a part of some value in the development of Pauline study, or were in some way typical. The fact that a work has been left unmentioned does not by any means necessarily imply that it has not been examined.

ALBERT SCHWEITZER.

19th Sept. 1911.

CONTENTS

CHAPTER I

PAUL
AND HIS INTERPRETERS

PAUL
AND HIS INTERPRETERS

I

THE BEGINNINGS OF THE SCIENTIFIC METHOD

Hugo Grotius. Annotationes in Novum Testamentum. 1641–1646.

Johann Jakob Rambach. Institutiones hermeneuticae sacrae. 1723.

Siegmund Jakob Baumgarten. Unterricht der Auslegung der heiligen Schrift. (Instructions in the art of Expounding Holy Scripture.) 1742.

Johann Christoph Wolf. Curae philologicae et criticae. 1741.

Johann August Ernesti. Institutio interpretis Novi Testamenti. 1762. (Eng. Trans., Biblical Interpretation of the New Testament, Edinburgh, 1832–1833.)

Johann Salomo Semler. Vorbereitung zur theologischen Hermeneutic. (Introduction to Theological Hermeneutic.) 1760–1769.
Abhandlung von freier Untersuchung des Canons. (Essay on the free Investigation of the Canon.) 1771–1775.
Neuer Versuch die gemeinnützige Auslegung und Anwendung des Neuen Testaments zu befördern. (A New Attempt to Promote a Generally Profitable Exposition and Application of the New Testament.) 1786.
Latin Paraphrases of the Epistles to the Romans (1769) and Corinthians (1770, 1776).

Johann David Michaelis. Einleitung in die göttlichen Schriften des Neuen Bundes. (Introduction to the Divine Scriptures of the New Covenant.) 1750. (Eng. Trans. by H. Marsh, Cambridge, 1793.)
Übersetzung des Neuen Testaments. (Translation of the New Testament.) 1790.
Anmerkungen für Ungelehrte zu seiner Übersetzung des Neuen Testaments. (Notes for Unlearned Readers on his Translation of the New Testament.) 1790–1792.

Friedrich Ernst David Schleiermacher. Über den sogenannten ersten Brief des Paulus an den Timotheus. (On the so-called First Epistle of Paul to Timothy.) 1807.

Johann Gottfried Eichhorn. Historisch-kritische Einleitung in das Neue Testament. (Historical and Critical Introduction to the New Testament.) 3 vols. 1814.

Gottlob Wilhelm Meyer. Entwicklung des paulinischen Lehrbegriffs. (The Development of the Pauline System of Doctrine.) 1801.

Leonhard Usteri. Entwicklung des paulinischen Lehrbegriffs. (The Development of the Pauline System of Doctrine.) 1824.

August Ferdinand Dähne. Entwicklung des paulinischen Lehrbegriffs. (The Development of the Pauline System of Doctrine.) 1835.

Karl Schrader. Der Apostel Paulus. 1830–1836.

J. A. W. Neander. Geschichte der Pflanzung und Leitung der christlichen Kirche durch die Apostel. (History of the Planting and Guidance of the Christian Church by the Apostles.) 1832. (Eng. Trans. by J. E. Ryland, 1851.)

W. M. Leberecht De Wette. Erklärung der Briefe an die Römer, Korinther, Galater und Thessalonicher. (Exposition of the Epistles to the Romans (2nd ed., 1838), Corinthians, etc. (1841).)

H. E. G. Paulus. Des Apostels Paulus Lehrbriefe an die Galater- und Römer-Christen. (The Apostle Paul's Doctrinal Epistles to the Galatian and Roman Christians.) 1831.

THE Reformation fought and conquered in the name of Paul. Consequently the teaching of the Apostle of the Gentiles took a prominent place in Protestant study. Nevertheless the labour expended upon it did not, to begin with, advance the historical understanding of his system of thought. What men looked for in Paul's writings was proof-texts for Lutheran or Reformed theology ; and that was what they found. Reformation exegesis reads its own ideas into Paul, in order to receive them back again clothed with Apostolic authority.

Before this could be altered, the spell which dogma had laid upon exegesis needed to be broken. A very promising beginning in this direction was made by Hugo Grotius, who in his *Annotationes in Novum Testamentum* [1] rises superior to the limitations of ecclesiastical dogma. This work appeared in 1641–1646. The Pauline Epistles are treated with especial gusto. The great Netherlander makes it his business to bring out by patient study the simple literal meaning, and besides referring to patristic exegesis, cites parallels from Greek and Roman literature. He does not, however, show any special insight into the peculiar character of the Pauline world of thought.

[1] In the Amsterdam edition of the whole in 1679, the *Annotationes* on the Pauline Epistles (1009 pp.), with those on the other Epistles and the Apocalypse, form vol. iii.

In the ensuing period the principle gradually became established that exegesis ought to be independent of dogma. Pietism and Rationalism had an equal interest in promoting this result. The accepted formula was that Scripture must be interpreted by Scripture. This thought is common ground to the two famous works on exegesis which belong to the first half of the eighteenth century, the *Institutiones hermeneuticae sacrae* [1] of Johann Jakob Rambach, which is written from the stand-point of a moderate pietism, and Siegmund Jakob Baumgarten's rationalistically inclined " Instruction in the art of expounding Holy Scripture." [2]

On the soil thus prepared by pietism and rationalism it was possible for a philologically sound exegesis to thrive. One of the most important attempts in this direction is Johann Christoph Wolf's *Curae philologicae et criticae.*[3] This was regarded as authoritative for several decades, and even later is frequently drawn on by exegetes, either with or without acknowledgment. The merit of having gained the widest recognition for the principles of philological exegesis belongs to Johann August Ernesti, the reformer of the St. Thomas's School at Leipzig and the determined opponent of its famous " Precentor," Johann Sebastian Bach. His *Institutio interpretis Novi Testamenti* appeared in 1762.[4] It is on the plan of the " Hermeneutics " of Rambach and Baumgarten, and deals with grammar, manuscripts, editions, translations, patristic exegesis, history and geography as sciences ancillary to exegesis.

But Ernesti's work suffices to show that the undogmatic philological method did not in itself lead to any

[1] 1723, 822 pp.
[2] 1st ed. 1742 ; 2nd, 1745, 232 pp. (For title see head of chapter.)
[3] Bâle, 1741. Five vols., covering the whole of the New Testament. The Pauline Epistles are treated in the 3rd (820 pp.) and 4th (837 pp.). The full title is : Curae philologicae et criticae . . . quibus integritati contextus Graeci consulitur, sensus verborum ex praesidiis philologicis illustratur, diversae Interpretum Sententiae summatim enarrantur et modesto examini subjectae vel approbantur vel repelluntur.
[4] 135 pp. Later editions 1765, 1774, 1792, 1809. The last two were brought out under the care of Ammon.

result. Its author is in reality by no means free from dogmatic prepossessions, but he skilfully avoids those questions which would bring him into conflict with Church doctrine. In fact the use he makes of philology is more or less formal. He does not venture to treat the books of the New Testament without prepossession as witnesses from the literature of a distant period, and to show the peculiar mould in which Christian ideas are there cast in comparison with subsequent periods and with the period for which he writes. He did not realise that the undogmatic, philological method of exegesis must logically lead to a method in which philology is the handmaid of historical criticism.

His great contemporary, Johann Salomo Semler, ventures to give expression to this truth, and so becomes the creator of historical theology. In his theoretical works on the Scriptures and on exegesis—" Introduction to theological Hermeneutics " (1760–1769),[1] " Essay on the free Investigation of the Canon " (1771–1775),[2] " A new attempt to promote a generally profitable Exposition and Application of the New Testament " (1786)[3]—the Halle professor explains again and again what is to be understood by a " historical " method of exegesis. He demands that the New Testament shall be regarded as a temporally conditioned expression of Christian thought, and examined with an unprejudiced eye. In making this claim he does not speak as a

[1] Four parts. Parts i. and ii. form the first volume (424 pp.), part iii. = vol. ii. (396 pp.), part iv. = vol. iii. (396 pp.). Part i. is occupied with the general principles of exegesis, part ii. with the text of the Old Testament, parts iii. and iv. with that of the New Testament.

[2] Four volumes. The first (in the reprint of 1776, 333 pp.) : On the natural conception of Scripture. The second (in the first edition, 1772, 608 pp.) : On Inspiration and the Canon, Answers to criticisms and attacks. Third (1st ed., 1773, 567 pp.) : On the History of the Canon, Answers to criticisms and attacks. The fourth (1775, 460 pp.) is wholly occupied by an answer to the work of a certain Dr. Schubert.

This often mentioned but little read work does not therefore present exactly the appearance that might be expected from its title. The polemical replies occupy a much larger space than the orginal arguments.

[3] 298 pp. A striking and brilliantly written work.

disinterested representative of historical science, but makes it in the name of religion. If religion is to develop progressively and purify itself into an ethical belief, the special embodiments which it has received in the past must not lay the embargo of a false authority upon its progress. We must acknowledge to ourselves that many conceptions and arguments, not only of the Old Testament but also of the New, have not the same significance for us as they had for the early days of Christianity. In his work of 1786, Semler even demands that "for present day Christians there should be made a generally useful selection from the discourses of Jesus and the writings of the Apostles, in which the local reference to contemporary readers shall be distinguished or eliminated."

This theory of historical exegesis is carried out in dealing with the great Pauline Epistles. Semler points the way to the critical investigation of the Apostle's thought. He gives paraphrases of the Epistle to the Romans and the Epistles to the Corinthians, and attempts to make clear the content and the connection of thought by a paraphrastic and expanded rendering of each individual verse.[1] Exegesis is no longer to be encumbered with a panoply of erudition ; it is no longer to be interpenetrated with homiletic and dogmatic considerations, and to defer to the authority of the old Greek expositors, who, " when it is a question of historical arguments, had no better or clearer knowledge than we have ourselves." It must let the Scriptural

---

[1] *Paraphrasis Epistolae ad Romanos . . . cum Dissertatione de Appendice, capp.* xv. et xvi., 1769, 311 pp. (Dedicated to Johann August Ernesti.)

Paraphrasis in Primam Pauli ad Corinthios Epistolam, 1770, 540 pp. (Dedicated to Johann David Michaelis.)

Paraphrasis II. Epistolae ad Corinthios, 1776, 388 pp. Each of these works contains a preface of some length on the principles of historical exegesis. As a specimen of the paraphrase we may quote that of Rom. vi. 1 : Jam si haec est Evangelii tam exoptata hominibusque cunctis tam frugifera doctrina, num audebimus statuere, perseverare nos tamen posse in ista peccandi consuetudine, ut quasi eo fiat amplior gratiae divinae locus ?

phrases say openly and freely what they mean in their literal sense, and devote itself simply to that dispassionate, objective study of facts which has hitherto been too much neglected.

The importance of the paraphrases does not however consist, as might be supposed, in their exhibiting the distinctive character of the Pauline trains of thought in comparison with the views of the other New Testament writers. By his use of a paraphrastic rendering of the text Semler puts an obstacle in the way of his gaining an insight into the specifically Pauline reasoning, and unconsciously imports his own logic into the Apostle's arguments.

On the other hand, his brilliant powers of observation enable him to call attention to some fundamental problems of literary criticism. He is the first to point out that we do not possess the Pauline Epistles in their original form, but only in the form in which they were read in the churches. The canonical Epistle is therefore not, as a matter of *a priori* certainty, identical with the historical letter. It is quite possible, he argues, that the letters as read in the churches were produced by joining together, or working up together, different letters, and also that written directions and messages, which originally existed in a separate form, were attached in later copies to the Epistles in order that no part of the heritage left by the Apostle might be lost.

On the basis of considerations of this kind Semler arrives at the result that the fifteenth and sixteenth chapters of Romans did not belong to the original Epistle. The sixteenth is, in his view, a series of greetings which Paul—who, it is assumed, was writing from Ephesus—gave to the bearers of the Epistle to be conveyed to the churches which they would visit on their way through Macedonia and Achaia. In the ninth chapter of 2 Corinthians there is preserved, he thinks, a writing intended for another city in Achaia, which was only later welded into the Epistle to the Corinthians. From the fourteenth verse of the twelfth chapter of 2 Corinthians to the close of the thirteenth chapter we have to assume the presence of a separate writing, of later date than the original Second Epistle to the Corinthians. Thus Semler takes the first steps upon the road of literary hypothesis. Theology at first took little notice of these investigations. In the third edition of his " New Testament Introduction " (1777),[1] the great Göttingen philologist and theologian J. D. Michaelis treats the letters of the Apostle in a quite uncritical spirit, and does not enter at all into the literary problems ; in his " Translation " and " Exposition " of the New Testament [2] he follows the old tracks and makes no attempt to carry out the task which Semler had assigned to historical exegesis. In general the eighteenth century, after Semler, contributed very little to the investigation of Paulinism. Schleiermacher was the first to take a step forward, when, in a letter to Gass, he expressed his doubts as to the genuineness of 1 Timothy.[3]

Shortly before the battle of Jena—so he recounts in the preface—he had communicated his doubts to his friend, but had not got the length of setting them forth in a reasoned argument. " The battle—though indeed it ended all too quickly—the consequent unrest in the town, and even in the house, the confused hurrying to and fro, the sight of the French soldiers, which was interesting in so many ways . . . the still incomprehensible blow which struck our University even before you left, and the sad sight of the students saying their farewells and taking their departure,—these were certainly not the surroundings

---

[1] Johann David Michaelis, *Einleitung in die Schriften des Neuen Bundes*, 1st ed., 1750. In its successive editions this work dominates the theology of all the latter half of the eighteenth century ; at the beginning of the nineteenth it is superseded by Eichhorn's Introduction. The third edition (1777) contains 1356 pp. The Pauline Epistles occupy pp. 1001-1128.

[2] *Übersetzung des Neuen Testaments*, 1790, 566 pp. *Anmerkungen für Ungelehrte zu seiner Übersetzung des Neuen Testaments*, 4 vols., 1790-92. The Pauline Epistles are treated in vols. iii. and iv.

[3] Friedrich Ernst David Schleiermacher, *Über den sogenannten ersten Brief des Paulus an den Timotheus. Ein kritisches Sendschreiben an Joachim Christian Gass*, 1807. In his complete works this is to be found in the second volume of the first division, 1836, pp. 223-320.

in which to set up a critical judgment-seat. Although, on the other hand, you would perhaps have been more ready then, when all seemed lost, to give up a New Testament book, than you are now." The verbal promise then given but not fulfilled is now discharged in writing.

Schleiermacher bases his argument against 1 Timothy upon 2 Timothy and Titus. While the same general conceptions are present in the longer letter as in the two shorter ones, they are not there found in the natural connections in which they occur in the others. It makes the impression of being a composite structure, and in its vocabulary, too, shows remarkable differences from the remaining letters taken as a whole.

Strictly speaking it was not Schleiermacher the critic, but Schleiermacher the æsthete who had come to have doubts about 2 Timothy. The letter does not suit his taste. He fails to perceive that, so far as the language goes, the two other letters diverge from the rest of the Pauline Epistles in the same way as 1 Timothy, and that they also show the same looseness and disconnectedness ; only that, in consequence of their smaller extent, it is not so striking. And, most important of all, it escapes him that as regards their ideas all three letters agree in diverging from the remainder of the Pauline Epistles.

Schleiermacher's omissions are supplied by Eichhorn in his well-known Introduction.[1] He lays it down that the three Epistles are all by the same author, and are all spurious. His criticism deals first with the language and thought of the letters, which he shows to be un-Pauline ; then he argues that the implied historical situations cannot be fitted into the life of the Apostle, as known to us from the remaining letters and the Acts of the Apostles ; finally, he points to the unnaturalness of the relation

[1] Johann Gottfried Eichhorn, *Historisch-kritische Einleitung in das Neue Testament*, 1st ed., vol. iii., second half (1814), pp. 315-410.

Eichhorn points out that he had recognised the spuriousness of the three Pastoral Epistles, and had expressed his conviction in his University lectures before Schleiermacher published his criticisms of the First Epistle of Timothy.

between Paul and his helpers as it is represented by these Epistles.

The Apostle, he points out, gives them in writing exhortations and directions which on the assumption of a real personal acquaintance and a long period of joint work with them are in any case unnecessary, and become much more so from the fact that the letters look forward to an early meeting. From this Eichhorn concludes that " some one else has put himself in Paul's place," and he sees no possibility of the success of any attempt to defend the genuineness of the Epistles against the arguments which he has brought forward. In particular he gives a warning against the seductive attempt to save the genuineness of 2 Timothy by the assumption of a second imprisonment. No hypothesis, he declares, can in any way help the Pastorals, since they must be pronounced from internal evidence—because of their divergence from the remaining Epistles—not to be by the Apostle. This was a long step forward. The circle of writings which have come down under the name of Paul had undergone a restriction which made it possible to give an account of his system of thought without being obliged to find a place in it for ideas which already have a quite early-Catholic ring.

Ten years after Eichhorn's literary achievement, in the year 1824, the Swiss theologian Leonhard Usteri, a pupil of Schleiermacher's, published his " Development of the Pauline System of Doctrine,"[1] which is generally regarded as the starting-point of the purely historical study of Paulinism, the first attempt to give effect to the demands of Semler.[2]

Usteri wishes to show the subjective imprint and

[1] Leonhard Usteri, *Die Entwicklung des paulinischen Lehrbegriffs*, 1824, 191 pp. The editions of 1829, 1830, and 1832 were revised by the author, who died in 1833. After his death two more appeared (1834, 1851). Reference may be made also to Usteri's " Commentary on the Epistle to the Galatians," 1833, 252 pp.

[2] The first work which undertook to give an account of the Apostle's system of thought as such is Gottlob Wilhelm Meyer's *Entwicklung des paulinischen Lehrbegriffs*, 1801, 380 pp. The author has collected the material well, but does not know in what direction Paul's peculiarity lies.

enrichment which ordinary Christianity received at the hands of the Apostle, and he sees in the Epistle to the Galatians the outline of his whole doctrine. He does not, however, venture to give full recognition to the idea of a real antithesis between the Pauline conceptions and those of the primitive Apostles, and consequently is led to soften down the peculiarities of the former so far as possible. The spirit of Schleiermacher, which tended to level down everything of a historical character, influences the book more than the author is aware.[1] A peculiar interlude in the investigation of Paulinism was due to the Heidelberger H. E. G. Paulus.[2] He published, in the year 1831, a study of the Epistles to the Galatians and Romans, which was in reality an essay on the Apostle's system of doctrine. The work is undertaken entirely in the interests of a rationalism bent on opposing the reaction to orthodoxy.

According to the arguments of Paulus it is not the case that the letters speak of expiatory suffering and imputed righteousness. Paul cannot have upheld " legality " as against " morality " and have maintained an " unpurified conception of religion." The " chief sayings," the characteristic terms, are to be given a purely moral interpretation. The Apostle means that " faith in Jesus " must become in us " the faith of Jesus," and the narrower conception of righteousness must be enlarged into the

---

[1] Of the works which criticise Usteri and mark an advance in Pauline study the following may be named :—

Karl Schrader, *Der Apostel Paulus* ; vols. i., 1830 (264 pp.), and ii., 1832 (373 pp.), deal with the life of the Apostle Paul; vol. iii., 1833 (331 pp.), with the doctrine ; vols. iv., 1835 (490 pp.), and v., 1836 (574 pp.), contain the exposition of the Epistles.

August Ferdinand Dähne, *Entwicklung des paulinischen Lehrbegriffs*, 1835, 211 pp.

Mention may also be made of the chapter on Paulinism in J. A. W. Neander's *Geschichte der Pflanzung und Leitung der christlichen Kirche durch die Apostel*, 1st ed., 1832 ; 2nd ed., 1st vol., 1838 (433 pp.). Paul is treated in pp. 102-433 ; 4th ed., 1847 ; 5th, 1862. As typical of the exegesis of the period prior to Baur may be mentioned the Commentaries of W. M. L. de Wette on Romans (2nd ed.), 1838 ; 1 and 2 Corinthians, 1841 ; Galatians and Thessalonians, 1841.

[2] H. E. G. Paulus, *Des Apostels Paulus Lehrbriefe an die Galater- und Römer-Christen*, 1831, 368 pp.

conception of " the righteousness of God." The
" righteousness of God " betokens righteousness such as
it exists in God, and is demanded by Him in man's spirit
as its "true good," "the only real atonement which
brings us into harmony with the Deity." Thus a proper
interpretation enables us to discover in these writings
" the agreement between the Gospel and a rational faith."

The book appeared two or three decades too late.
The rationalism which it represents had had its day.
But there is something imposing in this determined
wresting of the Apostle's views. It is parallel to that
which was practised by the Reformation. The latter
interpreted the whole of Paulinism by the passages
on the atoning death, and ignored the other thoughts in
the Epistles. The Heidelberg rationalist starts from the
conceptions connected with the " new creature," which
were later to be described as the ethical system of the
Apostle, and interprets everything else by them.

The fact that the two views—the only ones which
endeavoured to grasp Paulinism as a complete, articulated
system—thus stand over against each other antithetically
is significant for the future. Critical study in the course
of its investigations was to come to a point where it would
have to recognise both views as justified, and to point out
the existence in Paul of a twofold system of doctrine—
a juridical system based on the idea of justification,
and an ethical system dominated by the conception of
sanctification—without at first being able to show how
the two are interrelated and together form a unity.

II

BAUR AND HIS CRITICS

Ferdinand Christian Baur. Die Christuspartei in der korinthischen Gemeinde. (The Christ-party in the Corinthian Church.) Appeared in the *Tübinger Zeitschrift für Theologie*, 1831 and 1836. Über Zweck u. Veranlassung des Römerbriefs (Purpose and occasion of Rom.), *ib.* 1836. Die sogenannten Pastoralbriefe. (The so-called Pastoral Epistles.) 1835.
Paulus der Apostel Jesu Christi (1st ed., 1845 ; 2nd ed., 1866–67). (Eng. Trans. by " A. P. " and A. Menzies, 1873–75.)
Beiträge zu den Briefen an die Korinther, Thessalonicher und Römer. (Contributions to the elucidation of the Epistles to the Corinthians, Thessalonians and Romans.) *Tübinger Jahrbücher für Theologie.* 1850–57.
Vorlesungen über neutestamentliche Theologie. 1864. (Lectures on New-Testament Theology.)
Vorlesungen über die christliche Dogmengeschichte. (Lectures on the History of Dogma.) Vol. i., 1865.

Albert Schwegler. Das nachapostolische Zeitalter. 1846. (The Post-Apostolic Age.)

Carl Wieseler. Chronologie des apostolischen Zeitalters. 1848. (The Chronology of the Apostolic Age.) On the Pauline Epp., 225-278.

Albrecht Ritschl. Die Entstehung der altkatholischen Kirche. (The Origin of the Early Catholic Church.) 1st ed., 1850; 2nd ed., 1857.

Gotthard Viktor Lechler. Das apostolische und nachapostolische Zeitalter. (The Apostolic and Post-Apostolic Age.) 1852. (Eng. Trans. by A. J. K. Davidson, Edinburgh, 1886.)

Richard Adalbert Lipsius. Die paulinische Rechtfertigungslehre. (The Pauline Doctrine of Justification.) 1853.

In the fourth number of the *Tübinger Zeitschrift für Theologie* for the year 1831, F. C. Baur gave to the study of Paulinism a new direction, by advancing the opinion that the Apostle had developed his doctrine in complete opposition to that of the primitive Christian community, and that only when this is recognised can we expect to grasp the peculiar character of the Pauline ideas.

The great merit of the Tübingen critic was that he allowed the texts to speak for themselves, to mean what they said. On the ground of the striking difference between Acts and Galatians regarding Paul's relation to the original Apostles, and in view of the divisions and contentions which reveal themselves in the Epistles to the Corinthians, Baur concludes that in the early days of Christianity two parties—a Petrine party or party of the original Apostles, and a Pauline party—stood opposed to one another, holding divergent views on the subject of the redemption wrought by Christ.

In the gradual adjustment of these differences he sees the development which led up to the formation of the early Catholic Church, and he traces the evidence for this process in the literature. He thinks he can show that the two parties gradually approached each other, making concessions on the one side and the other, and finally, under the pressure of a movement which was equally inimical to both of them—the Gnosticism of the early part of the second century—they coalesced into a single united Church.

The recognition of the character and significance of Gnosticism makes it possible for Baur to introduce a new kind of criticism. Before him it was only possible to arrive at the negative result that a writing was not by the author to whom it was traditionally ascribed. Now, according to him, it is possible to determine to what period it belongs. It is only necessary to show what position it occupies in the process of reconciliation of the two parties, and, especially, whether it deals with speculative error. This Baur calls " positive " criticism.

He applies it in the first place to the Pastoral Epistles, and argues that the heretics combated in them do not belong to primitive Christianity but are representatives of the Gnostic movement of the second century. By the " myths and genealogies " here mentioned are meant the great speculative systems which are known from Church history. The description given of the heretics is intentionally couched in terms which are neither too general nor too special, in order to sustain the fiction that the false doctrine arising at this later period only revives a movement which had already been attacked and defeated by Paul.

That neither the assumption of a second imprisonment, nor any other possible or impossible hypothesis, can restore to the Pastorals their lost genuineness is as firm a conviction with Baur as it was with Eichhorn.

In the course of his study of the Pastoral Epistles the Tübingen master had expressed the opinion that the criticism of the Pauline writings would probably not " come to a halt " with these Epistles. The results of his further study were offered ten years later (1845) in the brilliantly written work, " Paul the Apostle of Jesus Christ." He here treats first the life and work, then the letters, and lastly the system of doctrine. The result arrived at in his investigation of the documents is that only the Epistles to the Galatians, Corinthians, and Romans can be confidently used as sources. Compared with these four, all the others must be classed as " anti-legomena," " which does not at all imply the assertion that they are not genuine, but only indicates the opposition to which their claim to genuineness is in some cases already exposed, in others, may be exposed in the future, since there is not a single one of the smaller Pauline epistles against which, if the four main epistles are taken as the standard, there cannot be raised some objection or other." There are strong grounds for questioning the Epistles to the Ephesians and Colossians ; those to the Thessalonians and Philippians are to be suspected because of the small amount of dogma they contain. Baur's reason for taking up such a critical attitude towards the " smaller epistles " is that he is bound to see in the heritage which has come down to us from the Apostle, writings " which belong to the history of the party which based itself on his name, and refer to the relations of the various parties," and show us how Gentile Christianity softens down its principles and its peculiarities in order to meet the Jewish Christianity, which on its part was going through a similar process, in the unity of the early Catholic Church.

This radical view was attacked on all sides. It gave rise to a kind of reaction even within the sphere of scientific theology, and led to the calling in question of results which the labours of Eichhorn had brought into general acceptance. Thus Carl Wieseler prefaces his detailed study on the date of composition of the Pauline letters with the remark that he held all the thirteen letters which are attributed to the Apostle in the Canon to be authentic.

The Apostle's system of doctrine culminates, according to Baur's representation, in the doctrine of the Spirit. In the brilliant disquisitions of this section it is not so much the historian who speaks as the pupil of Hegel. Paulinism is in its own way an announcement of the unity of the subjective spirit with the objective spirit. It is only from this point of view that a consciousness of freedom such as is found in the Apostle of the Gentiles can exist. His doctrine is concerned with union with Christ and with God by faith, from which comes Spirit. " Righteousness " is " the proper relation towards God, to place men in which is the highest duty of all religion."

Baur does not enter into the details of the Pauline doctrine of justification. Detail is in fact somewhat neglected in his treatment. Strictly speaking, he only includes that which can be in some way or other expressed in Hegelian thought-forms, and that in which Paulinism may be exhibited as representing absolute religion. Everything else is thrown into the background, and receives only a partial appreciation—or depreciation— in a separate chapter entitled " A special discussion of some subsidiary dogmatic questions." The characteristic stamp of the Pauline doctrine is largely obliterated. In particular, Paul's views about the " last things " and the angels are not allowed to become disturbingly prominent. Baur does not, indeed, hesitate practically to eliminate

them. The angelology he dismisses with the following
remark : " Of the angels the Apostle says little in the
letters which we have here to take into consideration,
and that little not dogmatically, but only metaphorically
and in current popular phraseology."

The Tübingen scholar, in fact, uses the language of
Paul in order to set forth an imposing philosophy of
religion instinct with Hegelian influence. He gives no
authentic account of the Apostle's thought. Nevertheless this book breathes the spirit of Paul the prophet of
freedom more fully than almost any other which has been
devoted to him. That is what gives it its remarkable
attractiveness.

A year after the appearance of Baur's " Paulus "—in
1846—Albert Schwegler published his work on the post-
apostolic age.[1] The founder of the Tübingen School had
hitherto only, so to speak, hinted at the phases of development by which the early Church grew up out of the
controversy between the two parties. Schwegler undertakes a more detailed description, and in doing so draws
the lines so sharply that, along with the greatness of the
construction, its faults become obvious. He has no
deeper knowledge of Paulinism to impart.

Schwegler's work had made it apparent from what side
the Tübingen position was open to attack, and on this side
Albrecht Ritschl proceeded to attack it in his well-known
work on the origin of the early Catholic Church.[2] The
first edition (1850) is primarily directed against Schwegler
only ; in the second (1857) he develops his opposition of

---

[1] Albert Schwegler, *Das nachapostolische Zeitalter in den Haupt-
momenten seiner Entwicklung* (" The Post-Apostolic Age in the main
Features of its Development "), 1846, vol. i. 522 pp., vol. ii. 392 pp.
In the writings which mark the course of the development of Paulinism
three groups are distinguished. To the first, the apologetic group,
belongs the First Epistle of Peter ; to the second, the conciliatory
writings, are to be reckoned the Gospel of Luke, the Acts of the Apostles,
the First Epistle of Clement, and the Epistle to the Philippians ; the
third is represented by the catholicising writings, the Pastorals, the
Letter of Polycarp, and the Ignatian Letters.

[2] Albrecht Ritschl, *Die Entstehung der altkatholischen Kirche, eine
kirchen- und dogmengeschichtliche Monographie*, 1850, 622 pp. ; 2nd ed.,
1857, 605 pp.

principle to Baur. He offers proof that the earliest
literature is not dominated by the negotiations for a
compromise between the two parties which was postulated by the Tübingen School, and at the same time he
attacks the basis of the whole hypothetical construction.
Baur, he urges, must have formed a false conception of
Jewish Christianity and Gentile Christianity, since, on
his view, it cannot be explained what was the common
element that held the two together. Had they only, as
the Tübingen School was obliged to assume, had
the external bond of profession of faith in Christ, it
would never be possible to explain why both parties felt
the need of approaching one another by mutual concessions until finally they coalesced in a single united
Church.

The extent of the doctrinal material common to both
must, Ritschl argues, have been much greater than Baur
represents. He has not discharged the first duty of a
historian of the Apostolic age, for this requires " that the
points should be clearly shown in which Jewish Christianity and Paulinism coincide." Baur had only given a
negative description of the Apostle's doctrine, because
he never gives any hint " that Paul in very essential
points held views which were common also to Jewish
Christianity."

The problem regarding the nature of the unity between
Paulinism and primitive Christianity is thus recognised
and formulated.

But it was not so easy for Ritschl to say exactly what
constituted the common element of doctrine, the existence
of which he postulated. That is especially evident in the
second edition of " The Origin of the Early Catholic
Church." He is then only willing to admit an " opposition of practice " between Paul and the original apostles ;
the area of this opposition is so restricted that " the
essential agreement in the leading ideas laid down by
Christ will be only the more clearly evident." But since
in Paulinism little enough is to be found of the " leading

ideas laid down by Christ " the proof of the " essential
agreement " remains a pious aspiration.

The only solid fact which Ritschl is able to adduce
is the expectation of the parousia. He assumes that
it formed a very important part of the common doctrinal
material, and inclines to believe that Paulinism and Jewish
Christianity agreed in an ideal-real expectation of the
Second Coming in order to make common cause against
Chiliasm, though the latter in its coarser form only
appeared later.

But in thus recognising eschatology Ritschl did not
take the matter very seriously. He uses the eschatology,
in fact, only in order to score a dialectical point against
Baur, who had taken too little account of it. In Ritschl's
" Justification and Reconciliation," where he later on
had occasion to give a positive description of Paulinism,
he avoided the faintest hint of any eschatological colouring
of the Apostle's ideas.

Another work which is occupied with the question of
the unity between Paulinism and primitive Christianity
is Lechler's " Apostolic and Post-Apostolic Age." [1] The
work is a prize essay in answer to the problem proposed by
the Teylerian Society in Holland, as to what constituted
" the absolute difference between the doctrine and attitude
of the Apostle Paul and that of the other Apostles," by
which the " so-called Tübingen School endeavours to
justify its hostile treatment of Christianity." Lechler
opposes his teacher, but is not able to make any advance
upon Ritschl in producing evidence of the common
elements in the two doctrinal systems.

---

[1] Gotthard Viktor Lechler, *Das apostolische und das nachapostolische Zeitalter mit Rücksicht auf Unterschied und Einheit in Lehre und
Leben* (. . . with special reference to their difference and unity in
life and doctrine), 1st ed., 1852 ; 2nd ed., 1857, 536 pp. The portion
dealing with Paul is pp. 33-154 ; in the 3rd ed., 1885 (635 pp.) Paul is
treated on pp. 269-407.

In the first two editions the whole of the Pauline epistles are regarded as genuine ; in the third the author no longer ventures to treat
the Pastorals as on the same footing with the other Epistles. The
very clearly and comprehensively stated problem is printed at the
beginning.

Among the works which controverted the Tübingen
view of Paulinism a prominent place belongs to an early
work of Richard Adalbert Lipsius on "the Pauline
doctrine of Justification."[1] Along with his scientific
purpose the author also pursues a practical aim. He
puts himself at the service of the anti-rationalistic reaction
which aimed at restoring the old evangelical ideas to
a position of honour, but in doing so did not grasp hands
with the orthodoxy of the seventeenth and eighteenth
centuries, but took as its starting-point the ideas which
it finds present in the New Testament. In giving an
objective presentation of the central Pauline doctrine
of justification he believes that he is offering to the
Protestantism of his time a view which it can adopt as
its own.

For the Apostle of the Gentiles, he argues, justification
is not a purely legal, forensic act, but also an ethical
experience. Faith is an ethical attitude which produces
an inward righteousness. What is really effectual in
redemption is the fellowship with Christ in life and death.
It is brought about by the Spirit of God and of Christ,
who unites himself with the believer and transforms his
personality.

Lipsius is the first to recognise the two trains of thought
in Paulinism, and to remark that the one is based upon
the juridical idea of justification, while the other has its
starting-point in the conception of sanctification—of the
real ethical new creation by the Spirit. He does not, as
had always previously been done, make everything of
the one and nothing of the other, but aims at showing
how they are brought together in the Apostle's thought.

The importance of the eschatological passages does not
escape him. He assumes that the thought of the parousia
gives an inner unity to the Apostle's ideas.

It is true that Lipsius did not succeed in fully dis-
charging the task which he laid upon himself. He
weakens down one set of ideas in the interests of the other,

[1] *Die paulinische Rechtfertigungslehre*, 1853, 219 pp.

and solders the two together externally by the use of
skilfully chosen expressions ; but it remains his great
merit that he was the first to recognise this duality in
Paul's thought. Had he not been pursuing a dogmatic
interest alongside of his scientific investigations he would
doubtless have come to still closer quarters with the
problem.

While his critics were at work Baur had not been idle.
From 1850 onwards he published in the *Tübinger
Jahrbücher für Theologie*, which had superseded the
Tübinger Zeitschrift für Theologie, a series of separate
investigations of the Pauline Epistles.[1] He had resolved
that the final results of his study of the Apostle of the
Gentiles, with which he had begun his work, and which
throughout his whole lifetime had been his favourite
study, should be set forth in a new edition of his Paulus.
This was to be the crown of his work.

But it was not to be. Death snatched him away from
his task when he had only just cast the first part into its
new shape. The second and most important, which was
to treat the " system of doctrine," he did not reach.[2]

To a certain extent a substitute for what was thus
lost was furnished by the " Lectures on New Testament
Theology," published by the master's son in 1864.[3] The
chapter on Paulinism is very striking in its brevity and
clearness, and shows a great advance on the work of 1845.
At that time Baur had examined and interpreted Paul's

---

[1] In 1850, *Beiträge zur Erklärung der Korinthesbriefe*, pp. 139-185.
Continued in 1852, pp. 1-40 and 535-574. In 1855, *Die beiden Briefe
an die Thessalonicher ; ihre Ächtheit und Bedeutung für die Lehre der
Parusie Christi*, pp. 141-168 (. . . their genuineness and their significance for the doctrine of the parousia of Christ). In 1857, *Über
Zweck und Gedankengang des Römerbriefs nebst der Erörterung einiger
paulinischen Begriffe*, pp. 60-108 and 184-209 ("On the Purpose and
the Argument of Romans, with a Discussion of certain Pauline Conceptions.")

[2] *Paulus der Apostel Jesu Christi*, 2nd ed., edited by Zeller, 1866–
1867, vol. i. 469 pp., revised by Baur; vol. ii. 376 pp. contains a reprint
of the chapter on Paul's doctrine from the first edition.

[3] *Vorlesungen über neutestamentliche Theologie.* Published by
Ferdinand Friedrich Baur, 1864, 407 pp. Pages 128-207 deal with the
doctrinal system of Paul.

teaching by the light of the Hegelian Intellectualism. Now he tries to grasp his ideas historically and empirically, and to describe them accordingly.

He discusses successively the Pauline views on : sin and flesh ; law and sin ; faith in the death of Christ ; law and promise ; law and freedom ; the righteousness of faith ; faith and works ; faith and predestination ; Christology ; baptism and the Lord's Supper ; the parousia of Christ.

Eschatology, which in the first edition was quite overlooked, receives here abundant recognition. Baur admits that the Apostle fully shared the faith of the primitive community in the nearness of the parousia, and was at one with it in all the conceptions referring to the End.

The Pauline theology as thus empirically apprehended has no longer the bold effectiveness of the speculatively constructed system of the year 1845. It becomes apparent in Baur, and increasingly evident in the work of subsequent investigators, that the self-consistency and logical concatenation of the system become obscured and disturbed in proportion as progress is made in the exact apprehension of the individual concepts and ideas.

III

FROM BAUR TO HOLTZMANN

MONOGRAPHS UPON PAUL

Adolf Hausrath. Der Apostel Paulus (1865, 172 pp.; biographical. 2nd ed., 1872, 503 pp.).

Ernest Renan. St. Paul (1869, 570 pp.; biographical and theological).

Auguste Sabatier. L'Apôtre Paul (1870, theological). (E.T. by A. M. Hellier, 1891.)

Otto Pfleiderer. Der Paulinismus (1873; 2nd ed., 1890; theological). (E.T. by E. Peters, 1877.)

Carl Holsten. Das Evangelium des Paulus (1st pt., 1880; 2nd pt., 1898).

NEW TESTAMENT INTRODUCTIONS

Eduard Reuss. Geschichte der heiligen Schriften Neuen Testamentes (5th ed., 1874). (E.T. History of the Sacred Scriptures of the New Testament, by E. L. Houghton. Edin. 1884.)

Christian Karl von Hofmann. Pt. ix. of "Die Heilige Schrift." 1881.

Heinrich Julius Holtzmann. Einleitung in das Neue Testament. 1885.

Bernhard Weiss. (Same title.) 1886. (E.T. by A. J. K. Davidson, 1887).

Frédéric Godet. Introduction au Nouveau Testament. 1893.

Adolf Jülicher. Einleitung in das Neue Testament. 1894. (E.T. by J. P. Ward, 1904.)

Theodor Zahn. (Same title.) 1897. (E.T. of 3rd ed. 1909).

WORKS ON NEW TESTAMENT THEOLOGY

Eduard Reuss. Histoire de la théologie chrétienne au siècle apostolique. 3rd ed., 1864. (E.T. by A. Harwood, 1872.)

Bernhard Weiss. Lehrbuch der biblischen Theologie des Neuen Testaments. 1st ed., 1868; 6th ed., 1895. (E.T. Edin. 1882.)

Christian Karl von Hofmann. Pt. xi. of "Die Heilige Schrift." 1886.

Willibald Beyschlag. Neutestamentliche Theologie. 1891. 2nd ed., 1896. (E.T. Edin. 1895.)

General Works on Primitive Christianity

Ernest Havet. Le Christianisme et ses origines (4 vols., 1884).

Karl von Weizsäcker. Das apostolische Zeitalter. 1886. (E.T. The Apostolic Age, 1894.)

Otto Pfleiderer. Das Urchristentum. 1887. (E.T. of 2nd. altered ed., see later.)

Studies on Special Points

Carl Holsten. Zum Evangelium des Paulus und Petrus. 1868.

Fr. Th. L. Ernesti. Die Ethik des Apostels Paulus. 1868.

Emmanuel Friedrich Kautzsch. De Veteris Testamenti locis a Paulo apostolo allegatis. 1869.

Franz Delitzsch. Paulus des Apostels Brief an die Römer in das Hebräische übersetzt und aus Talmud und Midrasch erläutert. 1870. (The Epistle of Paul the Apostle to the Romans translated into Hebrew and illustrated from Talmud and Midrash.)

Hermann Lüdemann. Die Anthropologie des Apostels Paulus. 1872.

Albrecht Ritschl. Die christliche Lehre von der Rechtfertigung und Versöhnung, vol. ii., 1874. (The Christian Doctrine of Justification and Reconciliation.) (E.T. of vols. i. and iii. only).

H. H. Wendt. Die Begriffe Fleisch und Geist bei Paulus. 1878. (The Meaning of the Terms Flesh and Spirit in Paul's Writings.)

Louis Eugène Ménégoz. Le Péché et la rédemption d'après St Paul. 1882.

Eduard Grafe. Die paulinische Lehre vom Gesetz. 1884. (The Pauline Teaching about the Law.)

Gustav Volkmar. Paulus von Damaskus zum Galaterbrief. 1887. (Paul, from Damascus to Galatians). A biographical study, with a critical comparison between the data of Galatians and Acts.

Alfred Resch. Agrapha. Ausserkanonische Evangelienfragmente. 1888. On the Question whether Sayings of Jesus have been preserved in Paul's Writings.

Otto Everling. Die paulinische Angelologie und Dämonologie. 1888.

Johann Gloël. Der Heilige Geist in der Heilsverkündigung des Paulus. 1888. (The Holy Spirit in Paul's Preaching of Salvation.)

Hermann Gunkel. Die Wirkungen des Heiligen Geistes nach der populären Anschauung der apostolischen Zeit und nach der Lehre des Apostels Paulus. 1888. (The Manifestations of the Holy Spirit according to the Popular View of the Apostolic Age and according to the Teaching of Paul.)

Eduard Grafe. Das Verhältnis der paulinischen Schriften zur Sapientia Salamonis. 1892. (The Relation of the Pauline Writings to the Book of Wisdom.)

Adolf Deissmann. Die neutestamentliche Formel " in Christo Jesu." 1892. (The New Testament Formula " in Christ Jesus.")

Richard Kabisch. Die Eschatologie des Paulus in ihren Zusammenhängen mit dem Gesamtbegriff des Paulinismus. 1893. (Paul's Eschatology in Relation to his General System.)

W. Brandt. Die evangelische Geschichte und der Ursprung des Christentums. 1893. (The Gospel History and the Origin of Christianity.)

Ernst Curtius. Paulus in Athen. 1894.

E. Bruston. La Vie future d'après St Paul. 1894.

Hans Vollmer. Die alttestamentlichen Zitate bei Paulus. 1895.

Ernst Teichmann. Die paulinischen Vorstellungen von Auferstehung und Gericht und ihre Beziehung zur jüdischen Apokalyptik. 1896. (The Pauline Views of Resurrection and Judgment and their Relation to the Jewish Apocalyptic.)

Theodor Simon. Die Psychologie des Apostels Paulus. 1897.

Paul Wernle. Der Christ und die Sünde bei Paulus. (The Christian and Sin in Paul's Writings.) 1897.

CRITICISM AND EXEGESIS

Bruno Bauer. Kritik der paulinischen Briefe. 1850–1851–1852.

Christian Hermann Weisse. Beiträge zur Kritik der paulinischen Briefe. 1867. (Contributions to the Criticism of the Pauline Epistles.)

H. J. Holtzmann. Kritik der Epheser und Kolosserbriefe. 1872. Die Pastoralbriefe. 1880.

Eduard Reuss. Les Épîtres pauliniennes (" La Bible," pt. iii.). 1878.

Georg Heinrici. Das erste Sendschreiben des Apostels Paulus an die Korinther. 1880. Das zweite, etc. 1887.

P. W. Schmiedel. Auslegung der Briefe an die Thessalonicher und Korinther in Holtzmann's " Handkommentar." 1891. (Exposition of the Epistles to the Thessalonians and Corinthians in Holtzmann's " Handkommentar.")

R. A. Lipsius. Auslegung der Briefe an die Galater, Römer und Philipper in Holtzmann's " Handkommentar." 1891.

WORKS OF A GENERAL CHARACTER, OR DEALING WITH COGNATE SUBJECTS

Emil Schürer. Neutestamentliche Zeitgeschichte. 1873. From the 2nd ed. (1886) onwards the work bears the title: Geschichte des jüdischen Volkes im Zeitalter Jesu Christi. (E.T. History of the Jewish People in the time of Jesus Christ. Edin. 1885.)

Karl Siegfried. Philo von Alexandrien als Ausleger des alten Testaments an sich selbst und nach seinem geschichtlichen Einfluss betrachtet. 1875. (Philo of Alexandria as an Expositor of the Old Testament, considered both in himself and in regard to his historical influence.)

Ferdinand Weber. System der altsynagogalen palästinenschen Theologie. 1880. The second edition (1897) bears the title Jüdische Theologie auf Grund des Talmud und verwandter Schriften. (Jewish Theology exhibited on the basis of the Talmud and allied writings.)

W. Gass. Geschichte der christlichen Ethik. 1881.

Theobald Ziegler. Geschichte der christlichen Ethik. 1886.

Edwin Hatch. The Influence of Greek Ideas and Usages upon the Christian Church (Hibbert Lectures for 1888).

Theodor Zahn. Der Stoiker Epiktet und sein Verhältnis zum Christentum. 1894.

Adolf Harnack. Dogmengeschichte, 3rd ed., 1894. (E.T. History of Dogma, 1894–1899). Die Chronologie der altchristlichen Literatur bis Eusebius. Vol. i., 1897.

PROBLEMS many and various confronted theological science when it attempted to carry forward Pauline studies from the position in which they had been left by Baur.

It was needful to clear up once for all the questions of literary criticism, to examine in detail the individual conceptions and trains of thought, to make clear the unity and inner connexion of the system, to show what rôle Paulinism had played in the development of early Catholic theology, and how far it was at one with primitive Christianity, and to solve the question whether the material employed in its construction was of purely Jewish, or in part of Greek origin.

In regard to the literary question a certain measure of agreement was in course of time attained. Baur had distinguished three classes of Epistles. In the first he placed, as beyond doubt genuine, Galatians, Corinthians, and Romans ; Ephesians, Colossians, Philippians, Thessalonians, and Philemon formed the second class, being considered uncertain ; the Pastoral Epistles formed the third class, and were regarded as proved to be spurious.

The views of the Tübingen master regarding the first class and the third were adopted by the majority of scholars of the next generation. No doubts were raised against the great Epistles ; the Pastoral Epistles were rejected. Holtzmann, in his work on the Letters to Timothy and Titus,[1] supplied a detailed argument in favour of this conclusion.

---

[1] *Die Pastoralbriefe kritisch und exegetisch behandelt,* 1880, 504 pp. Adolf Harnack (in *Die Chronologie der altchristlichen Literatur bis Eusebius,* vol. i., 1897, 732 pp.—on Paul, 233-239) is disposed to regard the personal notices of the Pastorals as genuine with the aid of the hypothesis of the second imprisonment.

Of the letters of the intermediate class, the first to the Thessalonians and that to the Philippians were by many rehabilitated as Pauline.   The second to the Thessalonians was rejected with increasing confidence.   A special problem was presented by the letters to the Colossians and Ephesians, both because of their evident mutual relationship and particularly in regard to certain parts of the Epistle to the Colossians which made a strong impression of genuineness.   Holtzmann offered a solution which gave general satisfaction.   He adopted the hypothesis that Colossians was based upon a genuine Pauline letter which had been worked over by a later hand.[1]   The redactor he identified with the author of the Epistle to the Ephesians.

While there was this general consensus in the critical camp, which was ratified in Holtzmann's " Intro- duction," [2] the most diverse opinions on special points are found.   Some attempts were made to save the

---

[1] *Kritik der Epheser- und Kolosserbriefe*, 1872, 338 pp.

[2] *Einleitung in das Neue Testament*, 1885 ; 2nd ed., 1886 ; 3rd ed., 1892. Second Thessalonians, Ephesians, and the Pastoral Epistles, spurious ; Colossians, worked over. A similar critical stand-point is occupied by Adolf Jülicher, *Einleitung in das Neue Testament*, 1894, 404 pp. The Pauline Epistles are treated in pp. 19-128.

A mediating position is taken up by E. Reuss, *Geschichte der heiligen Schriften Neuen Testaments* (5th ed., 1874, 352 pp. ; 6th ed., 1887). All that can be said in favour of the genuineness of the Pastorals and 2 Thessalonians is set forth with the greatest completeness, since the author is very reluctant to give up these writings. See the same author's *Histoire de la théologie chrétienne au siècle apostolique* (1852 ; 2nd ed., 1860, 2 vols., i. 489 pp., ii. 629 pp. Paulinism is treated in vol. ii., 3-262 ; 3rd ed., 1864). Mild polemic against Baur.   Another mediating work is Willibald Beyschlag's *Neutestamentliche Theologie*, 1891 ; 2nd ed., 1896. Only the Pastorals spurious.

A conservative stand-point is occupied by Bernhard Weiss, *Einleitung in das Neue Testament*, 1886, 652 pp. Paul and his Epistles occupy pp. 112-332. The Pastoral Epistles are saved by the hypothesis of the second imprisonment. 2 Thessalonians and Ephesians are held to be genuine (3rd ed., 1897, 617 pp.). Conservative also is Theodor Zahn, *Einleitung in das Neue Testament*, 1st ed., 1897, vol. i., 489 pp. Pauline Epistles, pp. 109-489. Ch. K. v. Hofmann in his *Einleitung* (pt. ix. of " Die Heilige Schrift," edited by Volck, 1881, 411 pp. Pauline Epistles, 1-200) proposes by means of the hypothesis of a liberation of the Apostle from his first imprisonment to make not only the Pastorals, but also the Epistle to the Hebrews genuine.   That 2 Thessalonians and Ephesians are genuine is for him self-evident. Frédéric Godet too (*Introduction au Nouveau Testament*, 1893, 737 pp.) regards all thirteen Epistles as genuine.

genuineness of the second Epistle to the Thessalonians. For some, the Epistles to the Colossians and Ephesians are genuine throughout and represent a later phase of the Pauline theology. Nor were there lacking attempts of all kinds to rehabilitate the Pastoral Epistles. Those who did not venture to defend them as wholes make a point of retaining at least the " personal references."

The presentation of the Pauline teaching was, however, hardly affected by the literary divergences. Not even the most conservative of the critics had the boldness to place all the letters which have come down under the name of Paul on a footing of equality. Even those who regarded the Epistles to the Ephesians and Colossians as genuine did not fuse ideas of these Epistles with the system extracted from the four main Epistles, but presented them separately ; and any who were not converted to the rejection of the Pastorals at all events took the precaution to give a separate chapter to the Pauline theology of these writings.[1] If only the personal refer- ences might be saved, these Epistles were as completely excluded from the presentation of the Pauline system as if they had been pronounced wholly spurious.

Thus it continued to be the case, as it had been with Baur, that, generally speaking, only the four main epistles were taken into account in describing the Pauline system. The only significant change was that the epistle to the Philippians began to be put on the same footing, and, with a few exceptions, scholars no longer hesitated to regard as Pauline the conception of the pre-existence of Christ which is expressed in the section on the incarnation and obedience unto death. It was realised that the main epistles also presuppose this view, even if they do not state it so explicitly.

There were, of course, as time went on, attempts to

[1] Typical in this respect is the procedure of Bernhard Weiss in his *Neutestamentliche Theologie* (1868). He treats the doctrine of the Epistles of the imprisonment and that of the Pastorals by themselves after he has developed that of the main Epistles, although he regards them all as Pauline.

explain the composition of the four main epistles and
Philippians as arising by the working up together in each
single epistle of two or more originals, but these were not
of any real importance for the study of the Pauline
doctrine.   It was only a carrying out of the task suggested
by Semler, when he pointed out that we have not got the
letters in their original form but only as prepared for
public reading by the early Church.   But the constitution
of the Pauline material is scarcely affected by the attempts
to reconstruct these originals.   They have a purely
literary interest.

Theology, so far as it was occupied with the study of
the Pauline system, did not allow itself to be at all dis-
quieted by the rejection of the whole of the Epistles
proposed by Bruno Bauer in his " Criticism of the Pauline
Letters." [1]   Nor was its confidence shaken by the hypothesis that the letters have been worked over to a very
large extent and in a very thoroughgoing fashion.
Christian Hermann Weisse's " Contributions to the Criticism of the Pauline Epistles," [2] which appeared in 1867,
where he sets forth the justification and the principles
of this method, scarcely attracted any attention, as
was indeed the case with almost all the theological work
of this writer.

The elucidation of the details of the Pauline doctrine
is vigorously pursued.   An empirical definition is attempted of the terms sin, law, conscience, justification,
redemption, election, and freedom.   A special interest
attaches to the study of the terms flesh and spirit.   After
Holsten had endeavoured to trace the significance of the
word flesh, Lüdemann—in a brilliant work published in
1872 — endeavoured to arrive at a clear idea of the
Apostle's anthropology and its place in his doctrine
of salvation.

There are, so runs his thesis, two conceptions of

[1] *Kritik der paulinischen Briefe*, 3 pts., 1850, 74 pp.; 1851, 76 pp.;
1852, 129 pp.; *Christus und die Cäsaren*, 1877, 387 pp.
[2] *Beiträge zur Kritik der paulinischen Briefe an die Galater, Römer
Philipper und Kolosser.*   Edited by E. Sulze, 1867, 65 pp.

" flesh " in Paul. The one agrees with the naive, simple Jewish linguistic usage, and means only the natural being of man. The other is much more precise and belongs to a dualistic system of thought. In it the flesh is defined as the necessary cause of sin and corruption and as the absolute antithesis to spirit. On close examination it appears that not merely two conceptions of " the flesh " existing side by side, but two different doctrines of man's nature, and consequently two different conceptions of redemption, are found in Paul.

According to the system which connects itself with the simpler, broader conception of the flesh, sin springs from the freedom of the will; the law is assumed to be inherently possible of fulfilment ; redemption consists in a judgment of acquittal pronounced by God which has its ground solely in His mercy ; righteousness is imputed ; the act which brings redemption consists in faith. This circle of ideas, which forms a self-consistent whole, is described by Lüdemann as the " Jewish-religious," the " juridical-subjective," doctrine of redemption. It has its source in reflection on the death of Jesus.

The other system of ideas is defined as the " ethico-dualistic." In contradistinction to the former it makes use of an " objectively real " conception of redemption. It presupposes the more precise, narrower conception of " the flesh," and regards sin as proceeding from it by a natural necessity. The law is the ferment of sin ; death the natural outcome of the flesh. Redemption can therefore only consist in the abolition of the flesh. It is based on the communication of the Spirit, which produces in the man a new creature and a real righteousness. The redemptive act takes place in baptism. The ideas of this second system are based on the Lord's resurrection.

The coexistence of a juridical and an ethical system of thought in Paul had been held by others before Lüdemann. What he did, however, was to follow out each separately into its details, and to endeavour to prove that all the contradictions and obscurities which are to be observed

in the conceptions and statements of the Pauline theology
find their ultimate explanation in the coexistence of two
different doctrines of man's nature and two different
doctrines of redemption.

Hitherto the doctrine of redemption which appears
alongside of the juridical had been described as " ethical."
He remarks that it is conceived not merely ethically, but
actually physically, and therefore defines it as ethico-
physical.   Further, he is of opinion that the two theories
are not co-equal in importance.   He holds that in the
ethico-physical " the real view of the 'Apostle " is set
forth, which only tolerates the other alongside of it, and
more and more tends to push it aside wherever in the
discussion Paul can count upon a thorough understanding
of the real essence of the matter.

In the Epistles the development, he thinks, takes the
following course.   The Letter to the Galatians knows only
the primitive Jewish system of thought with reference
to Christ's vicarious suffering and righteousness by faith ;
it does not advance to the bolder realistic doctrine of
righteousness.

In the Epistles to the Corinthians, according to Lüdemann, the Apostle does not make much use of dogma.
" The less advanced position of the church there may have
been one cause of this."   But the fundamental conceptions of the ethico-physical series of ideas begin to
appear in them.   Later on they attain to " constitutive
importance " and " force their way into the leading
dogmatic statements."   In the first four chapters of
Romans the old view still finds expression.   From the fifth
onwards the new tenets are developed fully and clearly.

This second series of ideas is not Jewish but Greek.
Lüdemann's view is that Paul, " in the attempt to give
dogmatic fixity to the doctrine of salvation, presses on
beyond the horizon of the Old Testament consciousness
and is carried in the direction of Hellenism." [1]   The latter

---

[1] Lüdemann was opposed by H. H. Wendt in his work *Die
Begriffe Fleisch und Geist im biblischen Sprachgebrauch*, 1878, 219 pp.

offered him a clearly-thought-out doctrine of man, in which the dominant idea was the antithesis of flesh and spirit, and made it necessary for him to think out a physically real doctrine of redemption.

Pfleiderer [1] also works out the two series of ideas, separating them scarcely less sharply than Lüdemann does. But he prefers to describe the series which runs parallel to the juridical, not as physico-ethical, but as mystico-ethical. Moreover, he does not admit that the ethical series expresses Paul's view more adequately than the other. He is of opinion also that the two sets of conceptions held an equal place in the consciousness of the Apostle from the first. By logically thinking out the Jewish idea of the atoning death, Paul was led—according to Pfleiderer—to the anti-Jewish conclusion that redemption is for all mankind, and that the law is consequently invalidated. With this view there is united another, the source of which lies in the Hellenistic anthropology. This is that redemption consists in the influence exercised by the Holy Spirit upon the fleshly creatureliness, in consequence of which sin and death are abolished. The beginning of this process is to be sought in the resurrection of Jesus Christ. In the close connexion of the Pharisaic and Hellenistic elements " lies the characteristic peculiarity of the genuine Pauline theology, which can only be rightly understood when these two sides of it both receive equal attention. "

That in Paulinism two lines of thought go side by side is recognised by almost all the investigators of this period. But in the importance assigned to each of them great divergences appear. Reuss makes the juridical ideas entirely subordinate to the ethical ; in Ménégoz the former are more strongly emphasised than the latter. No one except Pfleiderer holds them to be on. an exactly equal

---

At the suggestion of Ritschl he undertook to prove that the meaning of these two words confined itself " within the boundaries set by Old Testament usage," and that therefore the assumption of Greek influence was unnecessary.

[1] Otto Pfleiderer, *Das Urchristentum*, 1887.

footing. In general the ethical set of ideas is regarded as
the original creation of the Apostle, and is assumed to
represent the deepest stratum in his thought. Accordingly, it is generally also held that the doctrine of the
abolition of the flesh by the Spirit comes to its full development later than the other, which is based upon the
atonement and imputed righteousness. Lüdemann's
theory of a development within the Pauline doctrine is
adopted by the majority, though only in a less pronounced
form.

It should be mentioned that the first important
attempt to prove the existence of different phases in the
thought and life of Paul was made by Sabatier.[1] His
work *L'Apotre Paul* appeared in 1870, two years before
Lüdemann's study. At first the Apostle held, according
to the French scholar, a simple doctrine which can be
psychologically explained from his rabbinic training and
his conversion. At the time of his great controversies he
was compelled to work out for himself a philosophy of
history which would enable him to prove that the law
was only a passing episode in the history of salvation, and
that justification by faith had always lain in the purpose
of God. This doctrine takes a dominant position in the
Epistles to the Galatians, Corinthians, and Romans. In
the letters written during his imprisonment the Apostle
advances to a speculative, gnostic development of his
ideas. The coexistence of the juridical and ethical
series of ideas does not receive the same prominence in
Sabatier as in the later writers, who were influenced by
Lüdemann and Pfleiderer.

When all is said and done, there is in the works of this
period much assertion and little proof regarding the
development within Paulinism. One almost gets the
impression that the assumption of different stages of
thought was chiefly useful as a way of escaping the
difficulty about the inner unity of the system. This

[1] Auguste Sabatier, *L'Apôtre Paul, esquisse d'une histoire de sa
pensée*, 1870, 296 pp. (2nd ed., 1881 ; 3rd ed., 1897).

problem is, however, rather instinctively felt than clearly grasped. The scholars of this period do not feel it incumbent upon them to trace out the connexion in which these disparate sets of ideas must have stood in the view of Paul. They show no surprise at his passing so easily from the one to the other and arguing from each alternately, and they do not ask themselves how he conceived the most general ultimate fact of redemption which underlies both of them. They do not seek to arrive at a really fundamental view of the essence of Paulinism.

Their method of procedure in their presentation of the doctrine is itself significant. They do not trace its development from one fundamental conception, but treat it under dogmatic *loci*, as Baur had done in his New Testament Theology. The scheme is more or less closely based on that of Reformation dogmatics. It is therefore assumed *a priori* that the Pauline theology can be divided into practically the same individual doctrines as that of Luther, Zwingli, and Calvin. Really, however, a preliminary question arises whether this arrangement of the material does not introduce a wrong grouping and orientation into the Apostle's system, and whether it does not destroy the natural order and relative importance of the thoughts, falsify the perspective, tear asunder what ought not to be disjoined, and render impossible the discovery of the fundamental idea in which all the utterances find their point of union. This procedure is innocently supposed to be scientific ; as a matter of fact it leads to the result that the study of the subject continues to be embarrassed by a considerable remnant of the prepossessions with which the interpretation of Paul's doctrine was approached in the days of the Reformation.

It is not less prejudicial when others, as for example Holsten,[1] adopt an arrangement of the material suggested by modern dogmatics. As the Pauline theology has, if possible, less affinity with the latter than with the Reformation theology, the error is almost more serious.

[1] *Das Evangelium des Paulus*, pt. 2 (edited by Mehlhorn), 1898, 172 pp.

In general these scholars are quite unconscious of the decisive importance which attaches to the arrangement and articulation of the material. It has, indeed, always been weakness of theological scholarship to talk much about method and possess little of it.

Otto Pfleiderer, alone, is not entirely in this state of innocence. He has an inkling that the usual way of approaching the subject is not wholly free from objection. In the first edition of his Paulinism (1873) [1] he raises the question whether the " genetic method " is not demanded by the task of tracing out the organic progress of the development of dogma in its Pauline beginnings. Practical considerations, however, determine him " to arrange the matter very much according to the customary dogmatic *loci*, " while, however, at the same time giving as much attention as possible to the position of the dogma in the Pauline system." He fears that the carrying out of the genetic principle would lead to many repetitions, and would make it more difficult to get a general view of " the way in which the separate doctrines were connected with their bases."

In order to salve his conscience he gives at the beginning, " by way of an introductory outline," a sketch of the " organic development of the Pauline gnosis from its single root." This general view—it occupies twenty-seven pages—is the most important part of the whole book. The succeeding chapters treat of sin, flesh, character of the law, aim of the law, Christ's atoning death, Christ's death as a means of liberation from the dominion of sin, the resurrection of Christ, the Person of Jesus Christ, the Son of David, the Son of God and heavenly Christ, the appearing of Christ in the flesh, faith, justification, sonship, the beginning and the progress of the new life, the Christian Church, the Lord's Supper, the election of grace, the parousia, and the end of the world.

Lüdemann was prevented by the task which he had set himself from adopting the division according to *loci*.

[1] P. 31.

His object was only to investigate Paul's conception of
the fleshly man in its relation to his doctrine as a whole.
In this way he was led to arrange the ideas in their natural
order and, without strictly intending to do so, to give a
general account of Paulinism, which is almost entirely
free from the defective arrangement of other works,
permits something of the logical articulation of the
Apostle's circle of ideas to appear, and certainly penetrates
more deeply than the rest into the Apostle's world of
thought.

As the works of Reuss, Weiss, Pfleiderer, Holsten,
Renan, Sabatier, Ménégoz, Weizsäcker, do not aim at
understanding and showing the development of this
doctrine from a single fundamental thought, there are
no real divergences in the general view which they take
of the system. The differences of opinion with their
predecessors which the authors express in their text and
notes relate, in point of fact, only to details and minutiæ,
surprising as this may at first sight appear. The plan
and design of the system are in general everywhere the
same ; the differences regard only the mixing and application of the colours, and the question how far Greek
influences are to be recognised.

In going through these works one after another, one is
surprised to observe how great is their fundamental
resemblance. At the same time there is something
curiously " elusive " about them. At a given point
one might be inclined to think that one of the authors
was formulating a thought more clearly, or giving it
more exclusive importance than the others ; and one is
just about to note this as a special characteristic of his
view. A few pages later, however, or in a following
chapter, one finds additions or reservations which show
that he does not really think differently from the rest.
The differences lie not so much in the actual conception
as in the literary presentation, and in the manner in which
the material, which is essentially a whole, is parcelled out
among the different *loci*. There is thus nothing to be

gained by analysing the various conceptions one by one and comparing them with one another. Since there is no real difference of fundamental view, the comparison would lose itself in endless and unessential detail.

To the general impression of monotony is to be added that of complexity. At the end of each of these works one is inclined to inquire whether the author really means to ask the reader to regard what is here offered as representing a system of thought which once existed in the brain of a man belonging to early Christianity, and was capable of being understood by his contemporaries. All the arts of literary presentation are employed to subtilise the conceptions, to describe the thoughts with exactitude, and to bring connexion and order into the chaos of ideas. But the result gives no satisfaction. No real elucidation and explanation of Paulinism is attained. The resulting impression is of something quite artificial.

The welcome which these authors' works received from their contemporaries shows that the latter saw in them an advance in the knowledge of Paulinism. They felt them to be satisfactory. That only means that the readers' presuppositions and requirements lay within the same limitations as those of the authors.

What had been the result arrived at ? A description of the Pauline doctrine, a remarkably detailed description, but nothing more. That doubtless implied a certain progress. It did not, however, extend so far as the authors and their readers assumed. Both innocently supposed that in the description they possessed at the same time an explanation—as though the descriptive anatomy of this organism sufficed to explain its physiology. They were unconscious that they had so far only looked at Pauline thought from without, and had never gained any insight into the inner essence of the system.

In these works the Apostle's statements are quoted one after another, and developed in his own words. The authors think they have discharged their task when they have so arranged the course of the investigation that all important passages can be respectably housed.

The odd thing is that they write as if they understood what they were writing about. They do not feel compelled to admit that Paul's statements taken by themselves are unintelligible, consist of pure paradoxes, and that the point that calls for examination is how far they are thought of by their author as having a real meaning, and could be understood in this light by his readers. They never call attention to the fact that the Apostle always becomes unintelligible just at the moment when he begins to explain something ; never give a hint that while we hear the sound of his words the tune of his logic escapes us.

What is his meaning when he asserts that the law is abolished by the death of Jesus—according to other passages, by His resurrection ? How does he represent to himself the process by which, through union with the death and resurrection of the Lord a new creaturehood is produced in a man, in virtue of which he is released from the conditions of fleshly existence, from sin and death ? How far is a union possible between the natural man, alive in this present world, and the glorified Christ who dwells in heaven ; and one, moreover, of such a kind that it has a retrospective reference to His death ? The authors we have named do not raise questions of this kind. They feel no need to trace out the realities which lie behind these paradoxical assertions. They take it for granted that Paul has himself explained his statements up to a certain point—so far, in fact, as this is possible in the world of feeling to which religion belongs.

This self-deception is made the more easy for them by the fact that they are accustomed to clothe their own religious views in Pauline phraseology, and consequently they come to treat as the authentic logic of Paul, arguments which they have unconsciously imported into their account of his teaching. They fail to reckon with the possibility that the original significance of his utterances may rest on presuppositions which are not present to our apprehension and conception. For the same reason they all more or less hold the opinion that what they have to do with is mainly a psychological problem. They assume that the Pauline system has arisen out of a series of reflexions and conclusions, and would be as a whole clear and intelligible to any one who could succeed in really thinking himself into the psychology of the rabbinic zealot who was overpowered by the vision of Christ on the road to Damascus.

The writer who goes furthest in this direction is Holsten. In his work on the " Gospel of Paul and of Peter " [1] he describes how Paul, while he was persecuting the new faith, was, as a Jewish thinker, occupied with the thought of the offence of the cross and the alleged resurrection. While still a fanatical zealot " he constantly carried with him in his consciousness the elements of the Messianic faith, even though as negative and negated." By the keenness of his theological dialectic he was compelled to imagine what the alleged facts would really signify if the belief of the disciples were justified. The " principle of the Messianic faith " was, in him, " alive in greater definiteness than even in the consciousness of the followers of the Messiah whom he persecuted." The Messiahship of Jesus could not for him take its place as a hope and faith within the Jewish system of thought and religious life,

---

[1] *Zum Evangelium des Paulus und des Petrus*, 1868, 447 pp. In this work the author collects some of his earlier and later essays. The following are its component parts, " Paul's Vision of Christ " (1861), " Peter's Vision of the Messiah " (1868), " Contents and Argument of the Epistle to the Galatians " (1859), " The Significance of the word σάρξ (flesh) in Paul's System of Doctrine " (1855). The collection is dedicated to F. C. Baur, " who though dead yet lives." In the first part of the work *Das Evangelium des Paulus*, 1880, 498 pp., Holsten deals with the Epistle to the Galatians and the First to the Corinthians. The second part was intended to give an exposition of Romans and 2 Corinthians and to close with a systematic account of the Pauline theology. At Holsten's death only the closing section was found to be ready for printing. It was published in 1898 under the editorship of Carl Mehlhorn, and bears the title " Carl Holsten, Das Evangelium des Paulus, part ii., Paulinische Theologie," 173 pp. What was thus published is based on a manuscript prepared for his lectures in the winter session of 1893–1894, and on students' notes.

but necessarily implied the destruction of what he had hitherto held to be true. Thus the persecutor had in principle thought out for himself to its ultimate consequences the revolution which would result from the acceptance of the Messiahship of Jesus. And this he translated into word and deed after he had experienced the vision on the Damascus road.

Other writers take as the starting-point for their psychological arguments the passage in Romans vii., where Paul depicts the despair of the man who recognises that the law, although it is spiritual and was given with a view to life, can only in the fleshly man produce sin, condemnation, and death. What we there read concerning the struggle between the natural, powerful will of the flesh and the law, is, they think, written from the point of view of the pre-Christian consciousness of the Apostle. He had experienced this agony of soul, and it was by this that the Jewish religious attitude had been broken down in him. Therefore in his Gospel he does not desire to retain anything from the faith of his fathers.

These two main lines of psychological theory are followed for a longer or shorter distance in all the works of this period. Hand in hand with this psychologising goes a tendency to modernisation. The scholars of this period spiritualise Paul's thought. The transformation varies in extent for the different ideas. The statements about the atonement and imputed righteousness are the least affected by it. What is unintelligible in these is put down to the account of the Jewish Rabbinic mode of thought in which Paul is supposed to be held prisoner. On the other hand, the conceptions regarding union with Christ in his death and passion, and the new life in Him through the Spirit, are subjected to paraphrase and explanation until nothing of the realistic sense is left remaining. The question is not faced why Paul, if he wanted to say anything so " spiritual " and general as this, should have adopted so exaggerated, paradoxical, and materialistic a method of expression.

Whatever remains unexplained after the psychologising, the depotentiation, and modernisation, is referred to the peculiar character of the religious experience which the Apostle is supposed to have undergone in the vision on the Damascus road. What essential difference there was between this appearance of the Lord and those experienced by the other disciples is nowhere clearly worked out, not even by Holsten, who makes the most extensive use of this vision. It is simply taken for granted by them all that in the vision itself is to be found the explanation, not only of Paul's conversion, but also in some way or other of his call to be a missionary to the Gentiles and of the peculiar character of his doctrine.

All these accounts of his teaching agree in assuming that Paul's system of doctrine was in the main a purely personal creation of his own, and is in some way to be explained by the special character of his religious experience. The question whether in this way his integral connexion with primitive Christianity is sufficiently preserved receives but little attention. In none of these works is the investigation of the doctrinal material common to Paul and his opponents seriously taken in hand. The writers are content with the affirmation that both parties took as their starting-point the fact of the death and resurrection of Jesus, without entering into any consideration of the question how far Paul's reasonings, which they refer back to his inner personal experience, reproduce generally current ideas of primitive Christianity and simply carry them out to their logical issue.

The question which Ritschl had formerly forced on the consideration of Baur has therefore not been faced or solved. It is true the author of " Justification and Reconciliation " [1] thinks that he has not only raised the question but also answered it. He undertakes to explain all the Pauline doctrinal passages on the basis of

---

[1] Albrecht Ritschl, *Die christliche Lehre von der Rechtfertigung und Versöhnung*, 1874, vol. ii. 377 pp. On Paul, pp. 215-259 and 300-369.

Old Testament conceptions. In this way he hopes to work out the Apostle's real conception of the atoning death of Jesus, and of " righteousness," and believes that these will then, since they have been gained from the Old Testament, coincide with the primitive Christian views in all essential points.

Speaking generally, Ritschl's tendency is to make the differences between Paulinism and primitive Christianity as small as possible, and to find them, as he had already done in the " Origin of the early Catholic Church," not so much in his doctrine proper as in his attitude to certain practical questions. Ritschl employs the dialectical skill with which nature had richly endowed him to transform and shade off the doctrine of the Apostle of the Gentiles until it harmonises with the fundamental Christian teaching which he assumes for the earliest period and finds necessary for his dogmatics.

He entirely depotentiates the juridical series of ideas. Moreover, he refuses to admit that Paulinism constitutes a speculative system. He assumes that the Apostle moved in a free, untrammelled fashion among the various sets of ideas and felt no real need to combine them into a unity.

In addition to Ritschl, Bernhard Weiss [1] and Willibald Beyschlag,[2] in their New Testament Theologies, endeavour to make clear the relations between Paul and primitive Christianity from the stand-point of critical conservatism. In order to secure a broad basis for the primitive form of apostolic doctrine, they pronounce 1 Peter and the Epistle of James to be documents of the pre-Pauline period.

The writer who makes things easiest for himself is Von Hofmann.[3] For him there is no " Pauline system

[1] *Lehrbuch der biblischen Theologie des Neuen Testaments*, 1st ed. 1868, 756 pp. On Paulinism, pp. 216-507 ; 6th ed. 1895, 677 pp. On Paulinism, 201-463.

[2] *Neutestamentliche Theologie*, 1st ed. 1891 ; 2nd ed. 1896, vol. ii. 552 pp. On Paul, pp. 1-285.

[3] Ch. K. v. Hofmann, *Biblische Theologie* (vol. xi. of " Die heilige Schrift Neuen Testaments " ; edited by Volck), 1886, 328 pp.

of doctrine." The Apostle never uttered anything that did not belong to the common doctrine of Christianity, but " according to the difference of the occasion " brought into prominence this or that aspect of the saving acts of God or of the condition of salvation, and what he thus brought forward, now under one designation now under another, he sets forth now in this relation and now in that one. Therefore this writer, who was vaunted by the orthodox as a brilliant opponent of Tübingen errors, has no scruple in working up together the Pauline ideas along with those of the other New Testament Epistles into a single whole, which he offers as apostolic doctrine.

Another problem which is hardly apprehended in its full difficulty by the scholars of this period is that of the total neglect in the Pauline gospel of the proclamation of the kingdom of God and His righteousness which Jesus committed to His followers. They seem to feel no surprise at the fact that the Apostle, even where it would be the most natural thing in the world, never appeals to the sayings and commands of the Master. Many of them never touch on this question at all.

Resch, however, in his collection of extra-canonical Gospel-fragments, even undertakes to show that in the Pauline letters a whole series of otherwise unrecorded sayings of Jesus are embodied, and defends the hypothesis that the Apostle had taken them from a pre-canonical Gospel which ranked for him as an authority of equal value with the Old Testament. The enigma of the untraced quotation, " What eye hath not seen, neither hath ear heard," etc., in 1 Cor. ii. 9 ff., is solved by referring the " as it is written " to the written Gospel on which Paul draws.[1]

It is curious that most of these authors believe that they reduce the acuteness of the problem by pointing

---

[1] *Texte und Untersuchungen zur Geschichte der altchristlichen Kirche*, vol. v., 1888, part iv. Alfred Resch, " Agrapha. Ausserkanonische Evangelienfragmente gesammelt und untersucht," 480 pp. The " logia " numbered 13-46 he holds, on the evidence of echoes in the letters, to have been known to Paul. See pp. 152-243.

out in the Epistles as many reminiscences of Synoptic sayings as possible. That, of course, only makes the matter more complicated. If so many utterances of Jesus are hovering before Paul's mind, how comes it that he always merely paraphrases them, instead of quoting them as sayings of Jesus, and thus sheltering himself behind their authority ?

As for those who have some inkling of the problem, their one thought is to dispose of it as rapidly as possible, instead of first exposing it in its full extent. Among them is Ritschl, who here employs all the arts and artifices of his exegesis and dialectic. That Jesus and Paul did not at bottom teach the same thing is to this undogmatic dogmatist unthinkable.

In general the writers of this period are involved in the most curious confusions regarding the problem of " Jesus and Paul." They fail to perceive that these two magnitudes are not directly comparable with one another because they think of Paul in complete isolation, and not as a feature of primitive Christianity. The differences and oppositions which reveal themselves between the teaching of Jesus and that of Paul exist also as between the teaching of Jesus and that of primitive Christianity itself. The momentous development did not arise first with Paul, but earlier, in the community of the first disciples. Their " religion " is not identical with the " teaching of Jesus," and did not simply grow out of it ; it is founded upon His death and resurrection. The "new element" was not brought into Christianity by Paul; he found it there before him, and what he did was to think it out in its logical implications. The difference of teaching between Paul and Jesus is not a difference between individuals, it is—in almost its whole extent— due to the fact that the Apostle belongs to primitive Christianity.

In its false statement of the problem of Jesus and Paul the scholarship of the period after Baur shows that it has not yet succeeded in understanding the Apostle of the Gentiles as a phenomenon, an aspect, of primitive Christianity.

There is frequent mention, in all these studies, of the Jewish roots of the Pauline thought. They attempt to explain his views, so far as possible, from the materials given in the Law and the Prophets. Some authors had been inclined to assume that in regard to his conception of the Law he did not stand wholly upon Old Testament ground, in the sense that he sometimes means by it a narrower ceremonial code of temporary validity, and sometimes a universal ethical law which has not been invalidated by the death of Christ. These confusions were put an end to by a study of Edward Grafe.[1] He shows that Paul when he speaks of the law, alike when he uses the article or does not use it, always has in mind the whole legal code, and never varies from the conviction that this has been set aside by the death and resurrection of Christ.

That in Galatians the ritual aspect of the law, in Romans the ethical, is the more prominent, does not alter this fact. Nor is the consistency of the Apostle's view annulled by the fact that in many places he formulates the negative judgment quite definitely, while in others he softens it by an admission of the historical and ethical significance of the law.

That Paul's thinking follows the lines of Old Testament conceptions is self-evident. The only question is whether the motive forces which make their appearance in his gospel are derived in some way or other from the Old Testament Scriptures.

That is not the case. In working up the primitive Christian views he does not have recourse to the ideas of the ancient Judaism. Nowhere does Paul attach himself to these. He takes no ideas from the Old Testament with a view to giving them a new development,

---

[1] *Die paulinische Lehre vom Gesetz* (" The Pauline Doctrine of the Law "). Based on the four main Epistles, 1884, 26 pp. The second edition (1893, 33 pp.) is a revision of the first, but in the results arrived at both agree.

but uses only what he can take from it ready formed. His new discovery rests on a different basis. The Law and the Prophets serve only to supply him with the Scriptural arguments, positive and negative, of which he stands in need.

On the essential nature of the distinctively Pauline world of thought the Old Testament therefore throws no light. This negative result is not, indeed, everywhere clearly formulated. There are some students of Paulinism who simply ignore it. Heinrici, in the preface to his study of 2 Corinthians (1887), ventures on the assertion that in Paul the " spirit of Old Testament prophecy " triumphs over contemporary Judaism.

And he is not the only one who clings to the illusion that much help is to be gained from the Old Testament for the understanding of the Apostle's world of thought. By way of proof they cite every possible parallel, even the most remote. But the disproportion between the amount of the material offered and the smallness of the result established tells against them.

That Paul is a child of late Judaism only began to be generally taken into account when its world of thought was made known to theology by Schürer's " History of New Testament Times," [1] and Weber's " System of Palestinian Theology in the Early Synagogues." [2] But even after this most scholars shared a certain disinclination to recognise a real connexion between the Apostle's world of thought and that of late Judaism. Heinrici, who in

---

[1] *Neutestamentliche Zeitgeschichte.* In the second edition the work bears the title *Geschichte des jüdischen Volkes im Zeitalter Jesu Christi* (English Translation : " History of the Jewish People in the Time of Jesus Christ," Edinburgh, 1885). The second volume deals with the literature and the various currents of thought. There have since appeared a third and fourth edition.

[2] *System der altsynagogalen palästinensischen Theologie aus Targum, Midrasch und Talmud dargestellt,* 399 pp. (Edited after the author's death by Delitzsch and Schnedermann.)

The second edition (1897, 427 pp.) bears the title *Jüdische Theologie auf Grund des Talmud und verwandter Schriften* (" Jewish Theology described on the Basis of the Talmud and cognate Writings ").

The earlier literature is referred to in Hans Vollmer's *Die alttestamentlichen Zitate bei Paulus* (1895), 81 pp.

his study in the Corinthian Epistles gives great attention
to the question regarding the source of his ideas, definitely
denies that " the intellectual and religious forces of Late
Judaism exercised a dominant influence " on the Apostle.
He holds, like many others, that Paul, passing over his
own time, grasped hands with the classical Judaism of
the prophets, and that one source of his strength is to be
found in this fact.   This prejudice is to be explained by
the low estimation in which late Judaism had always
been held by theologians.   It was identified, without
examination, on the one hand with " fantastic apocalyptic
views," and on the other with a " soulless Rabbinism."

The admission, however, that Paul in the principles
of his exegesis was in agreement with Rabbinism was made
by theologians with comparative readiness.   This did
not carry with it the surrender of anything that had been
much valued, since the verbal comparison and contrast
of passages which he practises, and the illogical and
fantastic reasoning which appears in his arguments, had
always been distasteful to theological science.   It was
therefore rather welcome to it than otherwise, to find,
in consequence of the increased knowledge of parallel
products of late Judaism, an explanation of a weakness
which did not properly harmonise with the greatness of
this heroic spirit, in the influences to which he had been
subjected by reason of his theological education.[1]

Along with this was accepted the fact that, in common
with his contemporaries, he naively treats the Haggadic
embellishments of Old Testament stories as on the same
footing with the Scripture itself.   His assumption that
the Law was given by the angels (Gal. iii. 19), and his
reference to the rock that followed the children of Israel
in the wilderness and poured out water (1 Cor. x. 4), are
to be explained from passages in the Rabbinic literature.

---

[1] A typical utterance is that of J. Wellhausen (*Israelitische und
jüdische Geschichte*, 6th ed. 1907, 386 pp.), " Paul has not been able
to free himself from the Rabbinic methods of exegesis.   He employs
it in his arguments, especially in connexion with justification by faith.
But the inner essence of his religious conviction was not affected by it."

No thoroughgoing investigation was undertaken with a view to determining whether the Rabbinic principles suffice to explain Paul's method of scriptural argument. In general the view prevails that his " typological " and " spiritualising " (*pneumatisch*) interpretation goes beyond what can elsewhere be shown in Palestinian theology. It is true these two methods of exegesis, going beyond the simple literal sense, are not wholly unknown, but they only came to their full development in contemporary Alexandrian Biblical scholarship. For this reason it is proposed to assume that Paul had also received an influence from this side.

As examples of Alexandrian exegesis are quoted the interpretation of Hagar and Sarah as representing the earthly and the heavenly Jerusalem (Gal. iv. 22 f.), that of the water-giving rock as representing Christ (1 Cor. x. 4), and the argument from the threshing oxen to the preachers of the gospel (1 Cor. ix. 9 ff.).

One of the greatest problems of the Pauline use of Scripture is not mentioned in these works. It is assumed that the Apostle attached special importance to proving the Messiahship of the crucified Jesus. How then can we explain the fact that he never makes any use of the passage about the Suffering Servant of the Lord in Isaiah liii ? This fact is the more surprising because it may be taken as certain that the apologetic of the primitive Christian community gave this passage a most prominent place in its plan of operations.

A scientific attempt to adduce from the Rabbinic literature explanatory parallels to Pauline thought was made by Franz Delitzsch in 1870 in connexion with his Hebrew translation of the Epistle to the Romans.[1] The

---

[1] *Paulus des Apostels Brief an die Römer in das Hebräische übersetzt, und aus Talmud und Midrasch erläutert*, 1870, 122 pp.

At the beginning the author gives an interesting review of previous Hebrew translations of the whole New Testament or of single books. He also refers to the Rabbinic reasoning in the apostle's arguments. The illustrations from the Rabbinic literature, pp. 73-100, follow the translation.

He expects as a result of this translation that it will bring into

net result is not great. The parallels adduced are so uncharacteristic that they throw no new light on the Apostle's ideas.

No further considerable attempts were made in this direction. Nor did Weber's " Theology of the Early Synagogue " lead to any other important works being undertaken in that department. On the contrary, his sketch of the Rabbinic world of ideas makes it apparent that Pauline thought does not become any more intelligible by its aid than it is in itself, even though one parallel or another may be unearthed. Moreover, it is to be remarked that the discovery of such parallels would only become of importance if proof could be given that they really date from the beginning of the first century. Such proof is, however, quite impossible.

Of the " Rabbinism " of Paul's day we know practically nothing. Even the earliest strata of the literature which is at our disposal were not formed before the beginning of the third century A.D.[1] It consists of a codification of tradition carried out by the later Rabbinic scholasticism. How far it offers us a faithful representation of the ideas and character of Rabbinic thought at the beginning of the first century must remain an open question.

Even if Paul, in virtue of his dialectic and certain external characteristics, belongs to the world which this literature reveals to us, in regard to the content of his ideas and his creative force as a thinker he is not to be understood by its aid. To register this fact is, however, by no means to deny that he has his roots in the Jewish theology of his time, but only to say that he shows no affinity as regards the inner essence of his problems and

---

prominence the Old Testament, Rabbinic, and Hellenistic elements in the early Christian modes of thought and expression.

Earlier attempts to point out Rabbinic parallels to Pauline ideas were made by Lightfoot, Surenhus, Schöttgen, Meuschen, and Nork. Information about this literature will be found in Hans Vollmer's work (*Die alttestamentlichen Zitate bei Paulus*, 1895, pp. 80, 81).

[1] A good general idea of the Rabbinic literature as a whole is given by Bousset in his work *Die Religion des Judentums im neutestamentlichen Zeitalter*, 1903, 2nd ed., 1906, pp. 45-53.

ideas with what a later age offers us as the Rabbinism of the first century. It is possible, indeed it is in the highest degree probable, that many of his ideas for which no " Rabbinic " parallels can be adduced, nevertheless have their origin in the Jewish theology of his time. Who is to guarantee that the later scholasticism has faithfully preserved for us the Jewish theology which was contemporary with Christianity ? It may well have been more living in thought and more profound than the men of the after-time could understand, or their tradition preserve. The picture which they draw for us shows only a sun-scorched plain, but this yellow, wilted grass was green and fresh once. What did the meadows look like then ?

It is to be remembered that the Apocalypse of Ezra, which shows in its own way such depth, while it is derived from the Scribal theology of the first century, is as little to be explained from what on the basis of the later literature we think of as the Rabbinism of the period as are the Pauline Epistles. Had this writing not been preserved, it would never have occurred to anyone that at that time men belonging to the circle of the Scribes had been tormented in this way by the primary problems of religion, and had brought the questions arising out of them into such close relations with eschatology.

Further, it is to be taken into account that Palestinian Scribism, even though it was an independent entity, did not, at the time when it has to be considered in connexion with Paul, exist in absolute exclusiveness, but maintained relations with Jewish Hellenism. The latter worked on a basis of ideas which it had in large measure taken over from Rabbinism and held in common with the latter. This relationship becomes in the case of Philo clearly apparent. With him one can never tell where the " Rabbinist " ends and the Hellenist begins. But if the theology of the Scribes stood in any kind of relation with Jewish Hellenism, it cannot have been so poor in ideas and unspiritual as it appears in the later tradition.

Even the discourses of Jesus, in spite of the polemical picture which they give of it, create the impression that He had to do with a Rabbinism which was interested in really religious questions, even though it showed itself incapable of rising to the height of the simple piety to which His preaching of the Kingdom of God and the repentance necessary thereto made its appeal.

It seems therefore probable that the Epistles of Paul and the Apocalypse of Ezra, along with its satellite the Apocalypse of Baruch, are witnesses to a Rabbinism, or a movement within its sphere, of which the Rabbinic tradition which later became fixed in written form gives us no information.

What should we know of the moving forces of the Reformation as they manifest themselves in Luther's works of the year 1521, if we were dependent for our information on the Lutheran scholasticism of the sixteenth and seventeenth centuries? How would we think of the Reformation as a whole if we possessed only these witnesses? With all due respect to the vaunted faithfulness of Rabbinic tradition, which after all we are not in a position to check, was it capable of preserving the record of a period of living thought? Is an oral tradition ever capable of doing so?

The historical examples in which we are able to test the tradition of later generations by the reality which has subsequently come to light, are calculated to shake our faith in the assumption that it can do so. What did Beethoven's time know of the achievements of the period of Bach? Mention is made of the elaborate fugues which had their origin at that time; but that the eighteenth century had produced choral works of deep feeling and an elevation secure against change of fashion, was entirely unknown to the second generation after Bach, although there had been nothing to interrupt tradition.

Moreover, it ought not to be forgotten that we possess the history of Judaism only in fragments. As regards the political events of the first century we are comparatively well informed, but of the religious movements we know little, and what does come to our knowledge is so disconnected and self-contradictory that it cannot be combined into a single picture. The Baptist, Jesus, Philo, Paul, Josephus, and the authors of the Apocalypses of Ezra and Baruch cover together about two generations. They are at first sight as entirely different as if they belonged to widely separated periods.

The destruction of Jerusalem interrupts the continuity of development of the Jewish people and of its thought. Its life is extinguished. Hellenism dies out. There arises a Rabbinism which is no longer borne on the tide of great national and spiritual movements. It becomes ossified, and confines itself to mere unproductive commentating upon the law. From the past its tradition takes only what lies within the field of its own narrow interests. The problems and ideas which moved the earlier, many-sided period no longer come into view, but fall into as complete oblivion as if they had never occupied Jewish religious thought.

The scholarship of the period after Baur is indeed far enough from embarking on reflexions of this kind. It takes scarcely any notice of what remains of the Late-Jewish non-Hellenistic literature. Even the commentators make scarcely any use of the parallels to Pauline ideas and conceptions which are found in Enoch, the Apocalypse of Baruch, the Apocalypse of Ezra, and here and there in the Testaments of the Twelve Patriarchs.

It is nothing less than astonishing that the close affinities with the Apocalypse of Ezra do not receive any recognition. In this work there are elaborate discussions of the problems of sin, the Fall of our first parents, Election, the wrath, long-suffering, and mercy of God, the prerogative of Israel, the significance of the law, the temporal and the eternal Jerusalem, of the prospect of dying or surviving to the Parousia, the tribulation of the times of the End, and the Judgment. The close affinity between this writer and Paul strikes the eye at once.

Writers on Paulinism are, however, so obsessed by the idea that the teaching of Paul is a " personal creation " that they cannot bring themselves to accept the view that the religious problems which struggle for solution in his letters had also occupied his Jewish contemporaries or at least a section of them.[1]

The claims of Late Judaism on Paul were therefore taken to be discharged when his Rabbinic dialectic and exegesis, and to a certain extent his eschatology also, had been ascribed to it.

The chapter on the future-hope which connected Paul on the one hand with Judaism and on the other with primitive Christianity, is never omitted in any account of his teaching given by the scholars of the post-Baur period. In it is collected all that the Epistles have to say regarding the parousia, the resurrection, the judgment, and the Kingdom of the Last Times. The treatment, however, is by no means thorough. Scarcely anywhere is there an attempt to arrange the scattered notices in an orderly way and bring them into relation with one another. It is taken for granted that they are inconsistent with one another, as a necessary consequence of the fantastic character of the material. That Paul may have had a clear plan of the events of the End in which all his statements can find a place, is not taken into account. These writers therefore set no limit to the admission of inconsistencies, and draw a picture which is, to put it plainly, meaningless.

So far, it occurs to no one that the want of connexion may perhaps result from the fact that the separate

[1] Among the few scholars who stem the tide of conventional stupidity Frederick Spitta deserves a foremost place. In his printed works, no doubt—those in question are *Der zweite Brief des Petrus und der Brief des Judas* (1885, 544 pp.) and the studies *Zur Geschichte und Literatur des Urchristentums* (vol. i. 1893 ; vol. ii. 1896)—he is chiefly engaged in maintaining the general thesis that the earliest Christian literature shows much more dependence on the Late-Jewish than is generally admitted. A detailed proof of this kind for the Pauline letters has only been given in his exegetical lectures, which have not been published. The stimulus which he gave to others is clearly apparent in the literature of the nineties. Kabisch's study of the eschatology of Paul (1893) is partly based on the foundation which he had prepared.

statements have not been carefully examined in regard to what they actually mean, and to their mutual relations. It is taken as quite certain that the " simple " eschatology of 1 Thessalonians is superseded by the more complicated view of the Corinthian letters ; and these in turn are not the last stage in this "development" of the Apostle's thought. No attempt is made to get a clear idea in what order he thinks of the judgment and the resurrection of the dead, or as to whether he holds that there is one resurrection and one judgment, or a resurrection of the "righteous," and another besides, and whether he assumes this to be accompanied by one judgment or two.

The authors regard with a certain amount of self-satisfaction the way in which they have emphasised the importance given to the eschatology by Paul. In the chapter devoted to it they have certainly emphasised again and again, " with the utmost energy," the fact that he really " shared " the eschatological expectations of his time and admitted them to an important place in his creed. The chapter in question, however, only gets its turn after the whole " system of doctrine " has been safely housed in the earlier chapters without seeking any aid from the eschatology or even saying a word about it. As in the Church prayers of to-day, one catches an echo of it only at the end. This means that, when all is said and done, these writers regard it only as a kind of annexe to the main edifice of Pauline doctrine. That is a fact which their brave words about the importance attributed to it in their account do not alter in the slightest. None of these students of Paulinism asks himself whether there is an organic connexion between the eschatological expectations and the system as such, and whether the fundamental conceptions and concatenation of ideas are not somehow or other conditioned by the hope of the final consummation. It is simply taken as self-evident that eschatology can only form an incidental chapter in Paul's teaching.

The most natural course to follow in the investigation would have been to begin with the eschatology as the most general and " primitive-Christian " element, and then to have tried to find a path leading from here to the central doctrine of the new life in union with the dying and resurrection of Christ. This course is nowhere followed.

That is the more surprising as it is generally assumed that the " missionary preaching " of the Apostle took an almost purely eschatological form, and was scarcely distinguishable from the primitive-Christian preaching of repentance, the judgment, and the parousia.   The point to examine would therefore have been precisely how the " Pauline theology " grew out of the eschatology which Paul shared with primitive Christianity.   Instead of that, these writers begin with the " doctrinal system," and attach to that by way of appendix an account of the eschatology.   It here first becomes fully apparent what a misfortune it was for Pauline study in the post-Baur period that it kept to the method of presentation under *loci*, and consequently accorded eschatology, in principle, no greater importance for Paulinism than it had had for Reformation theology.

Bernard Weiss, agreeing in this with Havet, lays strong emphasis on the eschatology, and makes a beginning in the direction of an intelligent presentation of Paulinism. Instead of beginning, like the others, with the " doctrine of man," or with " sin and the law," he first sets forth " the earliest preaching of Paul as Apostle of the Gentiles," which he makes to consist of nothing but the proclamation of the judgment and the parousia.   But having got this length, he does not feel any need to point out the paths which lead from here to the " teaching of the four great doctrinal and polemical epistles."   He simply puts the two sections side by side, and even falls into the inconsistency of devoting another chapter to the eschatology at a later point.   The doctrine of Paul consists therefore for these scholars of a theology of the present and a theology of the future which have no inner connexion with one another. It is indeed cited as an achievement on his part that he turned the eye of faith from the exclusive contemplation of the " hereafter " to take in the present also. How he came to do so— he alone of this first Christian generation—to point to present " blessings of salvation " in addition to those of the future, is not explained. The co-existence of the two is simply noted as a fact.

How far the scholars of this period were from taking the Pauline eschatology seriously, is evident from the fact that they neglected to enquire into its connexion with that of Late Judaism. Otto Everling, who in 1888 took in hand to give an account of one of its main features, its angelology and demonology, was not able to refer to any previous work in this department.[1] A theologian to whom he spoke of his design answered that " one ought not to examine the birth-marks of a genius like the Apostle."

Everling brings forward the passages which speak of Satan, the angels, and the demons, one after another, and adduces parallels from Enoch, the Ascension of Isaiah, the Wisdom of Solomon, the Book of Jubilees, the Testaments of the Twelve Patriarchs, and the Apocalypse of Baruch. His review of the material shows in what a step-motherly fashion it had been treated by previous commentators of all shades of opinion.

In the result it appears that the Pauline statements about angelology and demonology have not sprung from his own imagination, but all have their earlier analogues in the Late-Jewish theology, or at any rate can be understood as inferences from the conceptions there laid down. It further appears that his statements stand in systematic connexion and mutually supplement one another.

In its main lines the Pauline doctrine of the angels shows us the following picture. Spiritual beings who, in accordance with the hierarchic arrangement adopted in

[1] *Die paulinische Angelologie und Dämonologie*, 1888, 126 pp.

Late-Jewish theology, are divided into various classes, played a prominent part at the giving of the law. From that time forward they acted as overseers of the chosen people, and also as the real powers behind the gods of the heathen. By the death and resurrection of Christ their power has been in principle abolished, although it continues to be still in some way exercised upon those who offer sacrifices to idols or submit themselves to the law.

Believers in Christ, however, stand over against them as a class of men who are liberated from their sway, and who possess a wisdom which understands better than their own the great events in which the history of the world is about to close.

These angelic existences feel that their domination is threatened, and fight with all the weapons at their command. It is at their instigation that the attempt is made to corrupt the Gospel by legalism ; all the difficulties which the Apostle encounters, all the corporeal sufferings which he has to bear, are to be attributed to them. It is on their account that women must be veiled when attending the services of the Church, since otherwise they run the risk of becoming the victims of their lust, as of old their mother Eve was seduced by the devil. Most dangerous of all is their skill in deception : Satan can disguise himself as an angel of light.

With the appearance of the Lord begins the decisive struggle which is to lead to the destruction of these powers. They are to be delivered up to judgment, to receive their sentence at the mouth of the saints, whom, until the parousia, they have still the power to harass with cunning and cruelty, though not to destroy.

" In its proper historical surroundings Christianity shows up in its true majesty," said Richard Rothe once. Everling drew from these words, which he placed at the beginning of his book, courage to make a thorough investigation of matters which had previously been timidly avoided because of their strangeness.

How wide-reaching was the significance of his synthetic

study he had hardly realised. His intention was to depict clearly and in vivid colours the imposingly fantastic Late-Jewish background of Pauline theology. The theology of his time took the same view. It accepted the offered gift somewhat constrainedly, but on the whole gratefully enough. If it had the impression that the background as thus restored, while no doubt "interesting," was somewhat too glaring and obtrusive, it remained confident that the "doctrinal system" which it throws into relief is not otherwise affected by it. The appendix-chapter on eschatology grows in size and acquires a certain connectedness. But there seemed no reason to fear that it might grow so vigorously as to overpower those into which the Pauline theology proper is neatly parcelled out.

In reality, however, there was quite sufficient reason for anxiety. Everling had shown that angelology and demonology were, as a matter of fact, component parts of Paul's cosmology. That they consequently also entered into his fundamental conception of redemption was a point which he had not especially emphasised. But the fact was written in giant characters across his work. From the moment when Paul's statements regarding God, the devil, the angels, and the world are apprehended in their organic connexion, it becomes abundantly evident that for him redemption, in its primary and fundamental sense, consists in a deliverance from the powers which have their abode between heaven and earth. It is therefore essentially a future good, dependent on a cosmic event of universal scope.

It at once becomes evident that the investigation of Paulinism must take as its starting-point these ideas as being of the most general character, and endeavour to show how the other statements regarding redemption are derived from them. Theological science was thus forced into the road which it had hitherto sedulously avoided. The deceptive character of the division of Paulinism under *loci*, by which it had long been kept in an unhappy state of subservience to Reformation and modern prejudices, now became apparent. But for all that theology held to the old way and was determined to cast out anyone who set foot upon the new. That is the explanation of the fate which befel Richard Kabisch's "Eschatology of Paul."[1] Kabisch had been considering the plan of a work on the Pauline Ethic, and in doing so had become aware that it was to a large extent conditioned by the eschatological expectations. Thereupon he resolved to begin with a preliminary study of the eschatology.[2]

"Salvation," so runs his argument, is thought of by Paul as "deliverance" from judgment and destruction. "Justification" and "reconciliation" are subservient to this deliverance and do not describe a state of salvation independent of it. The spiritual goods which are characterised by many theologians as the object of the Apostle's wrestling and striving are in reality only the anticipatory first-fruits of the blessedness which the future has in store. This blessedness consists in the believer's being freed at the parousia from the fleshly body in order to put on the heavenly robe of glory. Thus eschatology is the foundation both of the dogmatics and ethics of the Apostle.

Life and death are for him physical conceptions. Spiritual death and spiritual life in the modern religious sense are unknown to him. Even where, as in Rom. vi., he speaks of a dying and rising again which are not accompanied by any change in the outward and visible existence of the individual, he does not mean a spiritual dying and rising again but, inconceivable as it may

---

[1] *Die Eschatologie des Paulus in ihren Zusammenhängen mit dem Gesamtbegriff des Paulinismus* (. . . in its relations with the general conception of Paulinism), 1893, 338 pp. The work is dedicated to Friedrich Spitta. After a historical introduction, the principal passages which come into question are examined. After that the eschatology is developed according to its contents and motives, and in the process its relations with the various doctrines of the Pauline theology come up for discussion.

[2] He did not, unfortunately, follow it up with the work on the Ethics.

appear, a physical occurrence. Everything spiritual goes back to something corporeal. That is true also as regards the ethics. It is not from the consciousness of the " ideal possession of eternal life " that he infers the duty of walking in newness of life, but from the fact that one who shares the death of Christ must also share His resurrection. Both events have reference to the present. It is " a simple logical consequence " that we should walk in accordance with this physical newness of life in order to show that the fleshly, *sarkic*, body has been put off.

The new life of which Paul speaks as a present spirit is therefore based on the " repetition " of Christ's bodily resurrection, which is rendered possible by the *unio mystica* with him. It guarantees to the individual his indestructibility even though the corruptible world, to which his fleshly corporeity belongs, falls a prey to destruction. The believer will then have a part in the new world-substance.

Paul's soul is therefore thrilled with the eager desire for life, shaken with the dread of destruction. His faith, hope, and fear all revolve about one centre—the abolition of corruption and the bestowal of incorruption. His religion is a " will-to-live " in a large elemental sense. He yearns for redemption from the creaturehood which is under the sway of Satan and his powers, and from the body which they hold in thrall. The moment in which the relative positions of the world of spirits and the world of men are to be reversed, and a great final renewal of all things is to be brought in—that moment cannot come quickly enough for him. Therefore he seeks in some way to antedate it.

The future condition of existence is that of " glory." It is anticipated in the present life by the possession of the " Spirit " which belongs essentially to the heavenly light substance.

Thus Kabisch endeavours to explain the Pauline doctrine of the Spirit purely on the ground of the Late-Jewish metaphysic. A super-earthly substance enters into the corporeity of those who in virtue of the *unio mystica* with Christ have entered into the experience of His death and resurrection. It produces in them a new being, and gives them a claim to the future perfected glory, and this while their fleshly existence still continues to the outward eye unaltered.

The great paradoxes of Paulinism are here for the first time clearly pointed out and so described that their real eschatological essence appears.[1] But Kabisch did not succeed in explaining them. In what sense is a " repetition " in the believer of the dying and rising again of Christ possible ? How can it produce a reconstitution of their creaturely being while their fleshly existence continues outwardly as before ? To these questions Kabisch gives no answer.

In the account of the eschatological events and their issue it is shown that the blessings and anticipations referred to by Paul are also present in the Late-Jewish theology. That the Apostle expresses his views about the future world in disconnected fragments, apparently distributed fortuitously through the text, does not show that it was not clear and consistent in his own mind, but exactly the opposite. The eschatological remarks come in so naturally and without appearing to need

---

[1] The eschatological character of the Pauline mysticism is also pointed out by Paul Wernle in his suggestive study *Der Christ und die Sünde bei Paulus* (1897, 138 pp.), but he does not follow out the idea in all its consequences.

A certain recognition of the " physical " character of the doctrine of redemption is also arrived at by Adolf Deissmann. In his study, *Die neutestamentliche Formel " in Christo Jesu"* (1892, 136 pp.) he comes to the conviction that Paul had created the formula on the analogy of a linguistic usage already obtaining in non-biblical Greek, and intended in using it to indicate the relation to Christ as an existence within the pneumatic Christ which was to be locally conceived. He does not, however, think of explaining it from eschatology.

The old psychologising and spiritualising methods are in no way departed from by W. Brandt. In his work, *Die evangelische Geschichte und der Ursprung des Christentums* ("The Gospel History and the Origin of Christianity," 1893, 591 pp.; on Paul, pp. 515-524), he maintains that it was the visions of the disciples which first made Jesus into the Messiah. Paul, he thinks, "in his profound reflexion over his conversion, came to think of this revolution in his life as a dying and rising again of his inner man."

explanation just because this whole set of conceptions was to the Apostle so long familiar and self-explanatory, that he can draw on it whenever he wishes as easily as an educated European uses the multiplication table.

Strangely, however, Kabisch does not succeed in giving a clear and simple picture of the order and relation of the final events presupposed in the letters. He gets confused over the various resurrections and judgments, and finds the sole way of escape in attributing to the Apostle a resurrection of the righteous only, and not a general resurrection in addition. In consequence he is forced to the conclusion that the righteous enter the Kingdom without passing through a judgment, and that what is meant by the judgment is always the destruction of the wicked at the parousia.

That is to make the Apostle contradict not only Jewish apocalyptic, but his own utterances, since it is certain that the Epistles frequently make mention of believers appearing at the judgment.

The difficulties which Kabisch here encounters are significant. They show that it is not possible to understand the Pauline statements simply by the light of the Late-Jewish eschatology. What for the Apostle composed a simple picture remains for the writer who endeavours to describe his apocalyptic full of obscurities and contradictions. It is as if one or two conceptions were lacking which would have enabled him to " get out " his game of patience satisfactorily.

It is true Kabisch has not done everything possible in order to attain clearness. He has neglected to adduce for comparison the eschatology of the Baptist and of Jesus, and to examine how far the Pauline simplification of apocalyptic is here prefigured. He thus falls into the universal but none the less unintelligible error of failing to call the two most important witnesses to the Late-Jewish eschatological expectations. Are they the less so because they belong to the New Testament ? Further, he neglects, as do all the other writers, to consider what are the primary questions which the theory of the events of the End had to answer.

What happens at the parousia to the non-elect? And what to the elect who have not become believers because the Gospel message has not reached them? The ultimate fate of these two classes of men can surely not be the same? Do those who at the parousia do not enter into glory suffer " death " or " destruction " ? What is the relation between these two conceptions?

According to I Cor. xv. 26, death is only to be vanquished at the end of the Messianic kingdom. Is a general resurrection before that conceivable? Does it follow as a consequence of this triumph over death?

Since Kabisch does not raise these and similar questions, he does not find the path which alone can lead to the understanding of the logic of the events of the End. Undoubtedly, in the eschatology of a thinker like Paul, all these problems must have been considered and thought out. They form the implicit presuppositions which guarantee and make clear the inner logic of his scattered and seemingly disconnected statements.

Although he has not explained the paradoxes of the Pauline mysticism, nor succeeded in making clear the ground-plan of his eschatology, Kabisch's book is one of the most striking achievements, not only in the department of Pauline study, but in historical theology as a whole. For the first time since Lüdemann's investigation of the Apostle's doctrine of man, in 1872, the problem of the Pauline doctrine of redemption receives a new formulation.

The two works show a curious analogy. Their authors have a consciousness of the fact that the theology of the Apostle is a living organism, and are preserved by some good genius from splitting it up into Reformation or modern *loci*. They endeavour to grasp the thoughts and connecting links of the doctrine of redemption from a single point of view. Lüdemann makes the " anthropology " his starting-point, Kabisch the eschatology.

Both are led, almost contrary to their intention, to give a general account of Paulinism. Both see in the paradoxical statements about the abolition of the flesh in the union with the death and resurrection of Christ the centre of his doctrine ; both arrive at the result that what is in view is a really physical redemption.

In the explanation of the facts which they agree in observing they diverge widely. Lüdemann claims the Pauline doctrine of redemption as Hellenistic ; Kabisch endeavours to understand it on the basis of Late Judaism. Theological science cast out the innovator and held to the conviction that the Apostle's system of thought was Greek. It was acknowledged that he had made the eschatology of the Apostle intelligible ; but in the attempt to pass from the eschatology to the centre of the Apostle's system of doctrine, contemporary scholarship saw only an extreme onesidedness for which there was no justification in the documents, which deserved neither examination nor refutation, but simply rejection.

On what lines had theology developed and defended the theory of Greek elements in Paulinism ? In the first place, it is to be remarked that in regard to the extent and importance of the influence which is supposed to have been exercised, various groupings are to be observed among the different writers. Pfleiderer, Holsten, Heinrici,[1] Havet, and others see in Paulinism the actual first step in the Hellenisation of Christianity. They assume, as Baur also had taken for granted before them, that the ethical series of ideas, the series dominated by the antithesis of flesh and spirit, is derived from Greek influences.

Schmiedel,[2] in his commentaries, and Harnack [3] express

---

[1] Georg Heinrici, *Auslegung der Korintherbriefe* (1 Cor., 1880, 574 pp. ; 2 Cor., 1887, 606 pp.).

[2] P. W. Schmiedel, " Auslegung der Briefe an die Thessalonicher und Korinther," in Holtzmann's *Handkommentar*, vol. ii. section i. ; 1st ed., 1891 ; 2nd ed., 1892.

[3] *Dogmengeschichte*, 3rd ed., 1894, vol. i. On Paul, pp. 83-95. Friedrich Loofs in his *Dogmengeschichte* (1890, 443 pp.) takes up no definite attitude towards the Pauline problem. Reinhold Seeberg, too (*Dogmengeschichte*, first half, 1895, 332 pp.), does not go into the doctrine of the Apostle.

themselves with more reserve. According to the latter, Hellenism, no doubt, "had its share" in Paul. The Apostle of the Gentiles " prepared the way for the projection of the Gospel upon the Graeco-Roman world of thought," but he never gave to Greek ideas " any influence upon his doctrine of salvation." Lipsius,[1] Bernhard Weiss, and Weizsäcker do not take much account of borrowings from Greek sources, but are concerned to explain Paul from and by himself so far as possible.

It is not so easy as might be supposed to determine the attitude of the various authors towards the problem of the Hellenic influence in Paul. This is partly due to want of accuracy in the terminology. " Hellenistic " is used to mean both Jewish-Hellenistic and Greek in the strict sense. The authors frequently express themselves in such a way that it is not obvious whether they mean the one, or the other, or both together. Attempts to establish an accurate terminology, to confine " Hellenistic " to the meaning " Jewish - Hellenistic," and to use Hellenic for Greek in the full sense, have not succeeded.

But the want of clearness is not wholly to be put down to the account of the language ; it is partly due to the mental attitude of the writers. The problem really includes two questions. First, Was Paul under the influence of Jewish Hellenism ? Secondly, Did Greek thought in itself, apart from the alliance into which it had entered with Judaism, exercise any influence upon his views ? Instead of keeping these questions separate these writers constantly confuse them, and assume that they have proved the existence of Greek ideas in the

[1] R. A. Lipsius, "Auslegung der Briefe an die Galater, Römer und Philipper," in Holtzmann's *Handkommentar*, vol. ii. section i. 1st ed., 1891 ; 2nd ed., 1892. This commentator's position is indicated by the following remarks : " The great antithesis between flesh and spirit gradually forces out the Jewish conceptions one after another, though it is not right to say that Hebrew ideas are driven out by Hellenic ones. When Paul goes outside the circle of Old Testament views he does so in consequence of a deeper ethical grasp of the originally Hebrew antithesis between flesh and spirit, not by a borrowing of Greek ideas."

Apostle's system of doctrine when they have only discussed his relations with Jewish-Hellenism.

Sometimes one actually gets the impression that in this difficult question they intentionally make their discussions a little obscure and inconsistent, and are more concerned to conceal than to reveal their views, in order not to lay themselves open to attack.

The discovery and the grouping of their opinions is therefore associated with difficulties, and can never be carried out in a way entirely free from objection. Fortunately the discussion and decision of the question does not depend on drawing them up in three divisions, each under the banner of its particular view, and so putting them through their facings.

It suffices to note the fact that in the study of the subject from Baur onward the greatly predominating opinion is that Paul was not only influenced by Jewish Hellenism but also derived some of his ideas directly from Greek thought. It is also safe to assert that of all the writers in question—even though some of them take up an attitude of reserve to Pfleiderer's more thoroughgoing views, none of them denies the influence of Jewish Hellenism on Paul. The difference between them consists rather in the fact that some assume in addition to this what may be called " free " Greek influence, while others are sceptical on this point and think that the facts can be explained without this assumption.

It is to be expressly remarked that the latter do not try to arrive at an understanding of the essence of Paul's thought by a different method, but only to clothe the usual explanations in different words. This is the case with Weizsäcker.

The well-known account of Paulinism in his " Apostolic Age "[1] neither offers any new idea nor raises any new problem. Though he is in some respects more cautious than Pfleiderer, because he feels the difficulty of proving Greek influence more strongly than the latter, in other

[1] *Das apostolische Zeitalter*, 1886, pp. 105-151.

respects he is less exacting than Pfleiderer with his logical development of Baur's ideas, since he is content with explanations which do not satisfy Pfleiderer.

That Bernard Weiss in dealing with Pauline theology dispenses with the assumption of Greek influence is due to the fact that his investigation holds strictly to the lines of " Biblical theology," and on principle takes no account of anything beyond the borders of the Canon.

It is interesting to note that both Weiss and Weizsäcker deliberately avoid a discussion of Greek and Hellenistic influence on Paul, and confine themselves to an objective account of Paul's doctrine. Indeed, it may be remarked that in the study of the subject between Baur and Holtzmann the problem is never thoroughly discussed.

The question how far the alleged influences are proved or provable may be held over for the present, and in the first place we may interrogate Holsten, Pfleiderer and their followers as to what their view really means, and what they think they can explain by means of it.

At bottom the question turns on the antithesis of flesh and spirit. In the clearly defined form in which this antithesis presents itself in Paul, it is held that it must be regarded as Greek. This view had been expressed by Lüdemann, who was the first to develop it clearly. Independently of him, Holsten[1] and Pfleiderer brought it into general currency.

It is universally taken for granted that the dualism is derived from Platonism. Whether Paul took it direct from Greek sources or from Jewish Hellenism is not clearly explained. Lüdemann seems to assume the former, Holsten to imply the latter ; Pfleiderer is doubtless to be understood in the sense that both possibilities have to be taken into account, separately and in combination.

The psychological process is differently conceived by

---

[1] It is most clearly developed by Holsten on pp. 37 and 38 of the second part of his *Evangelium des Paulus*, 1896.

Holsten and by Pfleiderer. The former holds that Greek ideas were already in his pre-Christian period present to the mind of the Apostle, who had been in touch with Jewish Hellenism, but they had as yet played no part in his thinking. By his religious experience at the vision of Christ on the Damascus road they were called into activity and helped him to give form to his new knowledge. In this way Holsten thinks it possible to understand Paulinism as both a personal creation of the Apostle and at the same time a product of the influence of Greek ideas. The emphasis lies, however, on the personal creation ; the influence of the Greek ideas is thought of as subsidiary.

For Pfleiderer the process was more largely determined from without. Paul's conversion creates as it were a void in his Jewish consciousness. The thought-forms which he has hitherto used prove incapable of dealing satisfactorily with the implications of his new faith. So the Apostle is driven to have recourse to another system of ideas. He no longer remains indifferent to the ideas which stream in upon him from Jewish Hellenism and Greek thought. They become significant to him ; he allows them to exercise their influence upon him. In this way there arises a remarkable duality in his thought. Pharisaic and Hellenistic trains of ideas form two streams " which in Paulinism meet in one bed without really coalescing." By way of conjecture Pfleiderer several times advances the suggestion that Apollos the Alexandrian may have introduced the Apostle to the Alexandrian Platonism.

Heinrici, again, in his commentaries on the Corinthian Epistles suggests that the Apostle's doctrine is a synthesis of elements taken on the one hand from the Jewish prophets and on the other from Greek thought.[1] Paul, he thinks, reached back beyond Late Judaism to join hands with the ancient prophetism, and similarly rose

[1] Vol. i., 1880 ; vol. ii., 1887. See especially the Introduction and the Epilogue to vol. ii.

superior to Alexandrianism and drew direct from Greek
thought.   In both cases what he seeks is an ethical force.
That he possessed the insight and the power to find this
in the thought of the ancient world and to apply it to the
formation of a Christian system of thought was a great
spiritual achievement, pregnant with consequences for
the future development of Christianity.

One might have expected that these various views
would be worked out in detail.   That is not the case.
In the last resort none of these writers gets beyond the
general and simple assertion that the antithesis of flesh
and spirit is Greek.   But even this is not further explained
by means of parallels from Greek literature.   There is
no attempt to show in what sense Paul's utterances
become more intelligible in the light of these analogies
than they are in themselves.

" The Greek dualism," writes Holsten, " underlies
all the decisive elements of his thought, and makes itself
apparent in a series of individual traits."   Any one
who goes through his work in the expectation of finding
evidence adduced in support of this statement will be
disappointed.   It is as though the author had forgotten
as he went on writing what he had set out to do.

It is also matter for astonishment that no serious
attempt is made to extend the range of the Greek elements
beyond the single antithesis of flesh and spirit.   The
suggestion is no doubt met with that the pessimism,
the longing for death, and the ethical teaching of the
Apostle, belong essentially to the tone of thought prevalent
in the Hellenic world.   But these remain mere *obiter
dicta* which are not worked out in any way.

It is as though these writers one and all had an in-
stinctive feeling that their thesis, so long as it is kept
quite general, has an admirable air of credibility and
admits of being nicely formulated, but that when any
attempt is made to follow it out into detail it yields little
in the way of tangible results.   Paulinism is deceptive.
Its outward appearance is such that the assertion that

here Greek influences have been at work seems the most self-evident possible, but when this has to be shown in detail it leaves the investigator whom it has drawn on by its specious appearance completely in the lurch.

The curious thing is that Holsten, Pfleiderer, and their followers do not venture to formulate the unwelcome admission which may be read between their lines, but keep up the game with one another as if everything was going as well as heart could wish. They overdo their air of unconcern, as though from an uncomfortable sense that they might in the end lose confidence in their assertion, and so find themselves unable to explain how Paul arrived at his dualistic antithesis between flesh and spirit.

For this is what it all ultimately comes to. The assertion of Greek influence is a kind of pillared portico behind which they construct the edifice of Paulinism as they understand it. The style, however, is only maintained as regards the front. What lies behind that is styleless, neither Greek nor Jewish, without plan, without character, without proportion. Those writers who wholly or partially dissent from the assumption of Greek influences carry out the same plan with the same materials, and with the same unconcern as regards the style. The only difference is that they do not conceal it by building a special façade in front of it, whether it be that, like Harnack, they have a fuller sense of the difficulties, or, like Weiss and Weizsäcker, persuade themselves that Paulinism, according to their construction of it, looks sufficiently well as it is.

There is, however, one point on which Pfleiderer and his followers think that they can point to definite results of the influence of Greek ideas. They maintain that the Apostle's eschatological expectations have been transformed by them. This has reference to the passage in 2 Cor. v. 1 ff. in which Paul gives expression to his desire not to be " unclothed " but to be " clothed upon." The natural interpretation which is given by Bernard Weiss and others understands the Apostle as speaking of his eager desire to experience the parousia while still alive in the body, in order to share that transformation in which " what is mortal will be swallowed up by life," and not to have to pass through a time of waiting in an intermediate state of non-being or death.

Pfleiderer in his " Primitive Christianity " does not accept this explanation, but maintains that this passage and two others—Phil. i. 21 f. and iii. 8 f. [1]—imply a departure from the Pharisaic eschatological hope in which the Apostle's thought elsewhere moves. In this later period of his life, represented by 2 Corinthians and Philippians, he turns away—so runs the theory—from the primitive view of an intermediate state of death, followed by a subsequent resurrection, and comes to hold that his soul, immediately after his departure, will pass into the presence of Christ in order to dwell with Him. And Paul is more and more driven to adopt this view in proportion as his life is daily exposed to greater danger, and he has to reckon with the possibility of dying before the parousia takes place. Under the pressure of this inward anxiety, guided by Platonising Alexandrianism, illuminated by the Greek spirit, he creates—we are still following Pfleiderer—a spiritualising hope of future blessedness, which in the sequel becomes of the utmost value to Gentile Christianity by enabling it to reconcile itself to the delay of the parousia.

---

[1] In Phil. i. 21 f. the reference is to an inner struggle which the Apostle experiences. He desires to depart and be with Christ, which, indeed, would be much better, but he knows that to remain in the flesh is more needful for the sake of his churches. From this conviction he draws the confident conclusion that he will remain with them for their progress and joy in the faith.

In Phil. iii. 8 he declares that he has counted all things but loss in order to win Christ and be found in Him, to know Him and the power of His resurrection and the fellowship of His sufferings, to be conformed unto His death, if so be that he might attain (?) to the resurrection of the dead.

Both passages are certainly obscure, and do not to a literal interpretation yield any satisfactory meaning. One feels that the logic of these close-packed assertions is not self-evident, but must somehow depend on presuppositions of which the basis is not here given. It cannot, however, be maintained that the assumption of a spiritualising hope regarding the future makes all clear.

Pfleiderer believes also that he can show the course of the development by which the new conception was arrived at. In 1 Thessalonians, he thinks, the Apostle still rested unquestioningly in that notion of a corporeal resurrection which primitive Christianity shared with Judaism. But in the explanations in 1 Cor. xv. the influence of the Greek ideas becomes observable, while in 2 Corinthians and Philippians it becomes dominant.

This construction of the course of events is defended by Pfleiderer and his followers—Holsten here stands apart—with fanatical energy, as though they wished to make noise enough to distract attention from the fact that they have so very little else to point to in the shape of positive evidence of Greek influence in Paul.

What are the difficulties which are raised by the assumption of Greek ideas in Paul's doctrine ? They are many and various, and they grow greater in proportion as the new element in Paul is more strongly emphasised. Take the problem of explaining the dualism of flesh and spirit. It is assumed that this has been done when it has been declared to be Greek. But in doing so a duality has been introduced into Paul himself which creates many more difficulties than the dualism it was invoked to solve.

The Apostle is made to think Judaically with one-half of his mind and Hellenically with the other, and nevertheless is supposed to be capable of being conceived as a single integral personality. In the writings of Lüdemann and Holsten the difficulty does not yet appear in its full magnitude. They understand by the Jewish element especially the juridical series of ideas referring to the atonement and imputed righteousness. Holsten is, moreover, in a specially favourable position, because in the last resort he ascribes the origin of the system not so much to the influence of Greek ideas as to the inward experience on the Damascus road, which of course eludes analysis. If they are thus referred exclusively to the separate but coexistent juridical and mystical sets of

ideas, a Jewish and a Greek element can at need be
thought of as in some way or other combined in a single
consciousness.

But for Pfleiderer the conception of the Jewish element
has become much more comprehensive and vital, because
he appreciates the significance of the eschatological ideas.
The result of that is to make the opposition which has to
be recognised much more acute. And, nevertheless, it
must continue to be asserted that Paul was unconscious
of the inconsistencies!

If the difficulty could be got over by pointing to an
opposition of which the Apostle was conscious, and which
he had made an effort to reconcile, the position of the
theory would be much more favourable. But for that it
would be a necessary condition that he should somewhere
have expressed the consciousness that he bore two souls
within his breast,[1] and that the marks of compromise
should appear in his work as they do, for example, in
that of Philo. That, however, is not the case. He is
conscious of no opposition, and steps unconcernedly
from the one world into the other, turns back again to
the first, and keeps on doing this over and over again.
Where, according to Pfleiderer's view, he is venturing a
leap over the abyss, he has all the air of putting one foot
calmly before the other on a level road. We must,
therefore, take it to be the case that he had not the
slightest inkling of the opposition.

This conclusion seems to negate psychology and render
a historical comprehension of the Apostle impossible, but
Pfleiderer hardens his heart and boldly accepts it. There
remains, he says, " no alternative but to admit that Paul
kept the two different kinds of conceptions in his consciousness side by side but unrelated, and jumped from
one to the other without being aware of the opposition
between them."

There is, however, a further complication in the

---

[1] An allusion to the passage in *Faust*, " Zwei Seelen wohnen, ach,
in meiner Brust."—TRANSLATOR.

question. Pfleiderer holds that in 2nd Corinthians and Philippians a Greek spiritualising future-hope has displaced the Jewish Pharisaic hope. In the last period of his life, he maintains, the Apostle no longer believes in a corporeal resurrection, but in a presence of the soul with Christ which begins immediately after death.

But the new conception does not in fact displace the old, although it is diametrically opposed to it. Pfleiderer has to admit that Paul, even in the writings of the latest period, advances without misgiving the doctrine of the " awakening of the whole man from the sleep of death," just as if the new doctrine of " the presence with the Lord beginning immediately after death " were not in existence, although it is the outcome of long years of mental struggle.

Pfleiderer, however, is prepared to accept even this portentous fact also, and to go on contentedly believing that Paul lived in a kind of mental twilight which is at once Jewish-eschatological and Greek-spiritualistic. He expresses this euphemistically by speaking of the Pauline eschatology as " hovering between the Pharisaic hope of the here and the Greek hope of the hereafter." The way to a scientific understanding of Paulinism lies, therefore, for Pfleiderer through a *credo quia absurdum*.

By his assertions about 2 Cor. v. 1 ff. he had brought the assumption of Hellenistic ideas in Paul into a dangerous position. Previously when a student of the subject had stated it to be his view that the sharp antithesis of flesh and spirit was Greek, there was no way in which this belief could be countered. If he was, further, convinced that the Apostle's brain was so organised that he could at the same time think consistently along two separate lines, Greek-spiritualistic and Jewish-eschato-logical, without noticing their divergence and without ever mingling the two sets of ideas, a mind accustomed to work by the methods of historical criticism was similarly powerless against views arrived at as if by revelation.

Pfleiderer, however, makes the mistake of referring

to a matter of fact when he asserts that the Apostle's conception of a life after death became Hellenised. Thereupon controversy about the Greek element in Paul rages furiously over 2 Cor. v. 1 ff.—it was only now that controversy had become possible. The simple wording of the passage is against Pfleiderer, for its subject is not the soul's being "at home with Christ," but the Apostle's longing for the parousia. Pfleiderer himself would never have arrived at his exposition had it not been for the laudable desire to produce at last some tangible example of the influence of Greek thought upon the Apostle's ideas.

The point which Pfleiderer raised here was after all only a particular case in relation to the general question whether a Hellenistic influence is to be recognised in the Apostle's conceptions of the final state and the times of the End. It was in this wider aspect that Kabisch dealt with the problem in his work on the Pauline eschatology. His decision is in the negative. The much-discussed "development" of the views of 1 Thessalonians into those of 1 Corinthians xv., and of these again into those of 2 Corinthians and Philippians, is, he maintains, a delusion. The conception of the things of the End is a unity, and remains the same throughout.

To oppose this view Teichmann entered the lists.[1] In his over-confident zeal he plays the part of Polos in Plato's *Gorgias*.

He goes much further than Pfleiderer, and seeks to show that Greek ideas actually superseded the whole Jewish Eschatology of Paul. In consequence of the

---

[1] Ernst Teichmann, *Die paulinischen Vorstellungen von Auferstehung und Gericht und ihre Beziehung zur jüdischen Apokalyptik* (" The Pauline Conceptions of Resurrection and Judgment and their relation to Jewish Apocalyptic"), 1896, 125 pp. Akin to Teichmann's study is that of C. Bruston, " La Vie future d'après St Paul " in the *Revue de Théologie et de Philosophie* (Lausanne), 1894, pp. 506-530. The author maintains that Paul had never really held the conceptions connected with the resurrection of the dead at the parousia, but had always thought " spiritually " and assumed a passing into glory immediately after death. But while in his earlier writings he still used certain expressions borrowed from the " Rabbinic eschatology," later he quite abandoned these.

influx of new thoughts one antinomy after another arises in the Apostle's conception of the things of the End. To trace out and exhibit these in detail is the goal of Teichmann's endeavour.

He arrives at the following conclusions :—In I Thessalonians Paul still assumes that Christians will enter the kingdom of heaven with their *earthly* bodies. Not before I Corinthians xv. does he introduce the idea of a " transformation." He is then led to do so by the development of the Greek doctrine of flesh and spirit. In the second Epistle to the Corinthians he carries out this new conception to its logical issue. " The compromise which he had attempted in I Cor. is abandoned, and the result is that the conception of the resurrection of the dead is set aside." Along with the resurrection of the dead the Apostle also strikes out from his programme of the future the parousia. " For the expectation of the descent of Christ to earth he substitutes the entry of the believer into the heavenly world. A resurrection of the dead, a descent of Christ to earth, was now no longer necessary."

Not only so, but the conception of the judgment is also abolished. In the first place, Paul draws this inference " at least so far as Christians are concerned." That subsequently, in following out his ideas, " he should also arrive at the conception of universal blessedness, can in view of his universalism cause no surprise." " As all men were included in Christ at His resurrection, so all must receive the Spirit, they must all be made alive." The End does not, therefore, mean blessedness for some and destruction for others, but eternal life for all. But since eternal life depends on the possession of the Spirit, it must be assumed that those who are not believers at their death " come to faith in Christ in the period between the parousia and the delivery of all authority into the hands of God, and in consequence of this the Spirit is given to them."

Teichmann professes to have demonstrated the Hellen-

isation of the Pauline eschatology. What he actually
shows is what it would have become if it had really
undergone Greek influence.

Not one of his "results" can be proved from the Apostle's
letters. Where is there a single word to suggest that
the Apostle abandoned the conception of the judgment
and that of predestination to life or to damnation?
Where does he ever speak of universal blessedness?
Where does he hint at the possibility that mankind as a
whole is to be converted to belief in Christ between the
parousia and the delivery of all authority into the hands
of God, and will thereupon receive the Spirit? What
grounds are there for supposing that he gives up the
idea of the parousia as superfluous? In his zeal to discover antinomies and trace developments, Teichmann
forgets to take account of the most elementary facts.
He asserts, for instance, that in 1 Thessalonians those who
arise from the dead enter the kingdom of God in their
earthly bodies. But from the Jewish Apocalyptic and
from the teaching of Jesus it clearly appears that the
resurrection included within itself a transformation of
this creaturely corporeity into a glorified corporeity. It
would not do for Teichmann to remember this. He is
bound, even where he represents the Apostle as still
wholly under the sway of Jewish conceptions, to bring
him into an inconceivable opposition to these in order
that the transformation which is taught in 1 Corinthians
xv.—entirely in accordance with Jewish eschatology—
may be represented as derived from the Greek doctrine
of the Spirit.

Without intending it, he thus supplies the most
brilliant refutation of the theory of the Hellenisation
of the Pauline eschatology. He engaged battle on ground
on which Pfleiderer and his school had incautiously ventured forth in the heat of action, and he has to find by
experience that he is unable to make good a single position.
A Hellenisation of the eschatology is quite impossible
to prove. Kabisch turns out to have been right. The

Apostle holds on this point too vigorous and too clear a language.

But if that be so, the theory that the doctrine of flesh and spirit is Greek is itself most seriously imperilled. Teichmann felt, and therein he was more logical and consistent than the rest, that if there were any Hellenistic ideas in Paulinism they must necessarily have attacked and displaced the Jewish eschatology. Pfleiderer's view that the two could have subsisted side by side without— except in the case of 2 Corinthians v. 1 ff.—influencing and interpenetrating one another is an untenable theoretical hypothesis. From the whole range of the history of thought no analogy could be produced for this harmonious coexistence of two different worlds of thought.

A further difficulty of the theory of the Hellenisation of Paulinism arises from the fact that the Apostle's views have to be more and more spiritualised in proportion as the Greek element is emphasised. Lüdemann, overpowered by the impression of the documents, had expressly characterised the doctrine of redemption which is bound up with the dualism of flesh and spirit as not ethical but physical. Holsten and Pfleiderer do not venture to follow him in that. The Platonism which they seek to discover in Paulinism cannot be brought into connexion with a physical doctrine of redemption, but is thought of as the antithesis of the " crude Jewish ideas." The whole of the mystical teaching about dying and rising again with Christ, about the new creature and the influence of the Spirit, has therefore to be spiritualised.

This brings them into conflict with the natural, literal meaning of the Apostle's statements, in which the materialistic character of his conceptions maintains itself against all the arts of exegesis. The interpretation given by Pfleiderer and his school deprives them of their original meaning to an even greater extent than the modern interpretation in general does.

Most unfortunately for those who seek to spiritualise Paul, his doctrine of the Spirit in particular shows no trace of Greek influence. As though from an apprehension that they might be deprived of one of their most indispensable illusions, for thirty years after Baur the students of Paulinism had neglected to deal with this subject. At last in the year 1888 Gunkel undertook the task.[1] He investigates the influence of the Holy Spirit as conceived by the popular view of the Apostolic age, and according to the doctrine of the Apostle, and is obliged to come to the conclusion that a Greek element in the latter is not to be assumed.

The Apostle, according to Gunkel's exposition, takes over the primitive Christian view and accepts it in all points. His own doctrine merely represents an elevation, a development of what he found already present. He introduces—1 Cor. xii.-xiv.—an ethical judgment and valuation of spiritual gifts, which was new to the Christian community. While the latter had regarded " speaking with tongues " as the highest manifestation of supernatural power, he puts all the *charismata* on a lower footing than love. He gives a further development to the primitive Christian doctrine by attributing to the influence of the Spirit a large number of the characteristics of the Christian life which were not so regarded by the primitive community. Love, joy, peace, long-suffering, gentleness, kindness, faithfulness, meekness, chastity are, according to Gal. v. 22, fruits of His power. He generalises, therefore, in such a way that all Christian willing, feeling, knowledge, hope, and action proceed from the *pneuma*, which for the common view was only thought of in connexion with revelations and miracles.

---

[1] Hermann Gunkel, *Die Wirkungen des Heiligen Geistes nach der populären Anschauung der apostolischen Zeit und nach der Lehre des Apostels Paulus* (" The Manifestations of the Holy Spirit according to the Popular View of the Apostolic Age and according to the Doctrine of the Apostle Paul "), 1888, 110 pp. Shortly before that appeared the purely biblico-theological treatment of it by Johannes Gloël, *Der Heilige Geist in der Heilsverkündigung des Paulus* (" The Holy Spirit in Paul's Preaching of Salvation "), 1888, 402 pp. It keeps entirely to description and does not enter into the question regarding the origin and innermost essence of the Pauline doctrine. Pfleiderer's view is, however, called in question.

There is a further point in which, according to Gunkel, Paul raises to a higher level the view which he took over. By the possession of the Spirit the primitive Church was made certain that the end of the present age was at hand and the new age was about to dawn. For the Apostle the temporal relation becomes an inner one. The Spirit is for him the earnest of the coming kingdom of God. Already in the present he calls into being the future life in believers and gives them the certainty, and to some extent even the reality, of the life which is about to dawn for them.

The Pauline doctrine of the Spirit is therefore simply a development of the primitive Christian doctrine. That it was so long regarded as Greek is due, according to Gunkel, to the fact that scholars never examined it as a whole, but always confined themselves to the discussion of the dualism of spirit and flesh. This prevents the relation of the doctrine to the views of the primitive community, and especially its relation to the doctrine of the future age, from becoming apparent.

One very weighty theoretic objection to the admission of Greek elements in Paulinism is passed over by its defenders in complete silence. If the thoughts developed by the Apostle of the Gentiles had grown up upon the soil of Hellenism, the original apostles and those closely associated with them would certainly have been aware of this and attacked them on that ground. From the records, however, as we have them in the letters, it appears certain that they only reproached him with his attitude towards the law, and found no other point to object to in his teaching. The primitive Christian community at Jerusalem accused him of keeping back something from his churches ; it did not discover anything new and essentially foreign in his thought. In spite of the keenness of the struggle, it was never made a charge against him that he had " heathenised " the Gospel. That shows how completely out of the question the assumption of Greek influences was for his

opponents.   But the fact that his contemporaries discovered nothing of the kind in him forms a strong
presumption against any such theory when brought
forward in later times.

The objection which arises from the side of the history
of dogma tends to the same result.   Those who hold the
theory of Greek elements in Paul must, if they are to be
consistent, assert that he pioneered a path for the Gospel
into the Hellenic world and prepared the way for the
early Greek theology.   And they do so most emphatically.
Pfleiderer explains [1] that the Greek Church - theology
arose by the expulsion from Paulinism of its specifically
Jewish elements, and by the free development of its
" universally intelligible Hellenistic side."   The noble
Platonic idealism had a place in the doctrinal system
of the Apostle of the Gentiles, " and conferred on it its
capacity to win the Graeco-Roman world for Christianity."
" The understanding of Paulinism is therefore a fundamental condition for the understanding of the Early
Church."   And all the adherents of the theory, whatever
their precise shade of opinion, express themselves to the
same effect.

But the history of dogma holds a different language.
It has to record the fact, inconceivable as it may appear,
that on the generations in which Greek dogma was taking
shape Paul exercised no influence whatever.   Even
the external literary influence is very slight.   If one
sets aside the Epistles to the Ephesians and Colossians
it is not even possible to speak of a deutero-Pauline
literature.   The Pastoral Epistles and the second letter
to the Thessalonians profess to be written by the Apostle,
but contain not a single thought which is characteristic
of his teaching.   In the Epistle to the Hebrews, in
I Clement, in the Epistle of Barnabas, in the writings of
Ignatius, in the works of Justin, expressions occur which
show acquaintance with the Epistles of Paul, and may have

[1] *Urchristentum*, 1887.   Similarly Heinrici in his commentary on
2 Corinthians.

been influenced by him in respect to their wording ; but beyond that they show no trace of his conceptions or his spirit.

The remarkable point, therefore, is that the post-Apostolic writers, though they are acquainted with the works of the Apostle of the Gentiles, make no real use of them. His ideas remain foreign, lifeless, so far as they are concerned.

That is also shown by the fact that early Greek Church-theology is quite independent of him. It is concerned with the incarnation and resurrection of Christ and with regeneration ; Paul's speculations deal with the death and resurrection of the Lord, and he never speaks of regeneration. The underlying logic is in the two cases so different that the representatives of Greek theology, even if they wished to do so, could not appeal to the Apostle. No community of thought between him and Justin is to be discovered.

Even Baur had to learn how little Greek theology attached itself to Paul,[1] although he wished to derive it from a compromise between the Pauline and the Petrine Gospel. So long as he is carrying out his theory on the lines of the history of the Church and its literature, the mistake does not become so apparent, because the universalism and freedom from the law which gradually establish themselves are set down as Graeco-Pauline. In treating the history of dogma, however, where he is dealing exclusively with the development of the Greek conception of the Person of Christ and of the redemption effected through Him, he can, as a matter of fact, make nothing of Paul. He hardly mentions him.

What Baur was unwilling to acknowledge to himself, Harnack has irrefutably proved.[2] According to his

[1] F. C. Baur, *Vorlesungen über die christliche Dogmengeschichte* ("Lectures on the History of Dogma"), vol. i. From the apostolic period to the synod of Nicaea, 1865 (edited by Ferdinand Friedrich Baur).

[2] *Dogmengeschichte*, 1885, vol. i. ; 3rd ed., 1894 ; 4th ed., 1909. Wilhelm Karl, too, in his *Beiträge zum Verständnis der soteriologischen Erfahrungen und Spekulationen des Apostels Paulus* ("Contributions to the Understanding of the Soteriological Experiences and Speculations

showing there is no bridge leading from the Pauline
Gospel to the doctrine of the Early Greek Church. The
" history of dogma," strange as it may appear, only
begins after Paul. The forces which are there at work
have not been set in motion by him.

The same result is arrived at by Edwin Hatch in his
work on Hellenism and Christianity.[1] A trained philological scholar possessing great knowledge of and insight
into the late Greek and early Christian literatures, he
endeavours to describe in detail the process by which
Christianity became Hellenised. In doing so he does not
find it necessary to deal with Paul. For the points of
contact which he finds to exist between the two worlds no
examples are to be discovered in the letters of the Apostle
of the Gentiles. Hatch's observations lead him to make
the process of Hellenisation only begin with the second
century.

The history of dogma cannot, therefore, accept the
suggestion that Paul recast the Gospel in the moulds of
Greek thought. The process began later, and of its own
motion. It did not derive its impulse from a single
great personality, but began gradually and on all sides.
It was the Greek popular mind as represented by the
members of the Gentile churches which Hellenised the
Gospel for itself. Men like Ignatius and Justin bring this
work to a provisional completeness by combining the
current ideas into a primitive but in its own fashion
impressively clear and living system, and creating a
connexion between Christology, the conception of redemption and the doctrine of the sacraments ; the

---

of the Apostle Paul," 1899, 116 pp.), does not feel obliged to have
recourse to Greek thought in order to explain the Apostle's doctrine. He
offers a thorough and independent analysis of the system which in many
points is much superior to the ordinary view.

[1] Edwin Hatch, Hibbert Lectures on " The Influence of Greek
Ideas and Usages upon the Christian Church." The work was translated into German by Erwin Preuschen in 1892. Its divisions are :
(i.) Introductory, (ii.) Greek culture, (iii.) Greek and Christian Exegesis,
(iv.) Rhetoric, (v.) Philosophy, (vi.) Ethics, (vii.-ix.) Theology, (x.)
Mysteries, (xi.) Corpus doctrinae, (xii.) The Transformation of the
basis of Christian Unity : Doctrine in the Place of Conduct.

Fourth Evangelist carries this system of doctrine back into the preaching of the historic Jesus. These men received no kind of impulse from Paul. Of the work which he did they make no use. They know it, but it seems as if it were impossible for them to use it.

The recognition of the true state of the case begins when one gets rid of the seemingly so natural but in reality unjustified assumption that the universalism [1] and freedom from the law for which Paul fought his battles, imply a Hellenisation of Christianity and form the Greek element in his doctrine.

Ritschl and Harnack, in opposing this assumption of Baur and his successors, went to the other extreme. They maintained that universalism and freedom from the law were purely practical and separable views, which had, properly speaking, nothing to do with the fundamental ideas of the doctrine of redemption. In this way they succeeded, no doubt, in liberating the history of dogma from the prejudices of the Tübingen school ; but they did less justice to the Apostle's statements than those whom they were attacking, since on every page of his writings he implies an actual connexion between his doctrines and the practical views which he is defending. It is to be noted that Ritschl and Harnack never clearly explain why Paul holds a different view on these points from that of the primitive community.

Truth here appears as the synthesis of a thesis and anti-thesis. Universalism and freedom from the law do in fact belong to the history of dogma, but not in the way Baur thought. And they are in themselves practical views, but at the same time they claim to be logically derived from the system of doctrine. The presuppositions on which they are based have nothing to do with Greek thought ; it was purely by systematically thinking out to its conclusions the primitive Christian doctrine that Paul was led to his theories of the universal

---

[1] *i.e.* as used in this connexion, here and later, the belief in the universal destination of the Gospel, not in universal salvation.

destination of the Gospel and of emancipation from the law.

These are the facts as they lie clearly before us in the letters. But to register them is not to explain them. How, exactly, do these conclusions result from the logic of the primitive Christian belief as rightly worked out in the Apostle's mind? That is the form which the question takes as the next stage, after Baur, Ritschl, and Harnack.

The negative result that the Pauline attitude in regard to these points is not Greek is in any case established. And so too is the other result that the creators of Greek dogma did not take him as their starting-point, and cannot therefore have discovered anything Hellenic in him. They had no consciousness that he had already quarried and shaped the material which they needed for their edifice.

But if they did not recognise in him one who had made a beginning in their direction, it is more than questionable whether modern historical criticism is right in professing to find Greek elements in him. If so, it must be supposed to have a better instinct for what is Hellenic than the men who Hellenised Christianity.

In any case it has no right to talk at large about the significance of Paulinism for Greek Christianity, as though the history of dogma was not there to prove the contrary.

How do the Debit and Credit of the theory stand at this point? For the credit side, it claims that the dualism of flesh and spirit is of Greek origin, but it does not get beyond the general assertion. No serious attempt has been made to demonstrate the existence of Greek conceptions in the particular aspects of the doctrine, and to explain the pessimism, the desire for death, and the ethical teaching of the Apostle as derived from the non-Jewish world of thought. That the Pauline universalism and doctrine of freedom from the law are directly inspired by the Greek spirit it no longer has the right to assert.

In a single instance its defenders venture to point to the influence of Greek religious thought on the Apostle's views. They seek to show that his Jewish, eschatological conception of the future life and his view of the events of the End were in time entirely transformed by it, if not actually cancelled. But the attempt to prove this from the documents has not been successful.

Meanwhile the following difficulties appear. The theory is obliged to assume a dualism between Jewish and Greek elements in Paul, and to assert that on the one hand he never allowed the two systems of thought to coalesce, while on the other he never became conscious of their disparity; it has to attribute to him a capacity for combining contradictions, which allows him to maintain alongside of one another a spiritualistic doctrine of immortality and a crudely materialistic notion of resurrection without becoming aware of their incompatibility; it is logically forced to the conclusion that he set aside the Jewish eschatology, with its conceptions of judgment and condemnation, in favour of a doctrine of universal blessedness, whereas there is in the Epistles not a single hint pointing in this direction; it is forced, in order to make his statements appear " Platonic," so to spiritualise them that the natural sense of the words disappears; it must ignore the proved fact that his doctrine of the spirit, when taken in its full compass and not confined to the antithesis of spirit and flesh, is most naturally explained as a mere development of the primitive Christian view; it must meet the objection— which it never can do—that the original apostles never discovered anything of an essentially foreign, Greek character in Paul's views; it must, when confronted with the history of dogma, bend itself with what grace it may to the admission that Paulinism exercised no influence upon the formation of early Greek theology, and cannot therefore have been felt by the men who were concerned in that process as itself representing a first stage in the Hellenisation of Christianity.

The theory therefore explains nothing, but creates difficulty upon difficulty.

In view of this relation of its assets to its liabilities it would have no alternative but to declare itself bankrupt, had it not astutely refrained from keeping any accounts.

And so far we have considered the mere for and against. Even if the balance had here inclined in favour of the theory, that would not have proved anything. The ideas in question ought not to be considered as Greek until it had been shown that they actually were so. But this would require it to be shown that exactly corresponding ideas were to be found in the preceding or contemporary Greek literature, and that Paul betrayed some kind of acquaintance with this literature. The possibility that it was a mere case of analogy would have to be systematically excluded, so far as that is possible.

But such a method of proof has never been seriously contemplated by the adherents of the theory. In going through their works one is astonished to see how lightly they have treated their task. They have never properly collected the material ; it is much if here and there a point is thoroughly considered.

The assumption of Greek elements in Paulinism appeared something so self-evident, and indeed, if one desired to arrive at any understanding of him, so necessary, that from the first it came forward with an assurance which secured credit for it everywhere without its needing to produce adequate guarantees.

When Lüdemann in the year 1872 worked out clearly the dualism of flesh and spirit, he added, as a thing to be taken for granted, that it was Greek in character. His successors show a similar absence of misgiving.

In order to bring the question once for all to an issue, let us gather up and put to the test, along with the poor fragments of attempted proof, every consideration that can be cited in favour of the assumption of Greek elements in Paulinism.

The Apostle was born and grew up in Tarsus, the

" Athens of Asia Minor " as Ernest Curtius has called it.[1] In his native city, as Heinrici expresses himself, " rhetoric and Stoic philosophy were to be met with in the market-place." [2]

No limits are set to the estimate of what the child of the Diaspora may have absorbed, retained, and laid up in his mind from the intellectual life by which he was surrounded.

But just as large a place might be claimed for the contrary argument, which would lay stress upon the exclusiveness of strictly Jewish circles of the Diaspora in regard to the Greek culture by which they were surrounded.

Neither argument proves anything. A thousand possibilities on the one side do not produce a certainty any more than on the other.

The greater probability, however, is on the side of the assumption of exclusiveness. Although he lived in the middle of Hellenism, it is possible that Paul absorbed no more of it than a Catholic parish priest of the twentieth century does of the critical theology, and knew no more about it than an Evangelical pastor knows of theosophy.

The decision lies solely with his works.

The case is similar as regards the argument from his language. It is inconceivable, so writers like Heinrici and Curtius urge, that a language like Greek could be familiar to a man like Paul without causing a flood of ancient conceptions and ideas to stream in upon him. Heinrici, indeed, is prepared to decide the question on this ground alone, and concludes his exposition of the Corinthian Epistles with a close analysis of their vocabulary. This shows, he thinks, that Greek concepts and expressions far outweigh in number and importance the " specific-ally Christian " and those which show the influence of the Old Testament or the language of the synagogue.

---

[1] *Paulus in Athen.* Collected Essays, vol. ii., 1894, pp. 527-543. In this essay the author seeks to exhibit with some fulness the view, which seems to him self-evident, that the Apostle was filled with the Hellenic spirit.

[2] Preface to his Exposition of 2 Corinthians, 1887.

But in opposition to this, Schmiedel,[1] a not less thorough commentator, expresses himself as follows : " We must be on our guard against concluding too hastily from the predominantly Hellenistic character of Paul's language to a Hellenistic mode of thought. With a language of which one learns colloquially the current use, one does not by any means necessarily assimilate all the thought-forms of which it contains, so to speak, the geological record."

Here too, therefore, one argument is balanced by another.

A fact which seems to carry us a little further is the Apostle's exclusive use of the Greek version of the Old Testament. In a detailed study, of the year 1869, Kautzsch[2] showed that out of eighty-four quotations which occur in the Epistles thirty-four agree exactly with the Septuagint, thirty-six show small deviations, and ten depart from it more widely. Two others show a considerable difference, without, however, throwing doubt upon the author's acquaintance with the wording of the ordinary translation ; two others, again, from Job, differ from it entirely.

This investigation was carried further by Hans Vollmer[3] and brought to a provisional conclusion. According to him the deviations are to be explained by the fact that Paul did not use a single complete recension of the LXX, but had recourse to different editions for different books. In Job he had before him a version which shows affinity with the later Jewish translations. To explain the remaining peculiarities Vollmer brings forward a hypothesis. He is inclined to assume that the Apostle used Greek Scriptural anthologies in which

---

[1] Holtzmann's *Handkommentar*, 2nd ed. The Epistles to the Corinthians, p. 92.

[2] Emil Friedrich Kautzsch, *De veteris Testamenti locis a Paulo Apostolo allegatis*, 1869, 110 pp.

[3] Hans Vollmer, *Die alttestamentlichen Zitate bei Paulus . . . nebst einem Anhang über das Verhältnis des Apostels zu Philo*, 1895, 103 pp. (" The Old Testament quotations in Paul . . . with an Appendix on the Apostle's relation to Philo ").

separate passages were collocated, or freely combined with one another. In such collections—their existence is not demonstrable — various versions were, he thinks, used promiscuously. Perhaps the passage quoted as Scripture in 1 Corinthians ii. 9, which is not traceable in the Old Testament,—" As it is written, what eye hath not seen, nor ear heard, neither hath it entered into the heart of man, hath God prepared for them that love Him "—may be derived from an anthology of this kind.

It is in any case certain that the Apostle always makes use of Greek translations ; and it is further certain that he argues from peculiarities in their wording which for one who knew Hebrew, as he also certainly did, must have been recognisable as mistranslations. He therefore goes so far as to ignore the original.

Nevertheless these facts do not warrant us in drawing conclusions of a too far-reaching character. If he wrote in Greek at all he could not do otherwise than use the Greek translations which were familiar to him, and in the synagogues of the Diaspora were regarded as " authentic," as the Vulgate is for the Latin Church according to the decrees of the Council of Trent. That being so, it was out of the question for him, in making quotations, to introduce renderings of his own from the original.

In all historical cases of theological bilingualism the same fact is to be observed. Scripture is never " personally " translated, but always cited in accordance with a recognised version.[1]

That Paul should turn to account the mistakes of the version need not, in view of his exegetical principles, cause us any surprise. Whether he forces his thought

---

[1] The author has had occasion to observe this in Alsatian theologians and in himself. One who is equally familiar with French and German will never, either in preaching or in conversation, give his own version of Biblical passages, but will without exception keep to the traditional form in the language which he is using, and this even where he would be capable of giving a more exact rendering. And in preaching he will turn to account the peculiarities of the wording of the version, if it lends itself to his thought, and will even perhaps use an argument which goes against the sense of the original, which he is supposed to be acquainted with—exactly as Paul does.

directly upon the original, or gets it expressed by the
Greek version, comes to much the same thing. The fact
that he adopts the errors of the LXX and finds his account
in them does not make him a Greek. It only shows that
he belongs to the Jewish Diaspora. But does this imply
that he has his place in the Jewish-Hellenistic movement?

This assumption is often taken as so self-evident that
any examination of it appears superfluous. The defenders of the theory of Greek influence in Paul, therefore,
feel themselves dispensed from this duty and act accordingly.

Even those who, like Harnack, do not admit a more far-
reaching direct influence of Greek ideas upon the Apostle,
do not feel any doubt about his relations with Jewish
Hellenism.

But the sceptics of the self-evident, with whom science
can never dispense, must dare to be tactless enough to
put the question here also, " What is really proved? "
As we have to do with a characteristic literature which
lies before us with some measure of completeness, the
verdict cannot be difficult to arrive at.

Pfleiderer and his followers had all along asserted that
Paul in his eschatology and anthropology showed dependence on the Wisdom of Solomon, which doubtless
dates from the first century before Christ. Others
denied this. In an essay which appeared in 1892, Grafe
sought to sift the material and decide the question.[1]

As " crucial " instances for the relationship he thinks
the following may safely be taken : Romans ix. shows
affinity with Wisdom xii. and xv. in regard to what
is said of the Divine omnipotence and mercy ; in their
references to heathen idolatry the two authors coincide
in a remarkable way ; the views regarding the relationship
of body and soul which are implied in 2 Cor. v. 1 ff. find
a parallel in Wisd. ix. 15, where there is a reference to

---

[1] Eduard Grafe, *Das Verhältnis der paulinischen Schriften zur
Sapientia Salamonis* (" The Relation of the Pauline Writings to the
Book of Wisdom "), in the Theological Essays dedicated to Carl von
Weizsäcker on his seventieth birthday, 1892, pp. 251-286.

the earthly tabernacle which weighs down the thinking soul. The facts do not, according to Grafe, justify the conclusion that Paul is dependent on the pseudo-Salamonian Book of Wisdom, but he does regard it as having been made highly probable that the Apostle knew and had read the book.

It is not a clear " yes " that one hears in Grafe's essay. When it is quoted, however, by writers on Paulinism it gets a push towards the positive side which makes it say exactly what Grafe did not venture to assert.

Scarcely more productive is Vollmer's cast of his net into the works of Philo.[1] He thinks that, in view of the affinities pointed out by him, " the acquaintance of the Apostle with the works of the Alexandrian writer will have become less improbable to others besides himself."

But that is not the point at all. That Paul, a scholar of the Diaspora, would have been aware of the existence of so important a work as the Wisdom of Solomon, and would not have been wholly ignorant of its contents, is really self-evident. And is it likely that none of the writings of his older Alexandrian contemporary—Philo died probably about the beginning of the forties—would have come to his knowledge ? On the contrary, the most probable assumption is that he was acquainted with the whole of the earlier and later Hellenistic literature. Whether this can be more or less clearly proved by certain real or supposed parallels does not really matter.

The important point is that he does not use the ideas which are here offered to him. Jewish-Hellenistic theology is so characteristic a product that it can never

---

[1] *Über das Verhältnis des Apostels zu Philo*, an appendix to his work on *Die alttestamentlichen Zitate bei Paulus*, 1895, pp. 80-98. See also Carl Siegfried, *Philo von Alexandria als Ausleger des alten Testaments an sich selbst und nach seinem geschichtlichen Einfluss betrachtet* ("Philo of Alexandria as an Expositor of Scripture, considered both in Himself and in Regard to his Historical Influence"), 1875, 418 pp. In pp. 304-10 thoughts and passages are cited from Paul which are supposed to show affinity with Philo. The resemblance is, however, so general and colourless that it cannot be considered as proving anything. The author quotes the passages without drawing any conclusion.

be overlooked even where it is only a subsidiary element. But in Paul no trace of it can be shown. Its problems, its speculations regarding the Logos, Spirit, and Wisdom, its ethics, do not interest him ; he makes no use of its theories. On the other hand he is concerned with eschatology and with the person of the Messiah, which for it seem to have no existence.

The characteristic mark of Jewish Hellenism is that it brings the different ideas into an external juxtaposition without effecting their interpenetration. Whether it is a question of philosophical or other writings, of problems of ethics, or of the doctrine of God and the Divine administration of the world, the Greek element always shows up plainly in contrast with the Jewish, and can be clearly recognised as Platonic or Stoic. It is a case of mosaic work, better or worse executed as the case may be.

Any one who proposes to show that Paul was influenced by Jewish Hellenism ought, therefore, to begin by recognising that the union of the two worlds of thought which is supposed to have taken place in him is of an entirely different order from that found in other cases, inasmuch as a real synthesis is effected, and the problems involved are such as do not elsewhere occupy Jewish Hellenism, while on the other hand those which interest it are here left out of account. How much is left then by way of a common element ?

Paul's attitude towards Jewish Hellenism is one of indifference. From his letters, written as they are in Greek, we should never learn that in his time there existed a literature in which the old Jewish theology, using the universal language of the period, entered into discussion with Greek philosophy and religious thought, and formed an external combination with them.

All the proofs which are offered of his acquaintance with this literature only serve to render more unintelligible the fact that he is not in the slightest degree influenced by it.

The phrase-making by which theologians of the post-

Baur period disposed of Paul's independence in regard to Jewish Hellenism—so far as they became aware of it—is quite inept. Heinrici, as we have seen, maintained that he had risen superior to Alexandrianism.

It is to be remarked that the theoretic question whether he was never influenced by this movement, or whether the influence only ceased when he became a Christian, must remain open. In the latter case he must have put off along with what was specifically Jewish also what was Jewish-Hellenistic. It would then belong to the things which, according to Philippians, were formerly gain to him, but which now he counted dross, and had cast aside in order to gain Christ.

This latter view is inherently possible if one is prepared to take literally what the Apostle says about that radical breach with the past to which we can apply no standard of measurement, and which we are unable to conceive. But the other alternative—that he had never been influenced by it—is the more probable.

Practically both come to much the same thing. We know only the Christian Paul, and we find it to be a fact that in his letters no specifically Jewish-Hellenistic conceptions are to be found.

The " self-evident " is therefore once more negated by the facts.

We may call attention to a curious parallel. *A priori* the assumption might appear justified that the Apostle of the Gentiles would have taken from Jewish Hellenism material wherewith to Hellenise Christianity. In reality he did not do so. *A priori* it was to be expected that the creators of Greek theology would have taken from Paulinism material for the construction of their doctrines. In reality they did not do so. The three points which it seemed would allow themselves to be joined to form a triangle, lie, in reality, in different planes, belong to different systems, and have no natural relation to one another.

If Paul stands solitary, without receiving or exercising

influence, between these two factors in which Greek characteristics are manifest, it follows that he does not exhibit their common element. If he did not adopt Platonism and Stoicism in the convenient compound which Jewish Hellenism had mixed ready for him, it is antecedently little probable that he made use of the uncompounded substances in the form in which they are to be met with in Greek life and literature.

What are the possibilities of direct influences which have to be taken into account ?

It is to be remarked that Paul never gives the slightest hint that he is making use of something which is familiar to and valued by the Greeks in his churches. The Acts of the Apostles indeed pictures him as a preacher who in the Areopagus at Athens takes as his starting-point an inscription upon an altar, and quotes from the Greek poet Aratus the pantheistic saying that men are of the Divine race (Acts xvii. 28). But for this Paul, the author of Acts, must take all responsibility.[1]

The Apostle of the Gentiles who is made known to us by the Epistles wears a different aspect. In this sense he never became a Greek to the Greeks. We find in him no trace of any high estimation of heathenism and its thought. It is for him idolatry, nothing less nor more. His estimate is purely negative.

He can therefore hardly have intentionally taken over anything from Greek thought. It is possible, however, that he did so unconsciously.

The most obvious suggestion is to assume that this was the case in regard to ethics. What he says in Rom. ii. about conscience, which in the heathen takes the place of the law, might be based on ideas derived from Greek rationalism. But on close examination what we find here is not so much a positive valuation of natural ethical feeling, but rather the creation for dialectic purposes of something to serve as an analogue to the law. Paul's

---

[1] Ernst Curtius in the essay cited above defends the historicity of Acts xvii.

purpose is to prove that Jew and Greek are alike delivered over to sin ; consequently the position in the two cases, if an injustice on the part of God is not to be suggested, must be made as similar as possible.

The assumption of Greek ideas here is rendered improbable by the fact that Paul's ethic as a whole is not to be explained as Hellenic. Neither Gass nor Ziegler in their works on the history of Christian ethics have ventured any attempt in this direction.[1] In general the Pauline ethic has been little treated by the students of Paulinism of the post-Baur period. The only monograph dedicated to the subject took a form that was purely biblico-theological and without interest.[2] It is interesting to note that Kabisch, when he planned to work up the ethical material, found it necessary first to deal with the eschatology. That does not suggest the presence of Hellenic influences.

It has also been maintained with a certain confidence that the pessimism of the Apostle is Greek, because it recalls the view of the world which we find in the writings of Seneca and Epictetus.

Seneca was his contemporary. That the Apostle knew the works of this writer is not held by any one to be proved.[3] Epictetus worked at the end of the first century,

---

[1] W. Gass, *Geschichte der christlichen Ethik*, 1881, vol. i. 457 pp. On Paul, pp. 34-38. Theobald Ziegler, *Geschichte der christlichen Ethik*, 1886, 593 pp. On Paul, pp. 72-90.

[2] Fr. Th. L. Ernesti, *Die Ethik des Apostels Paulus*, 1868, 155 pp. ; 3rd ed., 1880.

[3] The Christian character of Seneca's thought was remarked as early as Tertullian, who in *de Anima*, xx., when he quotes a phrase from him, describes him as " saepe noster." Augustine and Jerome know of a correspondence between Seneca and the Apostle. From the literature we may mention the following works : Amédée Fleury, *Saint Paul et Sénèque. Recherches sur les rapports du philosophe avec l'apôtre et sur l'infiltration du Christianisme naissant à travers le paganisme*, 2 vols., 1853, 404 and 383 pp. Seneca is supposed to have drawn on Paul. At the end of the second part the correspondence between them is printed. The work is uncritical in character. Johann Kreyher, *L. Annaeus Seneca und seine Beziehungen zur Urchristentum* (. . . and his relations with early Christianity), 1887, 198 pp. Seneca is supposed to have had some relations with Christianity in Rome even before the Apostle's coming, and thenceforward to have entered into a close relationship with him. Charles Aubertin, *Étude*

was himself acquainted with Christianity, and was doubtless influenced by it, even if unconsciously.[1]

All that could come into question, even as a possibility, is that the Apostle might have adopted the same generally current ideas of his period which are expressed by these two writers.

The expressions which are quoted as parallel have only an external resemblance. They are not really analogous. The roots from which the pessimism springs are entirely different in the two cases.

In the philosophers it is purely a result of reflection on the conditions of the present life. Existence appears to Seneca a burden which one may at any time cast off— by suicide. For Paul the present world is evil because it is sinful, lies under the dominion of the angel powers, and is subject to corruption. He judges it, not in itself, but with reference to a new and perfect world which is soon to appear. The idea of suicide does not enter into his thoughts, indeed he dreads that he might be released from the present earthly existence before the parousia occurs.

Seneca's religion is resignation, Paul's is enthusiasm. The two may show verbal similarities, but no affinity of thought exists between them.

Further, the anthropology and psychology[2] of the Apostle are claimed as Greek. Pfleiderer lays great stress upon this point. He does not, however, offer any proofs.

What Paul has to say about man rests in the first place

---

critique sur les rapports supposés entre Sénèque et St Paul, 1857, 442 pp. All connexion between Seneca and Christianity is denied. In the work of Michael Baumgarten, Lucius Annaeus Seneca und das Christentum (1895, 368 pp.) no connexion between Seneca and Paul is admitted.

[1] See Theodor Zahn, Der Stoiker Epiktet und sein Verhältnis zum Christentum. A Rectorial address at Erlangen, 1894, 27 pp. The lecture offers proof that in spite of many resemblances of expression and in spite of his acquaintance with Christianity, the teaching of Epictetus contains nothing which really connects it with the new religion.

Inconceivable as it may appear, even the Meditations of Marcus Aurelius—of the second half of the second century—have been sometimes cited to prove the Greek character of Paul's religious thought.

[2] Theodor Simon, Die Psychologie des Apostels Paulus, 1897, 118 pp. A leisurely analysis of the material.

on ordinary observation and is of a self-evident character. The special features of his view which go beyond this are to be explained from eschatology and not from Greek thought. Anthropology and psychology, in the development which he gives them, have reference not to the natural man but to the redeemed man, who is risen with Christ, endowed with the Spirit, and already living in a supernatural condition. His conception of the natural condition of man is determined by reference to its actual abolition, and therefore has quite a different orientation from that of the Greek thinkers.

How do matters stand in regard to the assertion that his system contains Platonic elements?

What comes into question is not Platonism proper, but the religious modification and popularisation of it which later on, in the third century, came to completion in Neo-Platonism. What this philosophy has in common with Paul is the general desire for deliverance from corporeity. When it is more closely considered, however, characteristic differences appear.

Platonism as a religion has to do with the deliverance of the soul from its imprisonment in the body, Paul looks for the deliverance of the whole human personality. In the one case the antithesis is between soul and body, in the other between the supernatural body and the corruptible flesh. Platonic religious feeling desires release from all corporeity, what Paul hopes for is a different kind of materiality. He believes in a resurrection, Platonism in mere immortality. For him the fate of the individual is so bound up with cosmical, eschatological events that the new state of existence can only result from a cosmical revolution. Platonism knows nothing of a temporally conditioned redemption of this kind, but represents it as coming to pass immediately after death.

The materialism which is implicate in eschatology thus opposes a barrier to the Platonising of Paul's religious thought.

For his conception of spirit a parallel might be sought

in Stoicism, which teaches that a spiritual substance proceeding from God permeates the universe, including corporeal organisms, and manifests itself in man as the rational soul. Common to this philosophy and to Paul is the material conception of spirit. But the differences which it exhibits are of such a kind that there can be no question of the Apostle's dependence upon it. In the Stoic philosophy the spirit is identical with the rational soul; in Paul it is introduced as something new alongside of the latter, and ends by displacing it.

According to the philosophic conception it is active in the world from all eternity; according to the doctrine of the Apostle it first appears in the times of the End, and is only bestowed upon a limited section of mankind. The one view is a pantheistic monism, the other is a theistic dualism.

The Book of Wisdom and Philo are Stoic in their mode of thought, but Paul is not so.

It is inconceivable how the Stoic *heimarmene* can have been brought into connexion with the Pauline doctrine of predestination.

The philosophic conception of fate thinks of the world-process as an unbroken chain of cause and effect in which also the actions of living beings have their place. Pauline foreordination is a pure will-act of God, non-rational and non-moral, and has to do with the ultimate issues of existence, not with the vicissitudes of life. To see a connexion between the two doctrines of predestination is as unjustifiable as it would be to identify the cosmic conflagration of the Pauline eschatology with that of the Stoic theory.

Paulinism has, in general, a different spirit from that of the Stoa. Its author is moved by the fear of death and corruption and yearns for a new being. To the Stoic such ideas are, as " passion," contemptible. He reckons —as you may read in Marcus Aurelius—with the present world as the only one there is, and with the present life as the only one which he has to live.

Whatever views and conceptions are brought up for comparison, the result is always the same—that Paulinism and Greek thought have nothing, absolutely nothing, in common. Their relation is not even one of indifference, they stand opposed to one another. Had the Apostle been influenced by Hellenism in any shape or form, he could never have conceived his system in the way he did.

Nevertheless it is possible to understand how theology came to class his doctrine as Greek. The mysticism which enters into it bears a certain analogy to that which springs from Greek religious thought and feeling. Since Judaism, itself guileless of any mysticism, produced nothing of the kind, could not create out of itself anything of the kind, the only possible alternative seemed to be to explain it as due to Greek influences, and to explain the essential character of Paulinism in accordance with this hypothesis.

But this road leads to an impasse. In this way it is possible only to misinterpret the mysticism of the Apostle, not to understand it. Critical theology is confronted with the at first apparently inexplicable fact that there has arisen on Jewish-Christian soil a system of thought which externally has all the air of being a twin formation to that of Greek religious mysticism, but inwardly has nothing whatever to do with it.

The actual result of the study of Paulinism in the post-Baur period is therefore wholly negative, and it must become evident that it is so the moment any one attempts to substitute references and proofs for mere assertions. This the scholars of that period avoided doing ; they were prevented from making the attempt by the scientific instinct of self-preservation.

IV

H. J. HOLTZMANN

Heinrich Julius Holtzmann. Lehrbuch der Neutestamentlichen Theologie. 1897. Vol. ii., 532 pp. On Paulinism, 1-225.
William Wrede. Über Aufgabe und Methode der sogenannten Neutestamentlichen Theologie. (1897.) (On the Task and the Method of the so-called New Testament Theology.)

HOLTZMANN'S " New Testament Theology " was eagerly awaited on all sides. It was hoped that it would bring about a clearing of ideas such as had been produced in regard to questions of criticism by his " Introduction."

In the new work the author follows the method which seemed to him to have proved its usefulness in the former work. He lets every writer who has dealt with the subject have his say at the appropriate place, even though he runs the risk of not making his own opinion distinctly heard amid the strife of tongues.[1]

While in the " Introduction " the advantages of the method predominate, in the "Theology" its disadvantages are conspicuous. The former work dealt with a series of questions which are already formulated and can be answered with a clear yes or no. There is therefore some sense in taking the suffrages of the writers, living and dead. It leads up to a verdict which in a certain sense

---

[1] In connexion with the following remarks on questions of principle, see also W. Wrede, *Über Aufgabe und Methode der sogenannten Neutestamentlichen Theologie*, 1897, 80 pp.

The essay discusses the plan and arrangement of Holtzmann's work. On p. 32 Wrede remarks: "The treatment is far too much influenced by the desire to include all kinds of opinions from other writers. To a large extent my objections have to do with these methodological questions."

may be given forth as the objective result of the period under survey.

But when it is a question of the content of thought in the New Testament writings, the questions are not so clearly formulated. The continual hearing of opinions has not the same usefulness. On the contrary, the account of the subject becomes thereby only the more complicated and confused.

Here the result of Holtzmann's threading his own view through those of others is that neither the one nor the other stands out with any clearness. Undoubtedly, he knows the literature as no one else does, and has absorbed into his own mind and worked up all that it has to offer. But a clear view of the state of opinion is what he does not in the end succeed in conveying, since he intentionally omits to give a sketch and criticism of the works cited and contents himself with quoting passages from them.

This unfortunate atomistic method does not even allow the individual problems to appear as clearly as would be desirable. In the post-Baur study of Paulinism, various questions had come up one after another which, taken together, form its fundamental problem. The most natural procedure for one who intended to make critical use of the work already done would have been to sketch these in their full extent and then formulate them more exactly and exhibit their inner connexions.

But that is not the kind of treatment which Holtzmann aims at. He has the feeling that this is no longer necessary, and agrees with contemporary scholars in thinking that assured results have been attained in sufficient number to admit of a simple positive account of the system. In accordance with this view he feels it to be his duty to act as a critical camera, focussing the views on his lens and combining them into a picture.

One looks, therefore, in vain in his work for a fundamental statement and solution of the problems. They are mentioned where they happen to come up, and are there discussed in a fragmentary fashion. In addition to this the author's peculiarly subtle and delicately shaded method of exposition has to be reckoned with. Any one who is not familiar with it runs the risk of passing too lightly over these passages and failing to appreciate the significance which Holtzmann himself attaches to his remarks. What he intends to give is a General-staff map of the results of investigation. The heights and hollows are not shown as such, but represented by curves which are only later to be carried out in relief.

Holtzmann does not stand above the post-Baur study of the subject, but within it.

That is immediately evident from the fact that, speaking generally, he takes as the plan of his exposition the scheme, partially " Reformation," partially modern, which the head of the Tübingen school had used in his theology and left as a legacy to his successors. After dealing with the doctrine of man, law, sin, and corruption, he describes the " revolution " (conversion). Then follow Christology, the work of redemption, and the Divine righteousness. The close is formed by the chapters on the " ethical " material, the " mystical," and " eschatology."

The difficulties and errors which are involved in this division of the subject have not been escaped by Holtzmann any more than by others. At every step it is evident how unnatural is an arrangement of the material which leaves out of account the connexions inherent in the system. How much art is expended on breaking off the thread at a given moment, in order to take it up again in a later chapter ! How many unnecessarily fragmentary representations ! How many annoying repetitions ! How many references forward and backward ! Thus, for example, what Paul has to say of redemption is not developed connectedly but split up among a number of chapters. And the same thing happens with regard to the doctrine of the death and resurrection of Christ.

The division which he has taken over leads Holtzmann

to regard the Pauline teaching on redemption from the stand-point of the Reformation doctrine. Involuntarily he always thinks either of the individual man, or humanity, instead of the entity always present to the mind of the Apostle, the group of the elect of the last generation, who have been subjected to the influence of the death and resurrection of Christ. He quotes the acute remark of Schmiedel [1] that " the men who had sought (and found) in Jesus before His death forgiveness and peace of soul " are left out of account by the Apostle, but he does not go further into the problem which this suggests. The temporally conditioned character and the general point of view of the Pauline doctrine of redemption is, owing to the faulty division, practically overlooked.

Not less unfortunate is the plan on which the significance of the death and resurrection of Christ is dealt with. Having begun with the psychology of the natural man, and the man in process of conversion, Holtzmann endeavours to explain the facts by which redemption is conditioned from this starting-point. He asks what these two events, the death and resurrection, signified for Jesus and what they signified for the believers. Jesus is thereby proved to be the Messiah ; the influence upon believers is described on the basis of the classical passages in the Epistles. But the inner connexion of the two effects is not clear, and it is equally unintelligible wherein the saving significance of the death and resurrection consists.

Holtzmann is, in fact, still straitly confined to the Reformation and modern point of view, from which the twofold event of the death and resurrection of Christ is considered by itself, in isolation, and an attempt is made to get behind it by psychologising, and thus to discover how, according to the statements of Paul, it produced a complete change in God and man, and effected justification and reconciliation. This attempt overlooks the fact that on the Apostle's view it is primarily a cosmic

[1] Holtzmann, p. III.

event which alters the condition of the whole creation and introduces a new Age, and that everything else is only a consequence of this fundamental effect.

As Holtzmann, like his predecessors, has thus omitted to consider the most fundamental aspect of redemption as conceived by Paul, he is not concerned to trace out the most general conception of the effect of the death and resurrection of Jesus Christ. That is as much as to say that he, like the rest, is condemned to a mere descriptive treatment, using Pauline phraseology, and is practically unable to give any explanation.

This unfortunate result becomes apparent in regard to the question of the Law. He is unable to make it in any way intelligible how Paul was necessarily led, as a matter of reasoning, to the conviction that it was no longer valid. In the last resort he can only appeal to the unique character of the vision on the Damascus road. He assumes that this " brought to an issue in the zealous Pharisee not only a theoretic, but also an ethical crisis, terminating that painful condition of inner division which Paul pictures out of his own inmost consciousness when he speaks of the experiences which are associated with subjection to the law." " Previously," he continues, " the Pharisee had anxiously sought to conceal from himself, or to argue away, the fact that the law was impossible of fulfilment, and was therefore no way of salvation, but rather the contrary. There now rose upon this melancholy scene, strewn with the shattered fragments of attempts to gain righteousness, a new light streaming from the Christ, whom the legalists had delivered to death, whereas His being raised again by God guaranteed the actual presence of another way of salvation. Not only did his former legal service appear to him a life of sin, his Pharisaic rabbinism as foolishness, his attack upon the Messianic community as enmity to God, but even in his inmost being a crisis had taken place in consequence of which a tension, under which he had hitherto groaned, had suddenly been relaxed."

How do we know that Paul when he was still a persecutor of the Christians was suffering inward distress
from his experiences of the powerlessness of the law?
How did the vision of Christ bring about the resolution
of this tension? How, exactly, did it reveal a way of
salvation by which the abolition of the law was implied?

In themselves the vision of Christ, and the law, have
nothing to do with one another. What Paul received
in that moment was the conviction of the Messiahship
of Jesus. While other believers were content simply
to adopt this conviction, he proceeds to draw from it
in some way or other the conclusion that the law was
henceforth invalidated. Whether he did that at the
moment or only later, we do not know. What is certain
is only that he does draw this conclusion, though it is not
contemplated either in the thoughts of Jesus or in those
of the primitive community.

How he came to draw it is not explained by Holtzmann,
any more than by the scholars of the post-Baur period
generally. The assumption that the Apostle experienced
along with the vision an ethical crisis which set him free
from the law, is a psychological hypothesis about which
the letters have nothing whatever to say. It does not
even prove what it professes to prove. Exactly how the
abrogation of the law is supposed to be effected by the
death and resurrection of Christ is not obvious. It is to
be remarked, too, that Paul always treats the abolition
of the law as a logical conclusion, not as a psychological
experience.

In other connexions, too, Holtzmann often has recourse
to Holsten's expedient of taking what is unintelligible
in the Apostle's statements as accounted for by the
Damascus vision.

In this way the doctrine of the " new creature " is
made to go back to a " personal experience," and " a
perception so keen as to be apprehended by the senses,
of the destruction of the law of sin in the members."

" The complex of new ethical powers, motives, duties,

and aims . . . which formed itself in him has as its centre
the risen Christ who had appeared to him in that moment
as light, to be henceforth the vital centre and the guiding
star of his individual life. . . . Hence the ' new creation.'
It is a simple generalisation and application of this personal
experience to cover all analogous cases, since now all
baptized persons appear as, on the negative side, dead to
sin, on the positive side as walking in a ' newness of life '
corresponding to the resurrection."

So Holtzmann. Paul, however, never speaks of his
theory of the new creature as if he were expressing by it
the generalisation and objectivation of an inner experience, but represents it as being logically and actually
involved in the death and resurrection of the Lord for
those who believe in him, and regards his own renewal
as only a special case of the general law which operates
in all the believing elect.

That is just the characteristic and unintelligible thing
about Paulinism, that its creator does not seem to have
the faintest consciousness of holding up his personal
experiences as something to be imitated, but presents his
whole system as something that immediately and objectively grows out of the facts, something which can be
examined by the higher, but in its own way logical
understanding from which " gnosis " is derived.

To treat his Damascus " experience " as a source of
theoretic knowledge, as is done by modern theology, in
order to be dispensed from rendering any account to
ordinary or philosophic thought, would have been out of
the question for an unsophisticated mind such as his, and
indeed for the mental attitude of antiquity in general.

Of Paul's objective statements Holtzmann always,
in order to be able to interpret them, makes something
subjective.

This error in method—which he shares with scholars
of the post-Baur period generally—runs through the
whole of his undertaking.

He frequently takes occasion to point to the element of

" gnosis " in the Apostle's doctrine. At bottom, however, he is afraid that his doctrine may be too much considered as an intellectual construction. For that reason he provides a special section on " the religious character of the doctrine." " Paul's world of thought," he there tells us, " is, to put it in a word, not merely a product of intellection, it is antecedently to that a product of experience also ; in this it differs fundamentally from any of the artificially excogitated gospels of Gnosticism proper. . . . The first condition for any understanding of Paulinism is that we should not obscure the volcanic character of its origin by any method which implies the gradual addition of one grain of sand to another. The whole system of doctrine means nothing more nor less than the way in which the Apostle objectified to himself the fundamental decisive experience of his life and theoretically explained its presuppositions and consequences. The doctrine fits the experience with a theory."

How, then, does Holtzmann know that Paul is not after all a Gnostic pure and simple ? The whole character of his system makes him appear so. He himself claims to be one,[1] and is quite unaware that his doctrine is nothing more than the form given by the constructive imagination to a personal experience.

He knows no distinction between " gnostic " and " religious." What is religious is for him gnostic, and what is gnostic, religious. Any one who strictly distinguishes the two in him is modernising.

His mission to the Gentiles and his universalism are also, according to Holtzmann, to be explained directly from the vision at his conversion. The Christ who has won through to triumph by way of death, so Holtzmann explains, implies for the Apostle the purification of the Messianic idea from all the carnal elements which in Judaism still cling to it. In the exalted Christ he sees

---

[1] Cf. 2 Cor. xi. 6, where Paul speaks of himself as " inexpert in speech, but not in knowledge " ($\tau \hat{\eta}$ $\gamma \nu \dot{\omega} \sigma \epsilon \iota$). See also 1 Cor. i. 5, viii. 1 ; Phil. i. 9, etc. " Gnostic " is used above in the general sense of one who lays stress on theoretic religious knowledge.—TRANSLATOR.

also the head of the Church gathered out from both Jews and Gentiles.

How, exactly, does the vision at the conversion carry with it the elimination of the carnal elements which in Judaism cleave to the Messianic idea? Paul, it is true, sees a glorified Person; but the Jewish Son-of-Man Messiah also belongs to the supernatural world. Further, universalism is provided for in the eschatology of Late Judaism, and in that preached by Jesus, since it is assumed that among those elected to the Kingdom of God others will be revealed who do not belong to the people of Israel. Universalism is therefore involved in the Jewish conception of the Messiah. Whereas, however, Late Judaism and Jesus only represent it as realised in the coming supernatural Age, Paul antedates it and affirms that distinctions are already abolished in consequence of the death and resurrection of Jesus, and infers from this the justification and the duty of preaching to the heathen. The problem has therefore nothing to do with the " purification of the Messianic idea," and consists simply in the fact that the Apostle assumes this universalism to be already applicable to the present natural era, just as he also asserts that believers are already in a condition of resurrection life.

Holtzmann is not much concerned to show the connexion of the Pauline statements with Jewish theology and eschatology in order to arrive in this way at a new formulation of the problems. In fact he clearly betrays the tendency to make as little use as possible of eschatology in explaining the Pauline system of doctrine.

Kabisch's work is in the highest degree distasteful to him. He refers to it only occasionally, and with reserve. It is true he cannot avoid acknowledging that, " with all the exaggerations, monstrosities, and inconsistencies which may be pointed out " in its emphasising of the physical character of the conceptions and ideas associated with the dualism of flesh and spirit, the work embodies a sound idea. But he never so much as mentions that this

insistance on the " physical " is ultimately due to the
fact that all the conceptions and ideas are traced back to
eschatology. Any one who is not already acquainted
with Kabisch's fundamental idea will not learn it from
Holtzmann.

True to the Baur and post-Baur tradition, Holtzmann postpones the chapter on eschatology to the
end. That this arrangement does not contribute to a
satisfactory treatment of the ethics is not surprising.
The eschatological roots of the conception of predestination discussed in this chapter, or of the designation of
believers as " saints " are hardly visible. That the most
general ethical maxims of the Apostle are conditioned by
the expectation of the nearness of the parousia, and that
the ethical implications of the mystical dying and rising
again with Christ have also in the last resort an eschatological orientation, is never fairly recognised. Holtzmann finds himself, therefore, rather helpless when
he has to deal with points in which the eschatological
character of Paul's ethic comes most clearly to light.
In the directions given in 1 Corinthians vii. about married
and unmarried persons, about marrying or remaining
single, he finds a certain " hesitation." In a quite general
way, he is willing to assume that " the so closely bounded
view of the future explains why in this and other departments there was no complete development of the ethics."

This halting estimate of the ethical significance of
eschatology shows that Holtzmann regards the Pauline
ethical teaching from the modern point of view.

He is bound to take this course with regard to eschatology because he agrees with Pfleiderer and the rest in
admitting a comprehensive influence of Greek ideas upon
Paul, and is well aware that a man cannot serve two
masters.

Even in the Apostle's doctrine of man he finds a
Hellenistic factor alongside of the Jewish, and asserts
that the " emphasis rests on the former." Wherever
reference is made to the antithesis of flesh and spirit

he thinks that the influence of the Greek element is manifest. By regarding sin as implicate in the empirical nature of man " Paul abandons in principle the ultimate basis of the Jewish philosophy and ethic."

Greek, or to speak more precisely, Alexandrian, is the metaphysical background of his conception of Christ. According to Holtzmann, Paul never really goes back expressly to Daniel or the Apocalyptic Messiah. His own special view grew up, Holtzmann thinks, out of speculations allied to those of Philo about the two accounts of the creation and the heavenly and earthly Adam. The primary point for him is " the metaphysical hypothesis of the two classes of mankind " which stand opposed to each other as the " psychic " and the " pneumatic " creation.

That the " subjective," ethical interpretation of the work of redemption is based on Hellenistic ideas is for Holtzmann self-evident. It is not less certain for him that the idea of predestination is " borrowed " from the Book of Wisdom, and consequently " in one of the most conspicuous points of the Pauline world of thought its Hellenistic origin " must be regarded as proved. That the idea of predestination is inherent in eschatology, and that Jesus Himself makes use of it, is not taken into account.

The doctrine of baptism " comes to base itself entirely on the Hellenistic side of Paul's theology." In general, he transformed the two sacred ceremonies of primitive Christianity after the analogy of the Greek mystery-cults, and thus " opened up for the early Catholic Church a way " into which it was forced by the natural progress of events.

Holtzmann sees in Paul's system of thought the first, but at the same time a far-reaching Hellenisation of Christianity. The Apostle, so runs his verdict, " by bringing Hellenistic forms of thought to bear for the first time upon Christian conceptions, prepared the way for the passing over of the latter from the Semitic to the Hellenic world, and beyond this again to the modern world."

The influx of Greek ideas is thought of, as by Pfleiderer, as coming through the intermediary channel of Jewish Hellenism. The question whether any literary relationship to the latter can be detected in Paul is dismissed in a few lines. Holtzmann admits that " no tangible influence " of Philo's writings is to be recognised. He is, however, of opinion that Grafe has proved " with all the greater certainty " the Apostle's dependence on the Alexandrian Book of Wisdom.

Instead of giving a regular proof he confines himself, as his predecessors had done, entirely to general considerations, which he sums up in the following sentences : " In any case Paul was by birth and parentage a son of the Diaspora, and from his youth up breathed at any rate at times a Greek atmosphere. His letters show, in regard to vocabulary and rhetoric, sometimes even as regards tone of feeling and mental attitude, not a few surprising affinities with Greek thought. Some kind of communication from this side, and that not merely occasional or accidental, one must certainly assume. The only question which remains is in regard to the extent and intensity of this Hellenistic, or even it may be Hellenic, admixture, which became amalgamated with his Jewish scholasticism. This is certainly the point on which depend all the problems which Pauline study is called on at the present day to face. . . ."

With this the matter is disposed of—on the third page of the work ! Gunkel's and Kabisch's arguments to show that the doctrine of the Spirit is intelligible apart from Greek influences, are left out of account ; that Hatch in his " Influence of Greek Ideas " had nothing to say about any Hellenisation of the Gospel on the part of Paul is not mentioned. On the contrary there follows a profession of faith in Pfleiderer's doctrine that Paul in the course of his career even advanced to the Hellenisation of his eschatology. Holtzmann cheerfully and courageously defends this theory to its ultimate consequences, and holds that in Paul's dread of being found unclothed

(2 Cor. v. 3) his national mode of feeling and a Greek mode of thought " are combined in a fashion which no one would have dreamed of inventing."

The usually so cautious scholar goes in this case unhesitatingly forward. The difficulties which arise out of the assumed collocation and opposition of Jewish and Greek ideas fascinate instead of alarming him.

Here, as in some other points, Holtzmann betrays Kantian tendencies and instincts, and is inclined to exhibit the problems as antinomies. Paul's system of teaching, as it had shaped itself in the course of the study of the subject since Baur, appears to him a unique formation, since in it are combined two worlds of thought and two different sets of religious ideas which are supposed to hold each other in equipoise and mutually interpenetrate one another. He takes it to be his task to lay bare this remarkable construction in its minutest details, and to show how the most diverse thoughts sometimes conflict, sometimes stand in a state of tension, sometimes mutually limit, and sometimes supplement each other. If he succeeds in making clear the position and relation of the various strata of thought, the system, he believes, will become intelligible.

This idea runs through his whole treatment of the subject, and gives him courage to take over all the contradictions and compromises which scholars from Baur onwards have discovered, and even to add new ones in addition. He is especially interested in the questions regarding the juridical and ethical sets of ideas, the relation of the " popular " missionary preaching to the " system of doctrine," the antithesis between " theory " and " practice " in the ethics, and the inconsistencies of the eschatology.

In these discussions there is much penetrating observation. The picture, however, does not become clearer, but rather more confused.

His predecessors had done their best in their treatment of the subject to conceal its fragmentary character, and

when all was said and done had been content to put in
the foreground only a few leading ideas, which could be
brought under a single point of view. They worked with
perspective, light and shade. Holtzmann brings all the
detail into one line and places it under the same illumina-
tion. The fact that the system becomes in this way
much more complicated than it had already been made by
the scholarship of the period awakes in him no misgivings,
but increases his confidence, since he sees in it one of
those offences which needs must come.

Even the objection that so complicated a system of
doctrine could not have been understood in primitive
Christian times does not alarm him. He anticipates it by
declaring that the actual contemporaries and adherents
of the Apostle could neither understand nor imitate him,
even if they had wished to do so. How, indeed, could
they possibly have done so ! The whole of Paulinism is a
" systematisation of the Christ-vision " and a " generalisation " of that which the Apostle had experienced in his
own soul, and consequently ascribed to all who walk in
the same way as an experience which they must necessarily undergo. " What this man with his unique
spiritual endowment had experienced, felt, and thought
amid influences and surroundings which could only once
have arisen, could never be exactly in the same way
experienced, felt, and thought by any other man."

Holtzmann, therefore, like Harnack, accepts the saying
that no one ever understood Paul, with the sole exception of Marcion . . . who misunderstood him ! It is
not enough for him to regard the system, as had been
usual among scholars since Baur, as a personal creation of
the Apostle ; he goes the whole way with Holsten in
maintaining that the personal creation was nothing else
than the interpretation of a unique personal experience.

But that is to admit that no connecting links between
Paulinism and primitive Christianity can be discovered ;
and does not that really imply an abandonment of all
attempt to explain the Apostle's doctrine ? Is it under-

stood at all if it is not understood in relation to primitive Christianity ?

What right has any one to assert that it was unintelligible to his contemporaries ? Paul confidently ascribes to them an understanding of it. And how are we to explain the success which is evidenced by the establishment of the Pauline churches and the victorious struggle for freedom from the law ? Can the least understood of all early Christians have exercised the greatest influence ? These fundamental questions are not asked by Holtzmann. His confidence in the results already attained left no room for them.

What he aimed at he has successfully accomplished. He has worked up into one great symphony the themes and *motifs* of the Pauline scholarship of the post-Baur period, a symphony such as he alone, at once critic and artist, could have written. Even one who does not allow himself to be carried away by it will again and again take up the score with its subtle counterpoint and skilful instrumentation, and always find in it new beauties.

Never was Holtzmann so impressive—this was to be observed even in his lectures—as in his treatment of Paulinism. Here he could grip his hearers, because he wished to do so—he who usually showed a certain dread of allowing the feeling, the enthusiasm, which glowed in him, to become perceptible when he was dealing with matters of scholarship. The system as modelled by him lives because he has breathed his own life into it. But it is not historic.

He thinks to sift out and preserve what is of permanent value in the heritage left by Baur and his pupils, of whom he was proud to count himself spiritually one. In reality he leads up to a declaration of bankruptcy, and that especially in the powerful closing chapter entitled " Retrospect and Prospect."

Here he endeavours forcibly to combine into one whole the results of Pfleiderer, Holsten, and Harnack.

From Pfleiderer he takes over the view of the wide-

reaching Greek influence in Paulinism, and from Holsten
he takes the theory that the system had its birth in the
unique experience of the vision of Christ on the way to
Damascus.

Now these two views might at need be combined,
though it is not quite easy to show—and this difficulty is
constantly coming to light in Holtzmann — how what
is in one aspect a purely subjective experience, never
exactly to be repeated by any other, appears in another
aspect, by a kind of miracle, as Greek religious thought,
and thus becomes universally intelligible.

But into this synthesis Holtzmann tries to introduce
in addition Harnack's recognition that Paulinism had no
part in the formation of early Greek theology.

Now Holsten and Harnack again, on their part, might
be combined. The Pauline teaching, if it is referred
to a unique personal experience, might well remain for the
Apostle's contemporaries and successors a book with seven
seals.

But Pfleiderer and Holsten and Harnack cannot all be
brought together. If Paulinism was largely Greek, it
must have had some influence. How is it conceivable
that Greeks should not have recognised and understood
the Greek spirit ? The triumvirate planned by Holtzmann cannot, therefore, be brought to pass, even if Holtzmann is regarded as the connecting-link between Harnack
and Pfleiderer. In defiance of all the facts of the history
of dogma the last-named must assert an influence of the
Pauline system upon the growth of Greek dogma, since
he sees in Paul the first step in the Hellenisation of
Christianity.

Any one who shares his premises must also draw his
conclusions, and Holtzmann is not bold enough to do
that. He agrees with him in asserting the Hellenic
character of Pauline doctrine, in other respects he bows
to the facts of the history of dogma. But this means
that, however he may wrap it up in qualifying clauses,
he is asserting the impossible, namely, that Christianity

as Hellenised by Paul remained uninteresting and unintelligible to the Greeks.

The edifice which he constructs, therefore, breaks down
from within, even though he may be able for a time to
maintain it in outward appearance intact.

Thus there met in this universal critical spirit, which
examined all things and desired to do justice to all,
Baur and the history of dogma which took its rise from
Ritschl and was opposed to Baur, and held a new settle-
ment of accounts. Once more it was made manifest
that the question of Paul's relation to primitive Christianity on the one hand, to early Greek dogma on the other,
had not been solved, and that his teaching therefore had
not been understood.

V

CRITICAL QUESTIONS AND HYPOTHESES

Edward Evanson. The Dissonance of the four generally received Evangelists. (1792.)

Bruno Bauer. Kritik der Apostelgeschichte (1850). Kritik der paulinischen Briefe (Galatians, 1850; 1 Corinthians, 1851; remaining Epistles, 1852). Christus und die Cäsaren. Der Ursprung des Christentums aus dem römischen Griechentum (1877). (Christ and the Caesars. How Christianity arose out of the Graeco-Roman Civilisation.)

Albert Kalthoff. Die Entstehung des Christentums. 1904. (E.T. by J. McCabe, The Rise of Christianity, 1907.)

Allard Pierson. De Bergrede en andere synoptische Fragmenten. (The Sermon on the Mount and other Synoptic Fragments.) 1878.

A. Pierson and S. A. Naber. Verisimilia. 1886.

A. D. Loman. Quaestiones Paulinae. (Theol. Tijdschrift, 1882; 1883; 1886—written in Dutch.)

Rudolf Steck. Der Galaterbrief. 1888.

W. C. van Manen. Paulus, 3 vols. Vol. i. deals with the Acts of the Apostles (1890); vol. ii. with the Epistle to the Romans (1891); vol. iii. with the Epistles to the Corinthians (1896). The criticism of the Epistle to the Romans has been translated into German under the title " Die Unechtheit des Römerbriefs," by G. Schläger. 1906.

M. Friedländer. Das Judentum in der vorchristlichen griechischen Welt. (Judaism in the pre-Christian Greek World.) 1897.

J. Friedrich (Maehliss). Die Unechtheit des Galaterbriefs. (The Spuriousness of the Epistle to the Galatians.) 1891.

J. H. Scholten. Historisch-kritische Bijdragen. (Contributions to Historical Criticism.) 1882.

G. Heinrici. Die Forschungen über die paulinischen Briefe; ihr gegenwärtiger Stand und ihre Aufgaben. (The Critical Study of the Pauline Letters; its Present Position, and the Tasks which await it.) 1886.

J. M. S. Baljon. Exegetisch-kritische Verhandeling over den Brief van Paulus aan de Galatiërs. (Exegetic and Critical Essay on the Epistle of Paul to the Galatians.) 1889.

Wilhelm Brückner. Die chronologische Reihenfolge, in welcher die Briefe des Neuen Testaments verfasst sind. (The Chronological Order in which the Epistles of the New Testament were written.) 1890.

Carl Clemen. Die Chronologie der paulinischen Briefe. 1893. Die Einheitlichkeit der paulinischen Briefe. (The Integrity of the Pauline Epistles.) 1894. Paulus, 2 vols., 1904.

Christian Hermann Weisse. Philosophische Dogmatik (3 vols., 1855 ; 1860 ; 1862). Beiträge zur Kritik der paulinischen Briefe. (Contributions to the Criticism of the Pauline Epistles.) Brought out by Sulze in 1867.

J. M. S. Baljon. De Text der Breven van Paulus. 1884.

Daniel Völter. Die Composition der paulinischen Hauptbriefe. (The Composition of the chief Pauline Epistles.) 1890. Paulus und seine Briefe. 1905.

Friedrich Spitta. Untersuchung über den Brief des Paulus an die Römer. (Examination of the Epistle of Paul to the Romans—in his work, Zur Geschichte und Literatur des Urchristentums, vol. iii., 1st half, 1901.)

THOSE critics who reject the Pauline letters as a whole profess to have derived the impulse thereto from Ferdinand Christian Baur, to be his true because logically consistent disciples, and to bear the same relation to him as Schopenhauer did to Kant. This profession, which has always filled the " legitimate " Tübingen school with indignation, is in many points well founded.

Baur's criticism was occupied with the *Corpus Paulinum* which remained after the exclusion of the Pastoral epistles. In the ten remaining Epistles, which show a large degree of inner homogeneity, he professed to discover differences on the basis of which some were to be assigned to the Apostle, others to the school which took its rise from him.

Once the rights of such a criticism are admitted, nothing can prevent it from working itself out to its limit, and seeking to explain all the Epistles as products of a school which went under Paul's name.

The Tübingen master held that the Epistles to the Corinthians and that to the Ephesians could not both be from the same hand. But the differences between the former and the Epistle to the Galatians are in their own way scarcely less great, if one considers that the violent controversy about the law with which the latter is filled is never mentioned in the others.

The letters to the Romans and to the Galatians, on the other hand, deal partly with the same subjects, since they both treat of sin, law, and justification by faith. Nevertheless they are far from coinciding. For all their agreement in fundamental views they show remarkable differences in detail. Is it, if this line of argument be followed, after all so indubitably certain that the four main epistles are from the same pen ?

Is it certain that they are by Paul ? Strictly examined, Baur's assumption that they are so rests only on tradition, which in respect of the other letters he impugns. Has he then the right to rely on it so confidently as regards the main epistles ? In conformity with his own principles he ought to have felt himself obliged to exercise " positive criticism " here also, and would only have had the right to regard them as Pauline after it had been proved that they really belong to primitive Christian times and have the historical Apostle of the Gentiles as their author.

The assumption of the genuineness of the four main epistles is by no means so self-evident as it may seem to us in our simplicity. The Acts of the Apostles know nothing of any literary activity of Paul. It is only from Clement of Rome, Ignatius, and the Gnostics that we first hear of his Epistles. Justin and the remainder of early Christian literature are silent in regard to his writings. Supposing that the first Epistle of Clement does not belong to the first century, the earliest evidence for the Epistles comes from the second century. If the Ignatian letters are not genuine, Marcion, about the middle of the second century, is the first witness to an actual *Corpus paulinum* !

For any one who has to defend the ordinary view, the position is very far from being favourable. So far as outward evidence goes it is hardly more difficult to defend the theory that the letters originated in an inner circle of Gnosticism and were gradually given out under the name of Paul.

Moreover, Baur made larger concessions than he realised to the opinion which jeopardised his position, when he maintained that Paulinism represents a Hellenisation of the Gospel.

Is it probable that a single individual belonging to the primitive Christian community, immediately after the death of Jesus, by himself achieved this result ? Historical analogy is uniformly in favour of the view that developments of that kind have a gradual beginning, and are only accomplished in the course of two or three generations. It would therefore be inherently much more probable that Paulinism should be the work of a school which sought to reconcile Christianity with Hellenism. In any case a writer who regards it as Greek ought to face the difficulty of explaining it as at the same time belonging to primitive Christianity, and ought not to regard this hypothesis as self-evident, but as standing in need of proof.

These theoretic considerations regarding the basis of the views of Baur and his successors are so obvious that they were bound to come up sooner or later. The fact was that in one particular point the Tübingen master had held back from unprejudiced criticism and had foisted upon critical science the traditional belief. In doing so he had obeyed an instinct of caution. Those who proceeded further along the path of questioning and investigation arrived, some with satisfaction and some with dismay, at the result of declaring all the epistles to be spurious.

It was Bruno Bauer who about the middle of the nineteenth century opened the ball with his criticism of the Pauline letters.[1]

---

[1] *Die Apostelgeschichte*, 1850, 143 pp. Acts, it is argued, is a work of " free reflexion " in which various hands have had a part.

Kritik der paulinischen Briefe, part i., The Origin of Galatians (1850, 74 pp.) ; part ii., The Origin of 1 Corinthians (1851, 76 pp.) ; part iii., 2 Corinthians, Romans, the Pastoral Epistles, Thessalonians,

This work is not on the same level as his criticism of the Gospels.[1] The objections which have to be brought against F. C. Baur's views are not clearly developed nor completely stated. In what sense Paulinism is to be considered the work of a school with Greek sympathies within Christianity is not explained.

In addition to this, Bruno Bauer complicates his task by regarding not merely the doctrine of the Apostle of the Gentiles, but Christianity in general, as a creation of the Greek mind. It was not, however, until twenty-five years after the appearance of his criticism of the Pauline letters that he attempted to prove this in the confused work on " Christ and the Caesars." [2]

It was not Palestine, according to his thesis, but Rome and Alexandria which cradled Christianity. Palestine merely supplied the background for the picture which the first Evangelist undertook to create of the beginnings of a movement which really originated with Seneca and

---

Ephesians, Colossians, and Philippians (1852, 129 pp.). The greater part of the epistles were not written until after Acts. Certainly Galatians is later. 1 Corinthians is earlier than Acts, and is doubtless drawn from common sources.

The first to venture an attack on one of the main Epistles was Edward Evanson, *The Dissonance of the four generally received Evangelists, and the evidence of their respective authenticity examined* (translated into Dutch, 1796), who holds Romans, as well as Hebrews, Colossians, and Ephesians, to be spurious. Further information regarding this, as it seems, rather rare book would be desirable. Whether any great critical importance is to be attached to it remains questionable. [Evanson (1731–1805), a Cambridge graduate, vicar of Tewkesbury, adopted Unitarian views, and resigned his living in 1778. His grounds for rejecting Romans are, the difficulty about the existence of a church at Rome prior to Paul's visit, the number of greetings in chapter xvi., and supposed references to the destruction of Jerusalem in xi. 12, 15, 21, 22. The treatment of the Epistles is much slighter than that of the Gospels, where he shows some insight into the difficulties of what is now known as the Synoptic problem. The *Dissonance* made some stir, and was answered by Joseph Priestley in *Letters to a Young Man*, 1792-93, and by T. Falconer, Bampton Lecture, 1810.— TRANSLATOR.]

[1] See A. Schweitzer, *Von Reimarus zu Wrede*, pp. 137-159 (Eng. trans., *The Quest of the Historical Jesus*, pp. 137-160).

[2] *Christus und die Cäsaren*, 1877, 387 pp. What the diffusely told story of the Roman court has to do with the origin of Christianity has certainly never been quite clear to any reader. In attempting to describe its contents one is never quite certain whether the author's meaning has been rightly represented.

his adherents. Whether there ever was a Jesus or a Paul may be left an open question. It is in any case certain that the one did not utter the sayings which the Gospels put into his mouth, and that the other is not to be regarded as the author of the letters.

The Christian " community " arose among the oppressed, the slaves and Jews, of the great city. They formed associations and fostered in one another a yearning for the End of the Age, developed the Platonico-Stoic thoughts of Seneca into the sayings of the Sermon on the Mount, and invented for themselves their hero, Christ. The spirit of the new creation came from the West ; its framework was furnished by Judaism.

Judaism brought with it a tendency towards legalism. In the Flavian period the Greek ethical philosophy struck up an alliance with the law. This movement was opposed by the freedom-loving Gnosis. In the last years of Hadrian and the first half of the reign of Marcus Aurelius matters came to an issue. So far as the struggle took a literary form we have the evidences of it in the Pauline letters and the Acts of the Apostles. Galatians is the last of the letters, issued at the crisis of the struggle, and was directed against Acts, which appeared at the same time.

" The figure of this champion of a universal Church and freedom from the law of ordinances " must have been already known to the Church. What was new was the association with his name of an epistolary literature, the production of which occupied a series of earnest and able men for some forty years.

In the Acts of the Apostles Paul is co-ordinated with or subordinated to Peter, the representative of the Judaeo-Roman hierarchic tendency. That reflects the issue of the struggle. The freedom-loving party was defeated ; in the last quarter of the second century Catholicism became supreme in the Church.

No attention was paid to Bauer, and in part he himself was responsible for the neglect. The bitterness and the carelessness of his writing, the contradictions in which he becomes involved, the fantastic imagination which he allows to run riot, made it impossible for the few who read him to regard him seriously.

Nevertheless, in detached observations, and in some of the incidental ideas, he displays a critical acumen which has something great about it.

After dismissing him with a few sharp words, the Tübingen school and their successors enjoyed a respite of thirty years, so far as radical scepticism was concerned. At the end of that time Bauer reappeared, like a *Nero Redivivus*, in peaceful Holland.[1]

In a critical introduction to his study of the Sermon on the Mount, Allard Pierson examined the earliest witnesses for the existence of Christianity, and in doing so threw out the question whether the historicity of the main Pauline epistles was so completely raised above all doubt that they could be treated with perfect confidence as archives from the earliest period of the new faith.[2]

In the year 1886 he published, in association with the philological scholar, Samuel Adrian Naber, the *Verisimilia*. The book was not adapted to make a deep impression. It was too much the ingenious essay for that.

The two friends combined their efforts in order to show New Testament exegetes how much they had left unexplained in the Epistles to the Thessalonians, Galatians, Corinthians, and Romans, and how many problems, incoherencies, and contradictions appear when one reads these writings with an open mind.[3]

---

[1] A spiritual descendant of Bauer's who writes on popular lines is Albert Kalthoff (*Die Entstehung des Christentums*, 1904, 155 pp.). But neither as regards the problem nor its solution has he contributed anything to Pauline scholarship.

[2] Allard Pierson, *De Bergrede en andere synoptische Fragmenten*, 1878, 260 pp.; on Paul, 98-112. With his doubt of the Epistles the author associates a doubt of the Gospels, and asks whether Christianity as they represent it can have been founded by a historical Jesus.

[3] A. Pierson and S. A. Naber, *Verisimilia. Laceram conditionem Novi Testamenti exemplis illustrarunt et ab origine repetierunt*, 1886, 295 pp. The work gives a running analysis of the letters in the course of which very interesting questions are thrown out. Why is nothing

But instead of making a thorough examination of the problems and laboriously arguing the case with the other students of Paulinism, the authors at once proceed to suggest what appears to them a possible solution.   They claim to have discovered that the inconsistencies are due in the main to the presence of two strata of thought which have been worked together.   The one is of a sharply anti-Jewish character ; the other consists of milder and more conciliatory ideas.

If it be assumed, so runs their argument, that Christianity was in its real origin a Jewish sect which had liberal ideas in regard to the law and directed its expectation towards the Messiah, the antinomian sections of the Epistles represent documents of that period.

The present form of the letters is due to the fact that a later " Churchman "—the authors call him *Paulus episcopus*, and think that he may have served as model for the Paul of Acts—worked into them the second, milder set of ideas.

At the time when Pierson and Naber launched this hypothesis, A. D. Loman had just finished the series of " Quaestiones Paulinae " which he threw out in the *Theo-*

---

said about the earthly life of Jesus ?   Why is no trace of the influence of this Paul's thought to be found in history ?   Do the various characteristics and actions of his which are recorded show us a character which is at all intelligible ?

The authors assume that the Jewish movement which led up to " Christianity " at first had only to do with the Messianic belief in general.   Only later, through the blending of Greek myths with Isaiah liii., did the belief arise that the expected Messiah had already come and had passed through death and resurrection.

The analysis of the Pauline Epistles is followed by essays upon the Paul of Acts and some chapters on the Fourth Gospel.   The close is formed by an essay on the gradual origin of the conception of Christ in the New Testament.

The theory that Christianity developed out of an already existing Jewish movement is maintained also by M. Friedländer in his popular and unimportant work, *Das Judentum in der vorchristlichen griechischen Welt*, a contribution towards explaining the origin of Christianity (1897, 74 pp.).   The opposition between a conservative and a freer tendency as regards the law, which appear in the primitive Church, are here held to have appeared previously in the Judaism from which Christianity originated.

logisch Tijdschrift of 1882–1886.[1] The battle began in earnest.

Loman confines himself to dealing with the external arguments, and only proposes to examine how far the assumption that these letters were written by the Apostle in primitive Christian times can or cannot be proved from the early witnesses. His decision is negative.

But his calmly written yet wonderfully living study shook two other thinkers out of their security, and compelled them to carry on the work of destruction to a further point.

Steck[2] and van Manen[3] undertook the task of supplementing the external arguments, of presenting the internal arguments by means of an analysis of the letters, and of offering a detailed hypothesis regarding the origin of the Pauline literature.

[1] A. D. Loman, "Quaestiones Paulinae," *Theol. Tijdschrift*, 1882, pp. 141-185, 302-328, 452-487 ; 1883, pp. 14-51. 1886, 42-113 (Dutch). In the prologue he tells us about the first impression which Bauer's criticism of the Pauline epistles made upon him : " With an *Apage Satana !* I took leave of this antipathetic critic, firmly resolved to take no further notice of him." The order followed is to treat first the relation of Acts to Galatians, then to discuss the " necessary proofs " of the genuineness of this work, while the witnesses from the literature, and the history of the Canon, are examined later, in the second part, 1886.

[2] Rudolf Steck, *Der Galaterbrief nach seiner Echtheit untersucht nebst kritischen Bemerkungen zu den paulinischen Hauptbriefen* (" The Epistle to the Galatians examined with Reference to its Genuineness, with critical Remarks on the main Pauline Epistles "), 1888, 386 pp. The examination of Galatians goes only as far as p. 151 ; the remaining chapters deal with the order of the main Epistles, the relation of Paul to the Gospels, the quotations from the Old Testament found in the Epistles, the affinities with Philo and Seneca, the marks of later authorship, the external evidences from the New Testament and from early Christian literature. In conclusion, a hypothesis of the origin and development of Paulinism is sketched. The author tells in the preface the story of his conversion to the Dutch heresy. At first he dissented from Loman, but in the course of repeatedly treating the Epistle to the Galatians in his lectures he found to his dismay that he was gradually arriving at the theory of its spuriousness.

The views of Pierson, Loman, and Steck are critically examined by J. M. S. Baljon in his *Exegetisch-kritische Verhandeling over den Brief van Paulus an de Galatiërs*, 1899, 424 pp.

[3] W. C. van Manen, *Paulus*, 3 vols. (see head of chapter for particulars). The author describes on pp. 9-11 how he came to reject the Pauline Epistles.

In respect of external arguments the three scholars combine to urge the following considerations :—

Acts, they argue, knows nothing of any literary activity of Paul; and it tells us nothing of the conflicts which these letters, if we are to believe their own evidence, called forth.

When the Tübingen school set up the axiom that Acts is less trustworthy than the Epistles, they made things easy for themselves. There are weighty arguments to support the opposite opinion.

That the moment a mission to the heathen was undertaken the question of the observance of the law must come up is clear. The most natural thing to happen would be that it should come up for discussion on purely practical lines and should take the form : how much must the Gentile Christians take over of the Commandments in order that the Jewish believers might have table-fellowship and social intercourse with them ?

This is the form of the problem which Acts presupposes, and it gives us in the account of the so-called Apostolic Council a decision in accordance therewith.

The Epistle to the Galatians, on the other hand, asserts that the question of the validity of the law as such was raised at that time, and that Paul and the original apostles agreed to divide the spheres of their mission work into Gentile and Jewish. About the most pressing need, the establishment of a *modus vivendi* in mixed churches, nothing was done. This representation is much less natural than the other.

Nor is the case different in regard to the picture of Paul which these two sources give us. In Acts everything is clear and simple. The Apostle appears at first rather as an assistant to Barnabas, but afterwards makes himself independent, and maintains his position in relation to the original apostles by the force of his personality, in a free but not a hostile fashion.

In the letters, on the other hand, everything is unintelligible. Stress is laid on the fact that the Apostle of the Gentiles after his conversion has no intercourse with the original apostles and the Church, receives nothing whatever of the doctrinal tradition about Jesus, and draws his gospel entirely from revelation.

The statements regarding the external facts of his life are extremely confused. After his conversion he is said to have first spent three years in " Arabia " and then to have gone to Damascus, and from there, three years after his conversion, to have paid his " visit of ceremony " to the Church at Jerusalem, during which, however, he says that he saw only Peter, and James the Lord's brother. After that he spent fourteen years in Syria and Cilicia.

Who can form a clear picture of the journeys implied in the letters, or of the relation of Paul to his churches ?

Who can understand the character here presented ? Sometimes the Apostle is radical, sometimes conservative, sometimes bold, sometimes despairing ; in small things firm, in great things weakly yielding ; now violent, then again mild ; in all ways full of uncertainties and contradictions.

Far from arousing belief, the statements of the letters about the Apostle create difficulty upon difficulty and doubt upon doubt, if once one ventures to read them with an open mind. On the one side it seems as if a certain tendency to bring him into opposition with the original apostles made itself felt throughout, while on the other hand the traits are thrown together without any reference to an integral psychologically intelligible picture.

The most natural view is, therefore, that Acts represents what is historically most authentic, while in the letters an imaginary picture is drawn, exhibiting throughout the same tendency, but composed by various hands.

The external attestation in the early literature of a Pauline collection of letters, which is in any case not too brilliant, is further reduced by the radicals. The Ignatian letters are held—as they also are by the Tübingen school—

to be spurious ; and they endeavour to bring down the
first epistle of Clement from the time of Domitian to
the middle of the second century.[1] If all this is admitted,
the first attestation of the letters is that of Marcion.
What, then, is there to oppose to the view that they had
their origin in Gnostic circles and were only later forced
upon the Church ?

With this agrees, too, the fact that the Second Epistle
of Peter, which alone in the New Testament makes
mention of Paul's literary activity,[2] and which itself
certainly belongs to the period of the struggle with
Gnosticism, treats it as something in the nature of a
" gift from the Greeks." [3]

In any case, in view of the silence of Justin, the
Shepherd of Hermas, the *Didache,* and the *Epistle of
Barnabas,* the attestation of the Pauline letters is no
better than that of the Johannine literature.[4]

Great stress is laid on the fact that among the Gnostics
the Epistles existed in a shorter form than in the Church,
as appears from the reckoning which Tertullian holds
with Marcion.[5] If this shorter text can be reconstructed

[1] The first epistle of Clement mentions (xlvii. 1) " the letter of the
blessed Paul " to the Corinthians, has a direct borrowing from Romans
(xxxv. 5 = the catalogue of vices in Rom. i. 29-32), and in other respects
also frequently shows dependence on the main epistles. For the
detailed attempt to place it at a later date see Steck, 294-310.

[2] 2 Peter iii. 15-17, "And count the long-suffering of the Lord as
salvation, as also our beloved brother Paul, according to the wisdom
given to him, wrote to you, as in all his Epistles when he mentions
these things, in which no doubt occur some things which are difficult
to understand, which the unlearned and unstedfast wrest, as they do
also the other Scriptures, to their own destruction." (The German
follows Weizsäcker's rendering.)

[3] As in the present context this phrase might possibly be misleading,
it may be worth pointing out that it is simply an allusion to the famous
" timeo Danaos et dona ferentes," *Aen.* ii. 49.—TRANSLATOR.

[4] The puzzle in the case of Justin is that he uses Pauline phrases,
and therefore seems to know the Epistles, but never mentions their
author. According to Steck the explanation of this silence lies in the
fact that the Epistles are, for the author of the *Apology* and the *Dia-
logue,* mere literary works and not as yet Church books. The *Didache,*
the *Shepherd* of Hermas, and the *Epistle of Barnabas* show no certain
evidence of acquaintance with the Pauline Epistles.

[5] *Tertullian adversus Marcionem,* bk. v., goes through the Epistles
of Paul as used by Marcion in those " Antitheses " which are now
lost to us.

and proves to be the better, this would show that the Epistles passed from the hands of the Gnostics into that of the Church, and underwent in the process an expansion of a certain " tendency."

In the hope of showing this, van Manen in the year 1887 reconstructed the Marcionite text of the Epistle to the Galatians.[1] In regard to the other Epistles he does not attempt this, as Tertullian's indications are insufficient.

The examination of the internal arguments takes the following form. These " Ultra-Tübingen " critics analyse the letters and point out all the difficulties which come to light in the course of exegetical study. They triumphantly establish the fact that there are many seams and divisions between the various verses and sections, that an ethico-mystical doctrine is found alongside of the juridical doctrine of justification, that the view of the law is subject to remarkable vacillations, and that it is not possible to weld together the different parts of the Epistles to the Romans and Corinthians, to determine the proper address of the Epistle to the Galatians, whether to the district or the province, to decide whether Romans presupposes Jewish-Christian or Gentile-Christian readers, and various questions of that kind.

The next point is to discover, if possible, some kind of system in the difficulties, inconsistencies, and contradictions. Steck and van Manen profess to be able to show that there is such a system.

What the letters tell us regarding the conversion, the life and work of Paul is not, according to them, to be considered earlier and more authentic than Acts, but is

[1] *Theologisch Tijdschrift*, 1887, pp. 382-533, "Marcions Brief van Paulus aan de Galatiërs." The text thus arrived at is given on pp. 528-533.

Van Manen is also inclined to hold that early Church witnesses may be found for a shorter recension of Romans. See *Die Unechtheit des Römerbriefs*, 94-100.

A reconstruction of the Marcionite text of Galatians had already been undertaken by Adolf Hilgenfeld, *Der Galaterbrief*, 1852, 239 pp., pp. 218-234. He holds that it was not the original but a mutilated form.

based on information which either coincides with the reports there given or points to an earlier common source. The material supplied by Acts is worked up in the letters under the influence of a tendency.

The existence of a written Gospel is also implied. All the passages in the Epistles which recall sayings of the Lord, and what the Epistles to the Corinthians in particular have to tell us about the institution of the Lord's Supper and the resurrection of Jesus, make, they think, the impression of having been drawn from Luke, or an earlier Gospel which is one of his sources. Steck and van Manen are even inclined to hold that in Rom. ii. 16 and xvi. 25 the words " my Gospel " refer to a written Gospel, as indeed the Church Fathers also thought.

That the four main Epistles cannot all be from the same hand is, they think, manifest from the differences between them. Further, the order in which they were written can, these writers think, be recognised. This order does not agree with that generally accepted, since the Epistle to the Galatians is not placed before Corinthians and Romans, but concludes the series. Steck endeavours to give a detailed proof that it was written after Romans and presupposes the latter. Wherever in Galatians there appear gaps and obscurities, a glance at Romans always, he affirms, gives the desired explanation. The more strongly the opposition to the law comes to expression, the later is the writing in question to be placed in the series of the Pauline writings, in which a development is traceable.

Another point to which the " Ultra-Tübingen " critics attach importance is to discover criteria by which various strata can be distinguished in the main Epistles themselves. They propose to regard the Epistles to the Corinthians as fragments of Pauline literature which have gradually been worked up together into letters. In regard to the letter to the Romans, van Manen holds that it originally consisted, roughly speaking, of chapters i.-viii., and was only gradually extended to its present form.[1]

It is also, these critics consider, certain that a number of hands have been at work on the letters, and that the increasingly anti-Jewish tendency shows us the direction followed by the efforts of the Pauline school.

Steck and van Manen assume that the teaching represented in the Epistles is of a Greek character. They think they can show that the Pauline school were influenced by Philo and Seneca, and seek to explain Paulinism as an " attempt to spiritualise primitive Christianity."

Essentially, they think, it belongs to Gnosticism, since it sets aside the " authority of tradition " and derives all knowledge, without historical mediation, from the revelation of the Spirit, and conceives of this knowledge as a system. The deification of Jesus Christ which is represented in the letters is also to be regarded as Greek and Gnostic.

By these observations Steck and van Manen are inevitably led to the decisive consideration regarding " time and space."

Could a Christology of this kind come into being a few years only after the death of the historical Jesus ? Is an intense anti-Judaism in primitive Christian times intelligible ? Can Greek, Gnostical ideas be assumed to have existed in the first generation ?

Steck and van Manen deny that this is possible and demand a longer period for the transformation of which the evidence lies before us. Therefore the historic Paul,

[1] Even the letter consisting of chapters i.-viii. is not, according to van Manen, all of a piece, as is evident, he thinks, from the complicated opening salutation, the vacillating use of " Jesus Christ " and " Christ Jesus," and other peculiarities of detail. One or more treatises—on justification by faith, on the equal importance of the Gospel for Jews and Gentiles, on the significance of the law, on the sense in which believers are entitled to call Abraham their father even if they are not by birth of his posterity—may have formed the basis of the longer writing. Its close was probably formed by Rom. xv. 14-33. Later on, the essays which we have in chapters ix.-xi., xii.-xiv. and xv.-xvi. were worked in. The Epistle is supposed to have undergone several successive redactions.

if there ever was such a man, as is almost certainly the case, was not the creator of the Paulinism represented by the Epistles.

How, then, is the origin of the letters and the doctrine to be explained?

On the basis of the facts which they observe in the documents, and the consideration regarding the necessity of time and space, the " Ultra-Tübingen " critics throw out the following hypothesis.

Christianity, they hold, remained at first Jewish. But as time went on, and as it spread beyond Palestine, two different tendencies manifested themselves within it. One, as the result of contact with Gentiles, and no doubt in consequence of the destruction of the Jewish State, moved in the direction of attaching less and less import-ance to the law, while the other maintained the older stand-point.

In general the development, due to the influence of Graeco-Roman ideas, proceeded without a struggle. Its goal was a " catholicism " such as meets us in Justin.

Within this " Gnostic " party, however, there appeared a school which put the question of the relation to Judaism and the law in its most trenchant form, as a question of principle, and sought to bring it to a decisive issue.

Somewhere or other—perhaps in the Roman Church, perhaps in several places at the same time—where Gnostics and representatives of the older view were at odds, an open conflict broke out. The former party fought with literary weapons, dating back the controversy by means of an epistolary literature specially created for the purpose into primitive Christian times.

In the course of the struggle the antithesis became more and more acute. The climax is marked by the Epistle to the Galatians. Here a " Gnostic " endeavours, with the aid of the already existing Pauline literature, and depending more particularly on Romans, to defend the stand-point of liberal Gentile Christianity against a " Jewish Christianity " which, as it seems, was " making headway." "With all the force of his intellectual superiority" he scourges the tendencies of a period which was endeavouring to make Christianity once more Jewish.

The form of a letter to the Galatians was given to the work, according to Steck's hypothesis, "because the literary *genre* of Apostolic letters held an established position ; and since the churches at Rome and Corinth already had their Epistles, the Galatian province, familiar in connexion with the first missionary journey in Acts, suggested itself as the appropriate scene of the struggle, since it was there that the Apostle had first had to suffer from the persecutions of the Jews. As the Epistle to the Galatians followed on the three other main epistles, and the Epistle to the Romans had already selected as its time and place the last visit of the Apostle to Corinth, shortly before his arrest at Jerusalem, the time of the Roman imprisonment suggested itself as the situation of the writer to be implied in the Epistle. During his imprisonment Paul receives news of the threatened, and in part already accomplished, falling away of the Galatian churches from his Gospel, and feeling himself about to take leave of the world he directs to the wavering churches this letter as the purest and most intense expression of his heart and mind."

The main Epistles originated about the years 120–140. The elements from which they are worked up may be ten or twenty years earlier. A final redaction may have taken place even subsequently to 140.

Why, exactly, the school of thought which created this literature took Paul as its patron, it is, according to van Manen, impossible to explain. He holds that the historic Apostle had as little to do with Paulinism as John the Apostle with the theology of the Fourth Gospel. Steck, on the other hand, is inclined to admit the historical justification of this connexion. For him, it is to be held as certain that Paul was the first to " open the door of the Christian salvation freely to the Gentiles." The doctrine

of justification by faith must therefore already in some
shape or other have formed part of his preaching. Only
the strictly systematic and sharply anti-Jewish development of the doctrine was supplied by the later school.

Steck is therefore here, as on some other points, more
conservative and less " critical " than van Manen.
Nevertheless the differences are not very noticeable in
comparison with the extent of the views which they share.

Theology of the post-Baur period generally had
ignored Bruno Bauer ; it would willingly have treated
in the same way those who took up his work again.
Since this was not possible, and references to " wild
hypotheses " and " rash, wrong-headed critics " did not
completely suffice to dispose of them, the authorities
great and small had necessarily to undertake a refutation,
which they prudently confined to the most pressing and
the easiest points.

The discussions were for the most part carried on in
periodicals. A work on the other side of an importance
at all corresponding to those of Loman, Steck, and van
Manen was not forthcoming.[1]

---

[1] Steck in the introduction to his work gives references to the
articles which had appeared up to 1888. The chronicles of the following years appear in van Manen. At the head of the counter-movement
among critics in Holland stood J. H. Scholten. His work, *Historisch-
critische Bijdragen naar Aanleiding van de nieuweste Hypothese aan-
gaande Jesus en den Paulus der vier Hoofdbrieven* (" Contributions to
Historical Criticism with Reference to the latest Hypotheses regarding
Jesus and the Paul of the four main Epistles "), 1882, 118 pp., is directed
against Loman's arguments.

From the German literature we may cite G. Heinrici, *Die Forschungen über die paulinischen Briefe : ihr gegenwärtiger Stand und ihre
Aufgaben* (" The Study of the Pauline Letters ; its present Position,
and Task"). Lectures given before the theological conference at Giessen,
1886, pp. 69-120. Wilhelm Brückner, *Die chronologische Reihenfolge,
in welcher die Briefe des Neuen Testaments verfasst sind* (" The Chronological Order in which the Epistles of the New Testament were written "),
1890, 306 pp. (An essay which received the prize offered for the
treatment of this question by the Teylerian Society of Haarlem.)
" On the Chronological Order of the Four main Epistles, pp. 174-203.
Carl Clemen, *Die Chronologie der paulinischen Briefe*, 1893, 292 pp.
By the same writer, *Die Einheitlichkeit der paulinischen Briefe* (" The
Integrity of the Pauline Epistles "), 1894, 183 pp.

In these writings Clemen makes some concessions to the Ultra-
Tübingen critics. Thus, for example, he is prepared to put Galatians
after Romans and Corinthians. The mediating views here offered,

How far is it possible to refute their view ?

In the domain of the external arguments, the main strength of the revolutionaries, the position is not so favourable to them as Loman wished to represent it. The transference of the first Epistle of Clement to the middle of the second century is not possible.[1] The fact that Justin knew and used Paul's writings, while he does not name him, is not explained by the hypothesis that they did not rank for him as Church writings.[2]

The Marcionite text of Galatians reconstructed by van Manen is not better but worse than the canonical text.[3] If the Ignatian letters, as is now generally held, are genuine, the attestation of the Pauline Epistles is in much better case than was formerly supposed. That Acts says nothing about the literary activity of the Apostle has at most the value of an *argumentum e silentio*. It is not otherwise in regard to the fact that Acts has nothing to say of the conflicts between him and his churches. In regard to the question of priority as between its narrative and that of Galatians there is at least nothing certain to be said.

The position of matters is therefore that the Epistles to the Romans and Corinthians are witnessed to by the first Epistle of Clement at the end of the first century, but that neither the legitimate nor the illegitimate representa-

---

though sometimes interesting, need nevertheless no longer occupy us, as Clemen has in the meantime completely recovered his confidence and has contradicted himself. In the first volume of his *Paulus* (1904, 416 pp., examination of the sources) he pronounces that the four main epistles are to be regarded as entirely genuine, if only we may divide the second Epistle to the Corinthians into four. In addition to 1 Thessalonians and Philippians, even Colossians and 2 Thessalonians are to be regarded as from the Apostle's pen.

In the preface the author begs that he may not be held accountable for his views prior to his Damascus.

The second volume of the work, *Paulus. Sein Leben und Werken*, 1904, 339 pp., is in biographical form, and does not enter further into the problems of the doctrine.

A writer who takes the " Ultra-Tübingen " side is J. Friedrich (Maehliss). In his work entitled *Die Unechtheit des Galaterbriefs* ("The Spuriousness of Galatians "), 1891, 67 pp., he defends both the rights of radical criticism and of a " simplified orthography."

[1] See p. 128, *sup.*   [2] See p. 128, *sup.*
[3] See p. 129, *sup.*

tives of the Tübingen tradition can explain why Justin
and the remaining writers of the beginning of the second
century are not under the influence of these Epistles,
and, with the exception of Clement, do not even mention
them.

The hypothesis brought forward by Steck and van
Manen in regard to different strata within the Epistles
and the development which culminates in the antinomianism of the Epistle to the Galatians cannot be proved from
the texts; the evidence is read into them by the exercise
of great ingenuity.

But the negative observation which formed their
starting-point holds its ground. Ordinary exegesis has
not succeeded in getting rid of the illogical transitions
and contradictions and making Paul's arguments really
intelligible. The impression of a certain disconnectedness is not to be denied. But Steck and van Manen
have not succeeded in discovering the law and order
which ought to prevail in it, and showing how the chaos
arose in connexion with the creation of this literature.

Against the hypothesis of the origin of Paulinism in
the second century there lies the objection that it is built
on purely arbitrary assumptions. Whence do Steck and
van Manen know anything about anti - Jewish conflicts taking place at that time? There is no evidence of
any such thing in the contemporary literature; and the
writings of the apostolic Fathers make quite in the
contrary direction.

On the other hand, the general considerations which
led them to adopt this hypothesis have not been in any
way invalidated. The illegitimate Tübingen critics share
with the legitimate school the presupposition that Paulinism signifies a Hellenisation of the Gospel; they are also
at one with their adversaries in regarding this unproved
and unprovable assumption as proved. The difference
is that they do not follow the others in their second
exhibition of naïveté—that of regarding this Greek
religious faith as being coincident with primitive Christi-

anity, but demand space and time for a development of this character. But the two wrestlers have the same chain about their feet ; whichever of them throws the other into the water must drown along with him.

That they are both involved in the same fundamental view of Paulinism sometimes comes to the consciousness of the post-Baur theology and its radical opponents. In a momentary aberration of this kind Heinrici ventures to praise Bruno Bauer for having discovered the relationship of Paul to the religious life of the ancient world, and is prepared to see his weakness only in the inferences which he draws from this discovery.[1]

Steck, on his part, praises Heinrici's commentary on the Epistles to the Corinthians, in which the Hellenistic element is so excellently traced, and expresses the hope that the exegete and his party will consider carefully whether the composition of this work " does not stand in an even much closer relationship to Hellenism than had previously been supposed."

The more the theologians who derive from Baur emphasise the Greek element in Paulinism the more helpless they are against the " Ultra-Tübingen " critics. For it is after all merely a matter of clearness and courage of thought whether they venture to raise the question about space and time. The moment they take this step they are lost. Nevermore can they find the way which leads back through the green pastures of sound common-sense theology, but are condemned to wander about with the revolutionaries in the wilderness of flat unreason. Wearied with problems, they come at last, like Steck and van Manen, to a condition of mind in which the wildest hypothesis appeals to them more than rational knowledge, if the latter demands the suppression of questioning.

How is it conceivable that a man of the primitive Christian period could, in consequence of a purely practical controversy regarding the observance or non-observance of the law by Gentile believers, go on, as Baur and

[1] See pp. 114 and 115 of the work cited above, p. 134.

his successors represent—to reject the law on principle? How could it be possible that, at that time, doctrine should take a frankly Gnostic shape, and in deliberate contempt of the tradition of the historic Jesus, should, under the eyes of the men who had been His companions, appeal only to revelation?

That is the element of greatness in the "Ultra-Tübingen" critics, that they did not forget the duty of asking questions, when it had fallen out of fashion among other theologians. To show that their hypothesis is untenable is by no means to get rid of it, as accredited theology wished to persuade itself. A few squadrons of cavalry which were skirmishing in the open have been cut off ; the fortress has not been taken, indeed the siege has not even been laid.

The chronicle of the discussion between contemporary theology and the revolutionaries is quite without interest. As soon as the refutation on points of detail was finished, and the fundamental questions regarding time and place came on the scene, there remained nothing for it to do but to stammer, with an embarrassed smile, something about tradition, intuition, an unmistakable impression, the stamp of genuineness, and the like, and to break off the conversation as quickly as might be.

What it could or could not refute, and what the other party could or could not prove, followed necessary from the form which the problem had assumed. The construction of the illegitimate Tübingen critics answers, in reverse, to that of the legitimate school, like the reflection in a mirror to the object reflected. The presuppositions and the difficulties are the same in the two cases ; the two solutions correspond except that they go in opposite directions. Both recognise that not only a conflict of practice, but one involving theory and principle, for and against the law, is fought out in the letters. The legitimate school place it in primitive Christian times, but cannot show how it was possible at that period, and how it could break off so suddenly that in the post-Pauline literature there is not an echo of it, and it seems as though it had never been.

The illegitimate school represent the struggle as having occurred in the course of the second century, but can cite no evidence for this from the remaining literature, can point to no traces of the gradual growth of the opposition, or show how a struggle of that kind could break out at that time.

Both explanations labour in vain at the problem of the inexplicable neglect of Paulinism in the post-Apostolic literature.

Both parties assume as a datum that the doctrine of the letters is to be considered as a Hellenised Christianity. The one party represents the process which leads to this result as taking place in primitive Christian times, without being able to show how such a thing is possible, or how the Greek and the Jewish-eschatological elements mutually tolerated and united with one another.

According to the other party, the Hellenisation came about in the course of a long development. But they cannot explain why Paulinism shows an entirely different character from that of the Greek Christianity which appears elsewhere in the literature of the second century. They assert that it belongs to Gnosticism ; and are right in this so far as regards the form of the system. On the other hand they cannot allow themselves to consider seriously the difference between the doctrine of the letters and the fundamental views of the known Gnostic schools, or the hypothesis flies in pieces. The Gnostics were real spiritualists, opposed to eschatology, and denying a corporeal resurrection ; Paul is an eschatologist, looking for the parousia and the transformation of the body. Therefore the " Ultra-Tübingen " critics must either explain the Jewish eschatological element in the system in such a way as to spiritualise it, or else drop it out of sight.

And as a matter of fact the ominous word eschatology is, one might almost say, never mentioned in their works.

The parallel between what the one and the other construction can and cannot make intelligible goes through to the last detail. For both it is true that the ostensible solution in each case introduces openly or otherwise a new problem which arises out of the solution itself. The sum of what is explained and unexplained is the same for both.

At first sight the position of the legitimate successors of the Tübingen school is more favourable than that of the other party. They have tradition and natural impression on their side, and are able to regard the situation implied in the Epistles as historic, whereas their opponents are bound to show that it is fictitious. When subjected to critical examination, however, they are no better off, for they cannot give any proof that the main epistles can belong to primitive Christianity and to it only. When they declared again and again that the attacks of the radicals had served a useful purpose in inciting them to examine anew their results, and to make corrections where necessary, that was the mere cant of criticism. If they had dared to make an effort to understand the objection which Loman, Steck, and van Manen constantly repeated, and to consider whether they could really prove the Pauline origin of the main epistles, or whether they did not really by their conception of the doctrine make it improbable, they would have been bound to perceive that nothing could be done by revising and correcting ; it was a case of mutually exclusive alternatives.

As matters stood, they had to choose between being consistent but irrational, or rational but inconsistent. They chose the latter form of the dilemma and left the other to the radicals.

The Ultra-Tübingen critics on their part cannot escape the blame of raising the question in a one-sided purely literary form, and not concerning themselves with the thought contained in the Epistles, because they felt that herein lay the weak point of their undertaking. Instead of analysing the system, they made play with the catchwords Greek and Gnostic, and thought to have got rid in that way of the question regarding the essential character of Paulinism. If contemporary theology did not grasp the problem which was presented to it in its full significance, that was partly due to the pettifogging way in which it was formulated. The representatives of radical criticism were like criminals who cannot rise to the height of their crime !

For a time it almost looked as if a *modus vivendi* had been found between the successors of Baur's school and the radicals. Steck, who stood on the right wing of the revolutionaries, refused to give up the belief that the historic Paul had in some way or other fought a battle for freedom from the law, and might be indirectly claimed as the starting-point of the theology which reaches its full development in the Epistles. From this it was only a short step to the hypothesis that the Epistles were not wholly spurious but combined thoughts of the Apostle with later views.

A criticism based on the distinction of original and interpolated elements did not need to be now for the first time called into being. It already existed, and had indeed made its appearance contemporaneously with Bruno Bauer's. Like the latter it had been either talked down or left to die of neglect.

In the first volume of his " Philosophic Dogmatic " (1855), when speaking of the documentary sources of our knowledge of Christianity, Christian Hermann Weisse defines his attitude towards the Pauline Epistles and offers the results of a study extending over many years, which he had undertaken in opposition to the conservatives on the one side and the Tübingen school on the other.[1]

His method he himself describes as criticism based on style. A man like Paul, he argues, has so characteristic a literary style that it will serve one who has made himself

---

[1] Christian Hermann Weisse, *Philosophische Dogmatik oder Philosophie des Christentums*, 3 vols., 1855, 60, 62 ; vol. i., 712 pp. On the Pauline Epistles, pp. 144-147.

thoroughly familiar with it as an unfailing criterion of what is genuine and what is not. Such a method of criticism must of course be prepared to be accused of arbitrariness and subjectivity. But that is no great matter. The fruits will vouch for the goodness of the tree.

The standard of indubitably genuine Pauline style is furnished, according to Weisse, by the First Epistle to the Corinthians. It bears in all its parts the stamp of the most complete integrity and genuineness. The eye which has acquired due fineness of perception by the study of this writing discovers that only the Second Epistle to the Corinthians, the First to the Thessalonians, and that to Philemon, " can boast of preserving in the same purity the original apostolic text." The Epistles to the Romans, Galatians, Philippians, and Colossians " have interwoven in them a regular series of interpolations, which so far efface the genuine apostolic character of the style in many places as to render it unrecognisable, and have given rise to that difficulty of disentangling the meaning which has made Romans especially a *crux interpretum,* and by the forced artificiality, intrinsic falsity, and unnaturalness of these interpretations has made this Epistle the bane of theological study; of which, in virtue of the character of its fundamental ideas, it was fitted to be the most precious treasure." [1]

The whole of these interpolations are, he thinks, from one and the same hand, and go back to a time previous to the ecclesiastical use of the writings. The redactor cherished withal the most respectful awe of the Apostle's words, and has hardly deleted a single one of them.

What remains after the elimination of the secondary stratum in the Epistles to the Romans and Philippians

---

[1] On Romans see also vol. iii. of the *Philosophische Dogmatik* (1862, 736 pp.), pp. 263, 264.
The Epistle to the Ephesians, the Second to the Corinthians, and the First to Timothy, Weisse holds to be " entirely unapostolic "; in the Epistle to Titus and the Second to Timothy he is prepared to recognise as a possibility the genuineness of the personal notices.

does not prove to be an integral whole. The latter consists of two letters to this church, the second beginning with iii. 3. With the former there has been worked up a letter to a church in Asia Minor, consisting of ix.-xi. and xvi. 1-20.[1]

Weisse did not get the length of publishing the reconstructed text of the Epistles. When his pupil Sulze carried it through after his death,[2] the prophecy which the author had put on record in his " Dogmatics " regarding his undertaking was fulfilled. It met with " universal disbelief."

In part the cause of this ill-success lay in the one-sidedness of the principle maintained by the author. Weisse confines himself entirely to " stylistic criticism." While he recognises the possibility of a distinction between genuine and spurious based on the contents, the trains of thought, of the letters, he will have nothing to do with it.

With the controversy about the genuineness of the main Epistles there began a new era of " interpolation criticism." Daniel Völter, rendered confident by the professedly " assured results " of the criticism of the Apocalypse in regard to the distinction of sources, thinks to find in a similar procedure the solution of the Pauline problem, and hopes that it will be possible by " careful criticism " to separate the genuine from the spurious.[3]

He differs entirely from Weisse in seeking the criterion for the distinction of what is genuine from what is spurious in the subject-matter. What is simple and " plain "—

---

[1] In 2 Corinthians, which shows no evidence of interpolation, three different letters to this church are worked up together.

[2] Christian Hermann Weisse, *Beiträge zur Kritik der paulinischen Briefe an die Galater, Römer, Philipper und Kolosser* ("Contributions to the Criticism of the Pauline Epistles to the Galatians, Romans, Philippians, and Colossians"). Edited by E. Sulze, 1867, 65 pp. By way of introduction the pupil prefixes an essay on the principles of his master's " stylistic criticism."

In the reconstructed texts it is apparent that the author had spent on them, as he says in his *Dogmatic*, the " diligent work of many years." It is a piece of really skilled workmanship.

[3] Daniel Völter, *Die Entstehung der Apokalypse*, 1882, 72 pp. *Die Komposition der paulinischen Hauptbriefe*, 1890, 174 pp. The Epistles examined are those to the Romans and Galatians. *Paulus und seine Briefe. Kritische Untersuchungen zu einer neuen Grundlegung der*

the latter expression recurs again and again—is to be regarded as primitive-Christian and Pauline, but anything which has the appearance of being complicated or having the character of a speculative system is to be regarded as of later origin.

Thus wherever we find a highly developed Christology, speculations regarding the Spirit, and eschatology, strongly predestinarian views, and an advanced estimate of baptism and the Lord's Supper, we are, according to Völter, in the presence of interpolations. A further mark by which these may be recognised is an advanced antinomianism.

The doctrine of the historic Paul includes, according to this author, the following points : The central point in it is the death of Christ, regarded as an atoning death appointed by God and ratified by the resurrection. Man becomes partaker of its fruits by faith, and thus obtains justification by the forgiveness of sins, of which he is given assurance by the testimony of the Holy Spirit. Faith also includes within it, however, a " mystico-ethical partaking in the death of Christ." Therefore in the act of faith there takes place at the same time an inner conversion to a life well-pleasing to God, which causes the believer " to appear blameless on the day of Christ and makes him a partaker in the resurrection."

As regards the relation of the Epistle to the Galatians to Acts Völter takes over the conclusions, unfavourable to the former, of the radical critics. Consequently this work is spurious throughout. It only reproduces the ideas of the interpolators of the letters to the Romans and Corinthians, and pushes to an extreme the antinomianism there represented. It dates from near the end of the first century.

---

paulinischen Briefliteratur und ihrer Theologie, 1905, 331 pp. Here he deals with Corinthians, Romans, Galatians, and Philippians. The results arrived at in the previous book are, as a rule, taken over. Völter rejects the genuineness of 1 Thessalonians, and sees in the letters to the Colossians and Ephesians, and in the Pastorals, new " phases in the development " of Paulinism.

In the Epistles to the Corinthians—we are still following Völter—the interpolations are not very extensive.
The most important is the correction applied to the
original Pauline doctrine of resurrection, in 2 Corinthians
iv. and v., where the redactor has worked in his Platonico-
Stoic doctrine of immortality.

The Epistle to the Romans has been very extensively
interpolated.[1] The original writing was addressed to
Gentile readers. The interpolator, on the other hand, has
in view readers " who occupy an Old Testament stand-
point." That is connected with the far-reaching development which began at Rome after the Neronian
persecution. At that time, as is proved, Völter thinks,
by the Epistle to the Hebrews and the Epistle of
Barnabas, together with the first Epistle of Clement and
the *Shepherd* of Hermas, the Church at Rome " fell
back upon a religious stand-point determined by Old
Testament ideas." It is this " reduction of Christianity
to Jewish Old Testament religion, modified by Christianity," that the interpolator is concerned to combat.
In doing so he is forced to enter upon general speculations regarding the flesh, sin, and the law ; in order " to
defend the independence and superiority of Christianity "
he develops an antinomianism, according to which the
law had as its sole purpose, " by intensifying the misery
of sin, to prepare men for deliverance from sin and the
law, by the redemption which is in Jesus Christ. "[2]

Völter's work is one of the adroitest performances
in the whole field of Pauline study. It is not only that
it represents what is in its own way a brilliant synthesis
between Weisse and the radicals ; its main significance

[1] In its original form it consisted, Völter thinks, of the following
sections: i. 1, 5b-7, 8-17 ; v. 1-12, 15-19, 21 ; vi. 1-13, 16-23 ; chapters
xii. and xiii. ; xiv. 1-xv. 6 ; xv. 14-16, 23b-33 ; xvi. 21-24.

[2] Völter is also able to indicate additions which have taken place
subsequently to this redaction.
The interpolations in Philippians relate, according to him, chiefly
to Christology and eschatology. The author of these additions had
before him Romans and Corinthians in their interpolated form, and
was also doubtless acquainted with Galatians.

lies in the fact that it breaks off the barren literary-critical logomachy, and directs attention once more to the subject-matter.

Steck and van Manen had failed, once they went beyond the simple registration of inconcinnities in the text ; Völter lets the theological problems have something to say for themselves. He observes more clearly than any one had stated it before exactly wherein the complexity of the question of the law consists, and rightly refers it to the fact that some passages take for granted its observance by the Jews as unquestionably right and proper, and only seek to maintain the freedom of the Gentiles in regard to it, whereas others reject it in principle, in such a way that Paul would be obliged to maintain also the emancipation of the Jews . . . if the rules of logical inference are to be applied. As it is, however, there is a want of congruence between the negative theory and the limitation of the practical demand.

In an equally thoroughgoing fashion Völter deals with the problems of Christology and of the doctrine of the Spirit, and eschatology.

His solution is ingenious and elegant. Of the hypothesis which places the controversies about the law in the post-apostolic period only so much is taken over as is absolutely necessary. The connexion between Paulinism and Gnosticism is made as loose as possible. The eschatology has a certain importance given to it. Hellenic elements are not assumed to be present in the primitive doctrine ; on the other hand, a knowledge of the Book of Wisdom, Philo, Seneca and the Graeco-Roman philosophy in general is ascribed to the interpolators.

The criterion by which to distinguish what is genuine from what is not is ingeniously chosen. It is not particularly difficult to separate in the letters the parts which are mainly plain and practical from those which relate to an antinomian speculative system. The resulting division between original text and interpolations has a more natural and simple air than is the case in any of the other attempts to draw the line between them.

Nevertheless, it was scarcely possible that this work should contribute anything to the solution of the Pauline problem. It is built upon sand, for the argument on which everything is based is unsound.

Völter asserts that " simplicity " is the mark of what is genuinely apostolic and Pauline. Since when ? How does he know this ? How, if it were just the other way round, and the strange, the abstruse, the systematic, the antinomian, the predestinarian represented the original element, and what is simple came in later !

What he describes as the doctrine of the historic Paul has not a very convincing look. It has not the ring of what we find elsewhere in early Christian literature, but has a suspicious resemblance to the Good Friday and Easter-day meditations of the *Christliche Welt*.[1]

What does not strike the modern man and his theology as distinctly peculiar is gathered together and receives the stamp of approval as historic Paulinism ! Völter, like every one else, has failed to consider, or to grasp, that fundamental question as to what is primitive-Christian in the Apostle's teaching, which, since the encounter between Baur and Ritschl, had tacitly dominated the discussion and had been again forced on the theological centre-party by the radicals. Otherwise it would have been impossible that he, after promising a " cautious criticism," should have so incautiously decided that what is simple is what is primitive-Christian.

Apart from Völter, the criticism which claims to distinguish various sources and detect interpolations is of a more innocent and guileless description. It does not plunge into the depths of the Pauline problems in the attempt to reach the firm ground that has never yet been reached, but amuses itself by determining what and how many original writings of the Apostle may have been worked up into the canonical Epistles to the

[1] The well-known German religious journal.

Corinthians, Romans, and Philippians. This work, at which Semler had already made a beginning, is in itself necessary and interesting. The results, however, prove to be uncertain and contradictory, because the criteria by which the deletions, dissections, and combinations are determined, are always derived from subjective impression.

The one consolation in regard to them is that any importance which attaches to these results concerns almost exclusively the pre-canonical literary history of the Epistles and does not affect our knowledge of the Pauline system. The supposed interpolations are of a subsidiary character. The text as a whole is hardly seriously affected by them. The sense is scarcely altered by the dislocations and conflations by which one critic or another restores the original letters and releases the present-day reader from the tutelage of the so inconceivably astute redactor.

It remains to remark that most of the scholars who have occupied themselves with this work do not trouble themselves very much about the meaning and the connexion of Paul's statements, but are like surgeons who think more of their skill in handling the knife than of being quite sure about the diagnosis which is to direct the incision, and therefore not seldom fall victims to the temptation of having recourse to an operation in cases where it turns out to have been unnecessary or even injurious.[1]

As a work which stands much above the average of

---

[1] The labour of making an inventory of what has been done in this kind of criticism up to the year 1894 was undertaken by C. Clemen in his work, *Die Einheitlichkeit der paulinischen Briefe an der Hand der bisher mit Bezug auf sie aufgestellten Interpolations- und Kompilationshypothesen* (" The Integrity of the Pauline Epistles, with Reference to the Hypotheses of Interpolation or Compilation which have been applied to them "), 1894, 183 pp. He takes account also of all contributions to the Journals. This gives a special value to this laborious and unselfish work.

A survey of previous work in conjectural criticism is given by J. M. S. Baljon in *De Tekst der Brieven van Paulus aan de Romeinen, de Corinthiërs en de Galatiërs*, 1884, 189 pp.

the usual cutting-up hypotheses we may mention Spitta's work on Romans.[1]

He distinguishes in the canonical Epistle two writings, a longer one consisting of, in the main—allowing for incidental interpolations—chapters i.-xi. with fragments from xv. and xvi., and a shorter writing which is made up of chapters xii., xiii. and xiv., with fragments of xv. and xvi. The longer one, which is the older, is supposed to have been preserved entire, the shorter is of later origin, and it lacks the introduction.

The problem of the composite character of the main epistle in connexion with the address and similar questions, is solved by supposing that it is a working up of an earlier general treatise intended for Jewish Christians into a letter addressed to the Roman Gentile Christians.

The controversy about the much-discussed series of greetings in Rom. xvi. is disposed of by attaching this to the shorter epistle, which is held to have been written between the first and second imprisonment. It is true this solution can only find favour with those who have made up their minds to take upon them the burdensome hypothesis of the second imprisonment along with the complete or partial acceptance of the genuineness of the Pastoral epistles.

In working them up, the redactor is supposed to have followed the method of bringing in the arguments of the second letter in those places in the first where they seemed most appropriate. That he showed no remarkable address in this process is credited to him as a proof of his historical existence.

Holtzmann has nothing very complimentary to say about the representatives of the dissection and interpolation criticism. In his New Testament Theology he reproaches them with " straining out the gnat," and indulging in critical vivisection, instead of studying the

---

[1] Friedrich Spitta, *Untersuchungen über den Brief des Paulus an die Römer* (" A Study of the Epistle to the Romans"), 1901, 193 pp. In the work *Zur Geschichte und Literatur des Urchristentums*, vol. iii. part i.

currents and undercurrents of Jewish and Hellenistic thought which run side by side through Paul's work, and so becoming cured of their mania.

In connexion with this, it is, however, curious that he himself, when he was asked why he never lectured on the Epistle to the Romans, used to say that the composition of Romans was, in his opinion, too problematical for him to venture to deal with the Epistle, so long as he was not obliged to do so.

VI

THE POSITION AT THE BEGINNING OF THE TWENTIETH CENTURY

1899. **Paul Feine.** Das gesetzesfreie Evangelium des Paulus nach seinem Werdegange dargestellt. (Paul's Gospel of Freedom from the Law : a Study of its Growth.)

Paul Wernle. Paulus als Heidenmissionar. (Paul as a Missionary to the Gentiles.)

Heinrich Weinel. Paulus als kirchlicher Organisator. (Paul as a Church Organiser.)

Hermann Jakoby. Neutestamentliche Ethik. (New Testament Ethics.)

1900. **Arthur Titius.** Der Paulinismus unter dem Gesichtspunkt der Seligkeit. (Paulinism with Special Reference to Final Salvation.)

A. Drescher. Das Leben Jesu bei Paulus. (The Life of Jesus in Paul's Writings.)

Karl Dick. Der schriftstellerische Plural bei Paulus. (The Literary Use of the First Person Plural in Paul's Writings.)

Adolf Harnack. Das Wesen des Christentums. (Translated under the title " What is Christianity ? ")

1901. **Paul Wernle.** Die Anfänge unserer Religion. (Translated under the title " The Beginnings of Christianity.")

1902. **Otto Pfleiderer.** Das Urchristentum, seine Schriften und Lehren. (Primitive Christianity, its Documents and Doctrines.) Second, revised and extended edition. (Translated, 4 vols., London, 1906–1911.)

Paul Feine. Jesus Christus und Paulus.

G. F. Heinrici. Das Urchristentum. (Primitive Christianity.)

1903. **Georg Hollmann.** Urchristentum in Corinth. (Primitive Christianity in Corinth.)

Emil Sokolowski. Die Begriffe Geist und Leben bei Paulus in ihrer Beziehung zu einander. (The Conceptions of " Spirit " and " Life " in Paul, in their Relations to one another.)

Wilhelm Bousset. Die Religion des Judentums im neutestamentlichen Zeitalter. (The Religion of Judaism in New Testament Times.) Die jüdische Apokalyptik, ihre religionsgeschichtliche Herkunft und ihre Bedeutung für das Neue Testament. (Jewish Apocalyptic : its Origin as indicated by Comparative Religion, and its Significance for the New Testament.)

Paul Volz. Jüdische Eschatologie von Daniel bis Akiba. (Jewish Eschatology from Daniel to Akiba.)

W. Heitmüller. Taufe und Abendmahl bei Paulus. (Baptism and the Lord's Supper in Paul's Teaching.)

Martin Brückner. Die Entstehung der paulinischen Christologie. (How the Pauline Christology arose.)

1904. **Heinrich Weinel.** Paulus. (E. T. St. Paul: The Man and his Work, 1906.)

Ernst von Dobschütz. Die Probleme des apostolischen Zeitalters. (The Problems of the Apostolic Age.)

Maurice Goguel. L'Apôtre Paul et Jésus-Christ.

Alfred Juncker. Die Ethik des Apostels Paulus.

William Wrede. Paulus. (E. T. by E. Lummis, 1907.)

1905. **Hugo Gressmann.** Der Ursprung der israelitisch - jüdischen Eschatologie. (The Origin of the Israelitish-Jewish Eschatology.)

1906. **Paul Feine.** Paulus als Theologe. (Paul as a Theologian.)

P. Kölbing. Die geistige Einwirkung der Person Jesu auf Paulus. (The Spiritual Influence of the Person of Jesus upon Paul.)

Eberhard Vischer. Die Paulusbriefe. (The Pauline Epistles.)

Wilhelm Karl. Beiträge zum Verständnis der soteriologischen Erfahrungen und Spekulationen des Apostels Paulus. (Contributions towards the Understanding of the Soteriological Experiences and Speculations of the Apostle Paul.)

W. Bousset. Der Apostel Paulus.

1907. **Adolf Jülicher.** Paulus und Jesus.

Arnold Meyer. Wer hat das Christentum gegründet, Jesus oder Paulus ? (Who founded Christianity, Jesus or Paul ?)

A. Schettler. Die paulinische Formel " Durch Christus." (The Pauline Formula " through Christ.")

J. Wellhausen. Israelitische und jüdische Geschichte (6th ed.).

1908. **Carl Munzinger.** Paulus in Corinth.

Hans Windisch. Die Entsündigung des Christen nach Paulus. (The Purification of the Christian from Sin in Paul's Teaching.)

Reinhold Seeberg. Dogmengeschichte. (History of Dogma.) 2nd edition.

Wilhelm Walther. Pauli Christentum, Jesu Evangelium.

1909. **Adolf Harnack.** Dogmengeschichte. 4th edition.

Martin Dibelius. Die Geisterwelt im Glauben des Paulus. (The World of Spirits according to Paul's Belief.)

Johannes Weiss. Paulus und Jesus. (E. T. by H. T. Chaytor, 1909.) Christus: Die Anfänge des Dogmas. (Christ: The Beginning of Dogma. E. T. by V. D. Davis, 1911.)

Johann Haussleiter. Paulus.

R. Knopf. Paulus.

W. Olschewski. Die Wurzeln der paulinischen Christologie. (The Roots of Pauline Christologie.)

1910. **A. Schlatter.** Neutestamentliche Theologie.

R. Drescher. Das Leben Jesu bei Paulus.

Eberhard Vischer. Der Apostel Paulus und sein Werk.

Julius Schniewind. Die Begriffe Wort und Evangelium bei Paulus (The Meaning of the Terms " Word " and " Gospel " in Paul's Writings.)

1911. **Adolf Deissmann.** Paulus, eine kultur- und religionsgeschicht-liche Skizze. (Paul, A Sketch with a Background of Ancient Civilisation and Religion.)

Johannes Müller. Die Entstehung des persönlichen Christentums der paulinischen Gemeinden. (How the personal Christianity of the Pauline Churches arose.)

THE dawn of the twentieth century found Pauline scholar-ship in a peculiar frame of mind. The criticism of the Ultra-Tübingen critics had not succeeded in disquieting it, nor Holtzmann in reassuring it.

That the problems by which Loman, Steck, and van Manen were tormented were mere cobwebs of the im-agination was so completely taken for granted that in dealing with the Pauline teaching no further attention was paid to them. On the other hand, however, the problems previously recognised by critical scholarship had not been so completely solved by Holtzmann that they could be considered as done with.

The disquisitions in which in his " New Testament Theology " he resumed the results of the whole study of the subject since Baur, did not have the effect which he had expected. They were much discussed and much praised ; the massive learning and wide reading, the art of the literary treatment and the subtlety of the dialectic compelled admiration. But behind all this chorus of appreciation, a certain sense of depression made itself felt. People were dismayed to find that Paulinism was so complicated, and that the web of Paul's thought must be so delicately and cautiously handled if it was to be disentangled. Was the doctrine of the Apostle of the Gentiles really a product of such extremely intricate mental processes as it was here represented to be ?

The process of disillusionment did not go so far as to lead to the calling in question of the fundamental view there offered. But results were not put forward with the same confidence as before ; effort was directed rather to strengthen them by revision and correction.

It was in this frame of mind that Pfleiderer prepared the second edition of his " Primitive Christianity." [1] Whereas he had formerly taken for granted the influence of the Greek world upon Paul, as being something self-evident, he now feels obliged to offer proof of it, in a newly inserted chapter upon Hellenism, Stoicism, and Seneca, in order to arrive at the result . . . that his Greek education was in any case " a problematical possibility." While he had previously held that the combination of the Alexandrian Platonic doctrine of immortality with eschatology was the great work accomplished by the Apostle of the Gentiles, he now is inclined to see a spiritualisation of the future-hope already prepared for in Judaism, and quotes the Apocalypse of Ezra and Jewish Hellenistic literature in testimony of this.[2]

Fate willed that about the same time theology should be seized by the impulse of popularisation, and now found itself in the position of being obliged to offer assured, absolutely assured, results in reference to Paulinism. The most important works of this character are Paul Wernle's " Beginnings of Christianity " and Heinrich Weinel's " Paul." [3]

[1] Otto Pfleiderer, *Das Urchristentum, seine Schriften und Lehren,* 2nd ed., 1902, vol. i. 696 pp. On Paul, pp. 24-335. (Eng. trans. " Primitive Christianity," vol. i. pp. 33-471.)

[2] On this point Pfleiderer follows suggestions given by Teichmann in his work, *Die paulinischen Vorstellungen von Auferstehung und Gericht* (" The Pauline Conceptions of Resurrection and Judgment "), 1896, 125 pp. As a matter of fact he cannot any more than his predecessors give any proof of this evolution.

[3] Paul Wernle, *Die Anfänge unserer Religion,* 1st ed., 1901, 410 pp. On Paul, pp. 95-220. By the same author, *Paulus als Heidenmissionar* (" Paul as a Missionary to the Gentiles "), Lecture, 1899, 36 pp. Heinrich Weinel, *Paulus,* 1904, 316 pp. The book grew out of essays which the author published in the *Christliche Welt.* By the same author, *Paulus als kirchlicher Organisator.* (Inaugural Lecture.) 1899, 30 pp.

Other works from this popular literature are : Adolf Harnack, *Das Wesen des Christentums,* 1900, 189 pp. On Paul, pp. 110-118. Georg Hollmann, *Urchristentum in Corinth,* 1903, 32 pp. Paul Feine, *Paulus als Theologe,* 1906, 80 pp. Carl Munzinger, *Paulus in Corinth. Neue Wege zum Verständnis des Urchristentums* (" Paul in Corinth. New Ways of arriving at an Understanding of Early Christianity.") 1908, 208 pp. The author pictures the work of the Apostle in the Greek

The efforts of these writers are directed to bring the author and his thoughts into close relations with our time. It is not his theology in its subtleties and its contradictions that they seek to grasp and to portray, but his religion—what lies behind the system and the formula. In this way they hope to escape many difficulties over which Holtzmann had laboured, and to be able to bring out the fundamental and intelligible elements which in him had been rather to seek.

Wernle makes Paul discourse in the character of the great missionary apologist; Weinel draws him as the preacher of the religion of inwardness, who as " Pharisee," " Seeker after God," " prophet," " apostle," " founder of the Church," " theologian," and " man," was all things in one.

The lively portraiture, quite different from the conventional works on the subject, found a ready welcome, and incited others to imitation.

In consistently emphasising the apologetic aspect of Paul's teaching Wernle brought up many ingenious ideas for discussion. Weinel, on his part, brought again to the consciousness of both theologians and laymen the poetic and emotional element in the Apostle's world of ideas.

But they found no new way of grasping and understanding him.

They walk in a shady path which runs parallel to the main road. But its pleasantness is associated with certain dangers, which they themselves, and those who followed them, have not always escaped.

When earlier writers on the subject modernised, they did so unconsciously. Wernle and Weinel, however, do

---

city in the light of analogies offered by modern missionary practice. Whether the new way really leads to a better understanding of primitive Christianity remains open to question.

As a special investigation of a point of detail at this date we may mention Karl Dick's work, *Der schriftstellerische Plural bei Paulus* (" The Author's ' We ' in Paul's Writings.") 1900, 169 pp. There are not many of these studies at this period since the tendency among theologians has been more to popularisation than to scientific research.

so on principle, and have no scruple about throwing light on what is obscure in Paulinism by the use of more or less appropriate catchwords of the most modern theology.

Not seldom they imagine they are explaining something when they are in reality only talking round the subject. In this way there enters into their treatment a kind of forced ingenuity, one might almost say flimsiness.

Their love of graphic description also sometimes becomes a temptation to them. They do not always remember to keep it within bounds, and sometimes allow themselves to fall into a kind of artificial naïveté. Wernle in particular delights to wield a pre-Raphaelite brush. He pictures the Apostle, for instance, in the evening at his inn, receiving visitors, exhorting and consoling them, weaving tent-cloth, busy with a letter, all at the same time. "Sometimes stones would come flying into the room as he was dictating—the Jews had set on the city mob to attack him. Many an abrupt transition in his letters may have had its origin in a violent interruption of this kind." [1]

Feine and Titius begin with a critical examination of previous views. They are not in this wholly disinterested, being in search of a Paulinism which has more to offer to modern religion, as they apprehend it, than the one-sidedly historical post-Baur liberalism. The result is that while they show themselves free from many of the presuppositions and prejudices which are common to the others, they are at the same time not in a position to put Paulinism on a new historical basis. They agree

[1] *Paulus als Heidenmissionar*, p. 36. Ernst von Dobschütz calls attention to the dangers of this method, which easily becomes unscientific in *Probleme des apostolischen Zeitalters*. (Five Lectures, 1904, 138 pp. See p. 61.) Paul Feine, *Das gesetzesfreie Evangelium des Paulus nach seinem Werdegange dargestellt*, 1899, 232 pp. *Jesus Christus und Paulus*, 1902, 309 pp. Arthur Titius, *Der Paulinismus unter dem Gesichtspunkt der Seligkeit* (2nd Part of the work *Die neutestamentliche Lehre von der Seligkeit und ihre Bedeutung für die Gegenwart*—"The New Testament Doctrine of Final Blessedness and its Significance for the present Time"), 1900, 290 pp. A. Schlatter, in his *NTle. Theologie* (Pt. ii. The doctrine of the Apostles, 1910, 592 pp. On Paul, 199-407), follows a conservative biblico-theological method like that of B. Weiss.

in opposing the separation of Paulinism from Primitive Christianity which is practised by Holsten and Holtzmann. They refuse to be converted to the unsatisfactory view that Paulinism, as being a so unique personal creation, must have remained unintelligible even to Paul's contemporaries. Before making up their minds to derive the whole of Paul's doctrine from the vision at his conversion and the influence of Greek ideas, they propose to examine it in reference to the conceptions which connect it with Jesus, with primitive Christianity, and with Judaism.

Consequently they are loth to admit Greek elements and the resulting duality in the Apostle's thought. Feine maintains that in the Apostle's mind before his conversion, Greek ideas were only present in so far as they had already been adopted by Pharisaism. Titius " will not deny that there is a touch of Hellenism in the great Apostle," but is far from seeking to explain the doctrine of flesh and spirit and the mysticism connected with the " new creation " purely from this point of view. On the other hand both of them assign a large part in the formation of Paul's doctrine to his Jewish consciousness, and consequently are led to a comprehensive recognition of eschatology.

In his examination of the individual views Titius always takes the future-hope as his starting-point— indeed his book begins with chapters on God and eschatology. He shows that redemption, in the most general conception of it, is a liberation from the present evil world and a deliverance looking to the world which is to come, and that justification was originally bound up with the thought of the judgment at the parousia. Instead, however, of systematically carrying out the analysis in this fashion, he breaks off and begins to work up the historical material which he has brought to light on the lines of the problems, definitions, and distinctions of modern theology, because, as the very title of his book shows, he undertakes his investigation with a view

to showing the significance of New Testament teaching
for the present day. In order to portray the "religious
life" he makes it a principle "not to hesitate to turn
aside from the highway, to which the technical terms
serve as sign-posts." Thus he comes finally to discover
everywhere that Paul clarified the doctrines which he
took over and transformed them into ethico-religious
teaching and subjective experience. From "the edifice
of eschatologico-enthusiastic thought, most closely connected with it but unmistakable in its distinctive
character," he sees, to his satisfaction, "the spiritual
life of the new religion" showing forth.

Here also, therefore, as with Wernle and Weinel, there
is conscious and intentional modernisation, in order to
discover the religion of Paul behind his theology.

One difference there is, however. The others brought
to this undertaking a certain naïveté and enthusiasm
which enabled them to see the modern and the historical
the one in the other. Titius is an observer with a keen
eye for the really historical. He holds past and present
side by side but separate, and must apply a mighty effort
of will and understanding and do violence to his feelings
in order to bring them into connexion. Out of these
inner pangs a book has come to the birth which in matters
of detail is full of just and suggestive remarks, but as a
whole is unsatisfactory.

The problem of the relation of Paul to Jesus stands for
Titius and Feine as the foreground of the interest. Both
hold the view that the connexion is a much closer one
than criticism had hitherto been prepared to admit.
The indifference which the Apostle professes regarding
"Christ after the flesh" is not to be understood in the
sense that he had no concern with His teaching. In his
detailed monograph Feine endeavours to prove that Paul
shows himself familiar with the words and thoughts of
the historic Jesus, and in his eschatology, doctrine of redemption, ethics, attitude towards the law, and conception
of baptism and the Lord's Supper, only carries to a further

point of development what is already present or fore-shadowed in the teaching of Jesus. Titius set himself the same task, and believes himself to have proved " to how great an extent the Apostle bases his views on the thoughts of Jesus, attaches himself to them, and further develops them."[1]

This result is opposed by Maurice Goguel,[2] who offers a thoroughgoing defence of the usual view. He is pre-pared to admit that Paul knew more of the life and teach-ing of Jesus than his Epistles show ; but a fundamental difference in doctrine is, he thinks, not to be denied, and he finds that it consists in the fact that the one preaches " salvation," the other the way of obtaining it. In his utterances about redemption through the death and resurrection of Christ, the parousia, Christology, Church and sacraments, Paul expresses, according to Goguel, views which go much beyond the horizon of the historical Jesus. A point of contact is only to be found in the simple ethical teaching. In reference to the law, Jesus prepared the way for what the Apostle of the Gentiles accomplished, without fully measuring the far-reaching consequences of his attitude.

The problem which theology since the time of Baur had always avoided now therefore came at last to dis-cussion. Goguel's essay did not indeed greatly elucidate the matter. That the thesis of Feine and Titius goes far beyond what the material warrants was not difficult to prove. On the other hand, it had, in justice, to be conceded to them that they had shown that there was

---

[1] R. Drescher, too "Das Leben Jesu bei Paulus" in *Festgruss an Stade*, 1900, pp. 101-161, is of opinion that the letters, rightly understood, offer us "an imposing amount of material" on the life of Jesus. The author thinks that wherever possible Paul referred to the teaching of Jesus ; and he fought his battle for freedom from the law with such confidence "because he knew that he had Jesus on his side."

It should be mentioned that J. Wellhausen takes up a similar standpoint. He gives it as his opinion, *Israelitische und jüdische Geschichte* (6th ed., 1907, 386 pp.), that Paul "was really the man who best understood the Master and carried on His work."

[2] *L'Apôtre Paul et Jésus-Christ*, 1904, 393 pp.

something in common between the fundamental conceptions of Jesus and Paul on which sufficient stress had
not previously been laid.

Goguel's sharp antitheses are at first sight more
convincing than the somewhat involved argument of
Feine, because he has the direct evidence of the text on
his side.   The difficulty, however, immediately makes
itself felt when he endeavours to make it intelligible
exactly why Paul was forced to create new conceptions.
He cannot point to any objective factors to account for
this development, and is consequently reduced to explaining everything psychologically.

From this exceedingly complicated controversy one
thing results with certainty, namely, that the problem,
in the form in which it is stated, is an unreal one.   The
statement of the problem which is here presupposed
leaves out of account the middle term, primitive
Christianity.

The credit of having expressed this clearly, and thus
put an end to the unprofitable wrangling about " Jesus
and Paul " and " Jesus or Paul," belongs to Harnack.[1]
If, he writes in the 1909 edition of his " History of
Dogma," even in the first generation the religion of
Jesus underwent a change, it must be said that it was
not Paul who was responsible for this but the primitive
Christian community.   He is not, however, able to explain
why the Apostle of the Gentiles goes still further than
the primitive community.

The question of the peculiarly inconsistent attitude of
the Apostle towards the law is not elucidated by Titius
and Feine.

The ethics are treated in monographs by Jakoby and
Juncker.[2]   The former gives a detailed description.

---

[1] Adolf Harnack, *Lehrbuch der Dogmengeschichte*, 4th ed., 1909,
vol. i., 826 pp.   See p. 107.   To the same effect, Adolf Jülicher, *Paulus
und Jesus*, 1907, 72 pp.   See p. 34.
[2] Hermann Jakoby, *Neutestamentliche Ethik*, 1899, 480 pp.   On
Paul, pp. 243-406.   Alfred Juncker, *Die Ethik des Apostels Paulus*,
part i., 1904, 288 pp.
Among other monographs we have to notice Emil Sokolowski's *Die*

The latter tries to discover the fundamental principle, and naturally finds himself obliged to deal with the whole doctrine of redemption. In the method which he applies he recalls Titius. With historical insight he recognises, in his fine chapter upon the origin of the new life, that all the ethical conceptions of Paul are in one way or another of an eschatological and "physical" character. Later on he falls a victim to the temptation to modernise.

Thus he tries, for instance, to show that Paul did not think of the influence of the Spirit in man as analogous to a physical process, but, on the contrary, "regarded the feeling of thankful love towards God and Christ as the subjective root of the new way of life." So that we find here, too, the dread of recognising anything objective in the Apostle's views and the tendency, not indeed to fall into the "one-sidedly intellectual view," but to bring into the foreground the "specifically religious estimate of the Apostle's person and gospel."

It is no accident that the scholars of this period are so anxious to distinguish between theology and religion. This expedient covers dismay and apprehension.

Meanwhile the study of Late Judaism had been going its own way. The further it advanced the more evident it became that this was the soil on which the theology of Paul had grown up. Holtzmann's New Testament Theology had not availed to render theological science proof against the assaults which it was to experience in the next few years from this direction. The impression was too strong to be escaped. And when the results

Begriffe Geist und Leben bei Paulus in ihrer Beziehung zu einander, 1903, 284 pp. The author ascribes little importance to Greek influence in comparison with Jewish, and tries to explain what is peculiar and vital in the Apostle's views as due to his individual experience, especially the vision on the Damascus road.

Hans Windisch, Die Entsündigung des Christen nach Paulus, 1908, 132 pp. The difficulties raised for Paul by his mysticism are pointed out. It is shown that this, strictly speaking, makes it impossible for him to admit sin in the case of baptized persons. The eschatological character of the sacramental-mystical theory of deliverance from sin is strongly brought out. The author continues the investigation which Paul Wernle, in his work Der Christ und die Sünde bei Paulus (1897, 138 pp.), was the first to undertake. See p. 60 of the present work.

of the study were presented, with a certain provisional completeness, in Bousset's powerful book on " Jewish Religious Life in New Testament Times," it became certain that the apprehension had not been unfounded.[1]

The naïve spiritualisation of the theology as practised by Holsten, Pfleiderer, and Holtzmann—by the latter no longer quite naïvely,—was over and done with.[2] The recognition of a " physical " [3] aspect in Paul's expectations of the future was no longer sufficient. It had to be

[1] Wilhelm Bousset, *Die Religion des Judentums im neutestamentlichen Zeitalter*, 1903, 512 pp. Simultaneously appeared the same writer's work, *Die jüdische Apokalyptik, ihre religionsgeschichtliche Herkunft und ihre Bedeutung für das neue Testament* (" Jewish Apocalyptic, its Origin in the Light of Comparative Religion and its Significance for the New Testament." A Lecture, 1903.)

Eschatology receives special attention in the fine work of Hugo Gressman, *Der Ursprung der israelitisch-jüdischen Eschatologie* (" The Origin of the Israelitish and Jewish Eschatology "), 1905, 378 pp. The author takes up an attitude of some reserve in regard to the " religious-historical method," and seeks to determine in the case of every statement whether it can have arisen in Israel or must be regarded as having been introduced from without.

Paul Volz, *Jüdische Eschatologie von Daniel bis Akiba*, 1903, 412 pp., endeavours, somewhat unconvincingly, to give a sketch of Jewish conceptions of the future age.

Everling's investigations are continued, on modern lines, by a study of Martin Dibelius, *Die Geisterwelt im Glauben des Paulus*, 1909, 249 pp. (" The World of Spirits as conceived in Paul's Belief "). In addition to the Late Jewish passages the author cites also the Rabbinical and those suggested by the Comparative Study of Religion. The excursuses on the linguistic history of the subject are very instructive (pp. 209-232). On Everling, see pp. 55-57 of the present work.

[2] G. F. Heinrici's work, *Das Urchristentum*, 1902, 142 pp., still occupies the old stand-point. On Paul, pp. 71-101. For what he has to say against the " physical " in the doctrine of redemption, see pp. 95, 96.

W. Bousset, *Der Apostel Paulus*, 1906, holds that we shall never completely understand the Apostle's doctrine. We must make up our minds to the fact . . . . that in his letters we have before us only fragments of his spiritual life, the full wealth of which we can only vaguely imagine. The individual arguments of Paul look to us like erratic boulders ; only toilsomely and partially can we reconstruct the connexion of thought.

[3] Rendering *naturhaft*. Dr. Schweitzer has favoured me with the following note on this difficult concept, which from this point becomes prominent in the discussions. After consultation with him, the word has been rendered " physical," but placed in quotation marks to indicate the special use.—TRANSLATOR. " In the special sense in which it is here used *naturhaft* is intended to convey that it is not a question of a purely spiritual redemption, but that the whole physical and hyperphysical being of the man is thereby translated into a new condition. Body and soul are redeemed together ; and in such a way that not only the elect portion of mankind, but the whole world is completely transformed in a great catastrophic event."

admitted that his doctrine of redemption as a whole bore this character, and that the fundamental strain in his mysticism was not ethical but physical, as Lüdemann had declared as long ago as 1872 without suspecting the far-reaching consequences of his observation.

The only question now was how much had to be conceded to this alien system of thought which was endeavouring to draw Paul within its borders, and how much could be saved from it.

In this quandary theologians had recourse to the expedient of applying the distinction between " theoretical " (theological) and " religious " to the doctrine of the Apostle, as Holtzmann had already tried to do when he could no longer refuse to recognise its Gnostic, intellectualistic character.

The position became especially critical in view of the concessions which had to be made regarding the Pauline conception of baptism and the Lord's Supper. Up to this time, that chapter had given little trouble to theological science. It had been taken for granted that at bottom it could only be a question of symbolism. The doctrine of redemption on its ethical side found, it was thought, in the sacred ceremonies its cultual expression.

Holtzmann, too, in the section on " Mystical Conceptions " [1] (*Mysteriöses*) had still to all intents and purposes taken the same ground. Baptism and the Lord's Supper are, he explains, in the first place, acts of confession by which the death of the Lord is proclaimed. To this has to be added, in the case of the Lord's Supper, the significance of a communion meal, and in the case of baptism the value of a symbolic act. It creates, according to Romans vi., a mystical fellowship with the buried and risen Christ. " The outward symbol of complete immersion signifies and represents the disappearance of the old, fleshly man, the coming forth out of the water represents the forthgoing of a new, spiritual man."

Paul, Holtzmann thinks, puts the content of his

[1] *Neutestamentliche Theologie*, vol. ii., 1897, pp. 175-187.

" experience " into this ceremonial act, and thereby cuts it loose from the earlier view which had arisen from its connexion with John the Baptist.   Strictly speaking, he transforms both the cultus-acts, by bringing his new conception of Christianity into connexion with them in order to give it cultual expression.

Probably—we are still following Holtzmann—he did this under the guidance of analogies which he found in the Mystery-religions of the period.   The expressions which he uses at any rate remind us sometimes of the language which is associated with them.   This, then, was the point from which the later transformation began.   " It was, in fact, Paul who from an outlying, one might almost say a remote point of his system of thought, opened up for the early Catholic Church a road which it would, indeed, most probably have followed even without this precedent, which was given, as it were, merely incidentally and casually."

It is interesting to observe precisely what views are intended to be excluded by these guarded explanations. Holtzmann is concerned to emphasise the view that baptism and the Lord's Supper have in the Apostle's doctrine a rather subordinate importance, and that they are not real sacraments but quasi-sacramental acts. He deliberately avoids the plain issue, on which after all everything really depends, whether baptism and the Supper effect redemption or only represent it.

But those who came after him were obliged to raise this question, and so far as they were willing to respect the documents were obliged to answer that the sacraments not only represent but effect redemption.   Wernle remarks regretfully that the cultus-acts have in Paul a much greater importance than one would be inclined to expect, and that in certain passages he tolerates or even suggests " pagan " views.   Weinel is obliged to admit that alongside of the religion of inwardness which he has discovered in the Apostle's teaching, a sacramental religion, which is inherently opposed to it, from time to

time appears. " Sometimes," he writes, " it is faith
that brings the Spirit, sometimes baptism, sometimes it is
faith that unites with Christ, sometimes the Lord's
Supper." Titius feels himself obliged to give up the
symbolical interpretation of Romans vi., which for
Holtzmann still forms a fixed datum, and admits that
the atmosphere of this chapter is " supranaturalistic,"
and that the baptism there referred to is a real baptism
into the death of Christ and an equally real partaking in His resurrection. Feine, in *Jesus Christus and
Paulus*, insists that the sacramental character of the
cultus - acts described by Paul should be universally
acknowledged.

Heitmüller, in his work on " Baptism and the Lord's
Supper in Paul's Writings," [1] gives the old and the new
view side by side, and shows that it is the latter which
alone is justified by the documents. The mystical connexion which in baptism and the Lord's Supper is set
up between the believer and Christ is a " physico-hyperphysical one," and has as its consequence that the believer
shares *realiter* in the death and resurrection of Christ.

For the liberal conception of Paulinism this was a blow
at the heart. If redemption is effected through the sacraments, these are no longer an " outlying point " in the
Apostle's doctrine, but lie at its centre. And at the
same time the distinction between " theoretical " (theological) and " religious " is rendered impossible. A
doctrine of redemption which is thus bound up with
Mysteries which work in a physico-hyperphysical way
is in its essence purely supernaturalistic. [2]

---

[1] W. Heitmüller, *Taufe und Abendmahl bei Paulus*, 1903, 56 pp.

[2] How unwilling theology was to draw this inevitable inference is
to be seen from the works of Weinel and Heitmüller. They refuse to
go beyond the statement that the sacraments stand in sharp opposition
to the real " religion " of Paul, and think that they have solved the
problem by asserting that the Apostle of the Gentiles did not notice
the contradiction. Weinel remarks, " Paul himself is quite unconscious of the problem raised by the collision of the ' physical ' doctrine of
redemption of the Mysteries with the ethical doctrine of Christianity."
Heitmüller says, " These views of baptism and the Lord's Supper
stand in unreconciled and unreconcilable opposition with the central

The courage of theological thinkers was put to a severe test. When Baur and his followers made their profession of faith in unbiassed free investigation they could have had no inkling that it would become so difficult for a later generation to remain true to this principle.

To give up the distinction between " theoretical " and religious and to follow a purely historical method meant, as things stood at the beginning of the twentieth century, to be left with an entirely temporally conditioned Paulinism, of which modern ways of thought could make nothing, and to trace out a system which for our religion is dead.

At this crisis theology encountered in William Wrede a candid friend who sought to keep it in the path of sincerity. His *Paulus*, short and written in such a way as to be universally intelligible, appeared in the year 1904.[1]

The " theology," he writes, is in Paul not to be separated from the " religion." His religion is through and through theological ; his theology is his religion.

The theory which Holtzmann introduced in his " New Testament Theology," and which Wernle, Weinel, Heitmüller, Titius, and the rest had developed, thus came to an untimely end before it had left its nonage. It survived only seven years.

And then the second expedient—that Paul had thought out no system, but just put down his thoughts in any kind of fortuitous order—is set aside. The framework of the doctrine of redemption, Wrede declares, is very closely articulated. Further, it is not really complicated, but is at bottom quite simple, if once we take account of the thought-material out of which it is constructed and take the most general conceptions as the starting-point.

Redemption—this is, according to Wrede, Paul's train

---

significance of faith for Pauline Christianity, that is to say, with the purely spiritual, personal view of the religious relation which stands in the foreground of Pauline religious life and religious thought."

[1] William Wrede, *Paulus*, 1904, 113 pp. (In the series entitled " Religionsgeschichtliche Volksbücher.")

of thought—is not something which takes place in the individual as such, as the later Christian view was, but signifies a universal event in which the individual has a part.

It consists in the deliverance of mankind from the dominion of the powers which hold sway over this world. These powers have been destroyed by the death and resurrection of Jesus, as will become manifest at the parousia. Thus redemption is essentially an insurance for this future.

But it is even in the present real, though not visible. Christ is the representative of the human race. What happened to Him, happened to all.

" All men are therefore from the moment of His death set free, as He is Himself, from the hostile powers ; and all are by His resurrection transferred into a condition of indestructible life." The proof of this change is given by the Spirit. He represents in the redeemed the super-earthly life, as a " gift of the last times in which the powers of the world to come already exercise an influence upon the present existence."

This wholly " objective " conception of redemption is, Wrede admits, for our modern modes of thought rather impersonal and cold. " It takes place in a way which is wholly external to the individual man, and the events seem, as it were, to be only enacted in Christ."

Redemption is effected in the sacraments. " The ' physical ' transformation is effected by physical processes." Paul's thought moves, therefore, among crude, unsubtilised conceptions.

His statements about justification by faith and about the law are based upon this fundamental view, and represent merely the " controversial teaching " to which he was forced in order to maintain the cause of freedom from the law.

The material of his world of thought was, therefore, Jewish. What was the transformation by which it became Christian ?

Paul's conception of the Christ [1] was fully formed
before he came to believe in Jesus. At his conversion,
by the vision on the road to Damascus, the only new
element that he took up into his conception was that this
heavenly being had temporarily assumed a human
form of existence in order by His death and resurrection
to redeem mankind and to bring in the new order of
things. An influence of the teaching of Jesus upon the
theology of the Apostle to the Gentiles is not to be recognised. Wrede makes the gap between the two as
wide as possible, and insists that Paul's gospel must be
considered as independent of, and essentially different
in character from, that of Jesus.

The Apostle's adoption of the view that the end of the
law had come, is, according to Wrede, partly due to his
experiences at his conversion, partly to the exigencies·
of the mission to the Gentiles.

Of the value and the remarkable literary beauty of the
book it is impossible to say too much. It belongs, not
to theology, but to the literature of the world.

But one must not, in one's admiration, forget justice.
What is here set forth is not absolutely new. A view
of a similar character, and more closely reasoned, had been
put forward by Kabisch—Kabisch,[2] whom theologians
had passed over in complete silence, because they did
not know what to make of him. Wrede does nothing
else than to give to the presentation of the latter's discoveries the advantage of his literary skill, while at the
same time showing that the separation of " theory "
(theology) and " religion " which had barred the way to
their acceptance is not tenable. There is one thing which
is to be regretted in Wrede's book, and that is that the
terse popular method of presentation forbids any detailed
discussion of the problems. If the author had worked

---

[1] In the sense of the Messiah.—TRANSLATOR.
[2] How far Wrede was consciously influenced by Kabisch, and how
far he has the sense of creating something new, is not quite evident.
He reckons the book among the " very important studies on special
points," to which he refers in the bibliography, but he does not quote it.

out his arguments thoroughly, and replied to his opponents and predecessors, he would have been obliged to face many questions which, as it was, did not force themselves upon him.

What are the points that remain obscure ?

Wrede proposes to conceive the possibility of redemption in such a way that "mankind," in view of Christ's solidarity with the race by virtue of His earthly life, has a part in His death and resurrection. This view is, in this form, untenable. In Paul, salvation has not reference to mankind as a whole, but only to the elect. It is also questionable whether the idea of racial solidarity suffices to explain how the death and resurrection of Jesus can realise themselves in other men.

What is the basis of the mystical union with Christ ? To this question Wrede has given no answer.

Then, too, the inconsistent attitude of Paul towards the law was not explained by him. He does not even succeed in showing how the Apostle arrived at the idea that the law was no longer valid. The suggestion that it was in part through his experience at his conversion, in part through the exigencies of the mission to the Gentiles, is a mere expedient. Unless it is possible to explain Paul's attitude, with all its inner contradictions, as a logical and necessary conclusion from his system as a whole, it remains for us practically unexplained.[1]

Again, Wrede gives no scheme of the events of the End, although such a scheme obviously belongs to the "system."

It is not explained, either, how the death of Jesus can be interpreted at the same time as taking place for the forgiveness of sins. In general, the relation between the essential theology, as laid down in the mystical doctrine of redemption, and the "controversial doctrines" is not clear.

---

[1] C. von Dobschütz, *Probleme des apostolischen Zeitalters* ("Problems of the Apostolic Age," 1904, 138 pp.), does not enter in detail into the question regarding the genesis of the Pauline view of the law, although he treats Jewish Christianity and Gentile Christianity with some fulness.

In regard to the question of the relation of Paul to
Jesus, Wrede holds that they lived in two wholly different
worlds of thought.   This is connected with his view that
the Galilaean Master made no claim to the Messiahship,
but was first raised to Messianic dignity after His death,
and that this claim was then projected back into the
Gospels in the form that Jesus had made His rank known
to His disciples only, and had enjoined upon them to keep
silence until after His death.[1]   His preaching was, above
all things, ethical.   So far as concerns eschatology and
the meaning to be attached to His death, the Apostle of
the Gentiles received no impulse of a theological character
from Him.

Paul, therefore, created something essentially new,
which has, one might almost say, nothing to do with the
thought of Jesus, and also goes far beyond the conceptions of primitive Christianity.[2]

Thus for Wrede, as for Holsten and Holtzmann, the
doctrine of Paul is an isolated entity without connexion in
the past or influence upon the future.   And he, too, finds
himself unable to explain why the system thus remained
without influence.   That the " controversial theology,"
with its insistence on the atoning death, lost its significance when the question of the law ceased to be actual
may appear plausible.   But why did the mystical doctrine
of redemption get pushed aside instead of being further
developed ?   Its presuppositions—if Wrede's account of

[1] See the present writer's *Von Reimarus zu Wrede, eine Geschichte
der Leben-Jesu-Forschung* (1906, 418 pp.).   On Wrede, pp. 327-347.
(English translation, " The Quest of the Historical Jesus."   A. and C.
Black, London, 2nd ed., 1911.   On Wrede, pp. 328-348.)

[2] This thesis of Wrede's called into being a new literature upon
Paul and Jesus which attacked Wrede chiefly on the score of his one-
sidedness.

P. Kölbing, *Die geistige Einwirkung der Person Jesu auf Paulus*,
1906 (" The Spiritual Influence of the Person of Jesus on Paul ").
Adolf Jülicher, *Paulus und Jesus*, 1907, 72 pp.   Arnold Meyer,
Wer hat das Christentum begründet, Jesus oder Paulus ? 1907, 104 pp.
("Who founded Christianity, Jesus or Paul ? ")   Wilhelm Walther, *Pauli
Christentum, Jesu Evangelium*, 1908, 51 pp.   Johannes Weiss, *Paulus
und Jesus*, 1909, 72 pp.   *Christus : Die Anfänge des Dogmas*, 1909, 88 pp.
(" Christ : The Beginnings of Dogma ").

matters is correct—could hardly have been much altered in the next generation.

A valuable supplement in many respects to Wrede's views is offered by Martin Brückner's study of the origin of the Pauline Christology.[1]

The author offers a detailed proof that the Pauline Christology arose by the insertion of the earthly episode of the incarnation, dying and rising again into the already present conception of a pre-existent heavenly Personality.[2] Incidentally he gives an admirably clear account of the Jewish eschatology and its formation.[3]

He shows that the Jewish eschatology itself, in the Apocalypses of Ezra and Baruch, distinguished between the temporally limited Messianic Kingdom and the subsequent complete renewal of the world, and that, in conformity with this, two resurrections have to be recognised. One, in which only a limited number have a part, takes place at the appearance of the Messiah ; the other, the general resurrection, only follows at the end of the intervening Kingdom. The scene of the latter was pictured, he thinks, by Paul, as by his Jewish predecessors, as the land of Palestine, with the New Jerusalem as its centre.

It is interesting to notice how Wrede and Brückner, without themselves remarking it, have refuted one of the weightiest objections of the Ultra-Tübingen critics.

[1] Martin Brückner, *Die Entstehung der paulinischen Christologie*, 1903, 237 pp.

The work appeared some months before Wrede's *Paulus*, but the author, who had the opportunity of personal intercourse and the interchange of ideas with him, was acquainted with his method and fundamental views. As he is also an independent thinker, his work represents not only a supplement but a real advance.

[2] Viz. the Jewish conception of the Messiah.—TRANSLATOR.

[3] William Olschewski replies to Wrede and Brückner in his thoughtful but obscure and heavily written dissertation, *Die Wurzeln der paulinischen Christologie* (1909, 170 pp.) ("The Roots of the Pauline Eschatology"). He thinks that the origin of Christianity which they suggest does not explain the " characteristic and peculiar connexion of Christology with Pneumatology," and insists that in the Damascus vision is to be found the sufficient reason for " the intimately organic fusion " of the conception of Christ with that of the Spirit which operates through Him. In any case he holds it to be " false in principle and method to try to derive the roots of the Pauline Christology from the Jewish Apocalyptic Christology."

The latter had asserted that it was impossible that the
process of deification of the Person of Jesus could have
reached its completion within a few years, and had claimed
for it at least two generations. Now, however, it is
shown that it is not this process at all, but another, which
could take place in a moment, which has to be considered,
since it is only a question of the taking up of the episode
of the incarnation, death, and resurrection into the
already present and living conception of the Messiah.

The immediate effect of Wrede's presentation of matters
was that writers ventured more confidently to accept the
" physical " view of the Pauline doctrine of redemption,
and that the distinction between " theory " (theology)
and religion, where writers could not make up their minds
to do without it, was applied with moderation.[1]

[1] From the literature we may mention A. Schettler, *Die paulinische
Formel " Durch Christus "* (" The Pauline Formula Through Christ "),
1907, 82 pp.   J. Haussleiter, *Paulus*, 1909, 96 pp.   (Lectures, popular.)
R. Knopf, *Paulus*, 1909, 123 pp.   Eberhard Vischer, *Der Apostel
Paulus und sein Werk*, 1910, 143 pp.   By the same author, *Die
Paulusbriefe*, 1906, 80 pp.   A remarkably good, clearly and simply
written guide to questions of " Introduction."   Julius Schniewind,
Die Begriffe Wort und Evangelium bei Paulus (" The Meaning of the
Terms ' Word ' and ' Gospel ' in Paul's Writings "), 1910, 120 pp.
    Johannes Müller, *Die Entstehung des persönlichen Christentums
der paulinischen Gemeinden*, 1911, 306 pp.   A good analysis of
the general contents of Paul's gospel.   The theological system and
the mysticism of the Apostle are not explained.   The book is the
second edition of a study which appeared in 1898 under the title *Das
persönliche Christentum der paulinischen Gemeinden nach seiner Entstehung untersucht* (" An Investigation of the Origin of the Personal
Christianity of the Pauline Churches ").
    Adolf Deissmann, *Paulus*, 1911, 202 pp.   The book grew out of
lectures.   The author is opposed to the method of investigation which
aims at understanding the " System of Pauline Theology," and thinks
that in following these " doctrinaire interests " it would go further
and further astray.   For him Paul is primarily " a hero of the religious
life " for whom " theology is a secondary matter."   He holds that the
Apostle was more a man of prayer and testimony, a confessor and a
prophet, than a learned exegete and laborious dogmatist.
    His aim is, with the aid of reminiscences of two journeys to the
East, to " place the man of Tarsus in the sunlight of his Anatolian home,
and in the clear air of the ancient Mediterranean lands," and he believes
that when this is done " what previously tired our eyes, like a set of
faded and rubbed pencil sketches, becomes at once plastic and living
in its light and shadow."   This hope is by no means realised in his
work.   It appears here, as was also noticeable in the writer's earlier *Licht
vom Osten* (" Light from the East "), that he has a high appreciation of
local colour and the memorials of ancient civilisation, but when it comes

But he did not succeed in forcing on a thorough revision of previous views. Harnack, for instance, in the 1909 edition of the "History of Dogma" stands by his account of 1893, unshaken.[1]

Reinhold Seeberg[2] undertook in 1908 a very interesting attempt to walk in new paths, but does not deal with Wrede and his problems. He holds to the view that the Apostle did not create "a unified system," but that his thought moved amid a number of different sets of ideas, which for him were held together by "religion as an experience."

This neglect of Wrede's work does not mean anything ; it was simply that the history of dogma could make nothing of his view. It is significant, however, that among those who accepted his view in substance, no one made the attempt to carry it to victory by a comprehensive presentation of it on an adequate scale.

The cause of this lies in the peculiar difficulties which lie concealed in the scheme which he sketched out.

The fact is that the " physical " element which is to be recognised in Paul's doctrine is neither all of one piece nor wholly to be explained from Late Judaism. Strictly

---

really to explaining the ideas he is not able to draw nearly so much profit from them as he expected. And his contempt for " doctrinaire interests " revenges itself upon his treatment. It is obscure and confused, and does not get at the essence of the thoughts. In regard to Paul's mysticism Deissmann has applied new catchwords to old psychological considerations, but in nowise contributes to the explanation of it. After Wrede's *Paulus*, his book seems a kind of anachronism. It is, besides, not fitting that what professes to be a new view should be presented in the inadequate form of a collection of lectures.

[1] Adolf Harnack, *Lehrbuch der Dogmengeschichte*, 4th ed., vol. i., 1909, 826 pp. On Paul, pp. 96-107 (3rd ed., 1893).

[2] Reinhold Seeberg, *Lehrbuch der Dogmengeschichte*, 2nd ed., vol i., 1908, 570 pp. On Paul, 68-78. The first circle of ideas embraces the thoughts regarding flesh and spirit, the power of grace and the strength of sin, Christ and the new creation ; the second consists of the formulas which were created in opposition to Jewish Christianity ; the third has to do with the mystical body of Christ, in which the natural distinctions between men are abolished. On points of detail there are many discriminating observations. The first edition, of 1895, did not even contain any section on Paul.

The 4th ed. of Loof's *Dogmengeschichte* (1906, vol. i., 576 pp.) does not deal with the Apostle of the Gentiles, any more than the preceding editions.

speaking, it takes three different forms, of which one is peculiar to the eschatology, another to the mystical doctrine of redemption, and the third to the sacraments.

The " materialism " of the conception of redemption which is directed towards the future has to do with super-earthly powers, with judgment, bodily resurrection and transformation.

Somewhat different is the " realism " of the mystical doctrine of the new creation, which asserts that believers here and now experience death and resurrection in fellowship with Christ, and so put on, beneath the earthly exterior which conceals it, a nature essentially immune from corruption.

Different from this conception again is the sacramental, inasmuch as it represents in some inexplicable fashion an externalisation of it. What, according to the mystical doctrine, seemed to take place by itself without being connected with an external act, is here to be thought of as the effect of eating and drinking, and cleansing with water. The sacramental conception is a magical conception.

Of these three varieties of the " physical," only the first can be immediately explained from Late Judaism. For the two others it offers no analogy. Late Judaism remained true to its Judaic character in knowing nothing of either mysticism or sacraments.

On the other hand, these three varieties of the " physical " in the Paul's doctrine of redemption do not stand side by side unrelated, but seem to be somehow connected in such a way that the eschatological element dominates and supplies the basis of the other two. The most obvious procedure would have been to attempt to derive the mystical and sacramental conceptions from the eschatological, as being the root-conception.

A beginning in this direction had been made by Kabisch when he attempted to exhibit the connexion between eschatology and the mystical doctrine of the real dying and rising again with Christ.[1]

---

[1] On Kabisch see above, pp. 58-63.

But in doing so he did not take into account the sacraments. It was just these, however, which seemed to make it *a priori* impossible to explain Paulinism exclusively on the basis of Late Judaism. Therefore Wrede and his followers seek other sources. They try to explain the system, not solely from the side of eschatology, but from that of " Comparative Religion," and hold that it betrays the influence not only of Late-Jewish but also of Oriental ideas generally, such as are found in the Mystery-religions.

No doubt the first question which here arises is whether the methods of Comparative Religion are essentially applicable to the explanation of Paulinism.

To apply the methods of Comparative Religion means to study the individual religions, not in isolation, but with the purpose of investigating the mutual influences which they have openly or covertly exercised on one another.

At bottom, therefore, it is a necessary outcome of the application of scientific methods generally, and it only received a special name because theological scholarship so long shut its doors against it.

Under this distinctive name the method attained to influence and honour in connexion with the critical study of the Old Testament and the Graeco-Oriental cults. In the former department of study it made an end of the prepossession that Judaism had developed entirely by its own inner impulses, and showed how much material of a generally Oriental character it had adopted. In particular it showed that Late-Jewish Apocalyptic is full of conceptions from the Babylonian and the Irano-Zarathustrian religions, and represents a combination of universal cosmological speculations with the future-hope of the ancient Jewish prophetism.[1]

In the comparative study of the heathen religions it became apparent that the Mystery - religions, which

---

[1] A sifting and a survey of results is offered in the closing chapter, " Das religionsgeschichtliche Problem " (448-493) in Bousset's book, *Die Religion des Judentums im neutestamentlichen Zeitalter*, 1903 (" The Religion of Judaism in New Testament Times ").

entered on their conquering progress westwards about the
same time as Christian Gnosticism, combined Greek
religious feeling and a Greek cosmogony with Oriental
cultus-ideas.

In both these cases it is a question of contacts and
influences which were due to political and cultural relations, and produced their effect in the course of extended
periods of time and under favourable historical circum-
stances.   The method cannot simply be applied without
more ado to the explanation of the ideas of an individual
man, since most of its presuppositions would not here be
valid.   In the case of religions, syncretism can work
its way in and develop ; in the case of individuals it can
only be recognised in a very limited degree.   The taking
over and remoulding of foreign conceptions is a process
requiring numbers and time.   The individual comes
into question only so far as he is organically united with
a community which is active in this way, and allows its
instincts to influence him.

Paul belongs to Late Judaism.   Whatever he received
in the way of influences such as Comparative Religion
takes account of came to him mainly through this channel.
The suggestion that apart from this he might be personally
and directly affected by " Oriental " influences calls for
very cautious consideration.   In particular we ought to
be very careful to guard against raising this possibility
to a certainty by general considerations regarding all
that the child of the Diaspora might have seen, heard, and
read.   The question can only be decided by what we
actually find in the Epistles.

It is further to be remarked that Late Judaism was
no longer in his time so open to external influences that
any and every kind of religious conception which was
floating about anywhere in the Orient could necessarily
impose itself on Paul's mind through this medium.   The
period of assimilation was, speaking generally, at an end.
The new material had been—before Paul's day—worked
up along with the old into a set of Apocalyptic conceptions,

which, in spite of the elbow-room which the heterogeneous ideas necessarily claimed for themselves, did form a system, and appeared from without as relatively complete and self-sufficing. The Oriental material has been poured into Jewish moulds and received a Jewish impress.

A still further point is that any one whose thought moves in the Apocalyptic system created by the books of Daniel and Enoch is not so much exposed to, as withdrawn from, the action of free Oriental influence. He is already saturated with those elements in regard to receptivity which the Jewish mind possesses and the tendency to assimilation, and possesses it not as something foreign to himself but as Jewish. Apocalyptic tends to produce in him immunisation as against further syncretistic infection.

This assertion is susceptible of historical proof. Late Judaism stands, even before the beginning of our era, apart from the Oriental religious movements. And it continues unaffected by them. Not one of its representatives was concerned in the syncretistic movement. Philo seeks to rationalise Judaism by the aid of Platonico-Stoic philosophy, but he gives no place to the religious and cultual ideas by which he was surrounded in Egypt. It is as though they had no existence for him.

To apply the comparative method to Paul would, therefore, generally speaking, mean nothing more or less than to explain him on the basis of Late Judaism. Those who give due weight to the eschatological character of his doctrine and to the problems and ideas which connect it with works like the Apocalypse of Ezra are the true exponents of " Comparative Religion," even though they may make no claim to this title. Any one who goes beyond this and tries to bring Paul into direct connexion with the Orient as such commits himself to the perilous path of scientific adventure.

Considerations of that kind were not taken into account by Wrede and his followers. But even if they had become conscious of the difficulties in the way of the application of the method to Paul, they could not have acted otherwise.

In spite of all theoretical warnings this path had to be followed.

If once the mystical doctrine of the dying and rising again with Christ is recognised to be " physical," and the view of baptism and the Supper to be sacramental, and if it is a further datum of the question that Late Judaism knows nothing of mysticism or sacraments ; and if one is not content to assume that the Apostle has created or invented this non-Jewish element out of his inner con- sciousness ; there is at first sight no alternative but to make the attempt to explain it from conceptions and suggestions which are supposed to have come into it from without, from some form or other of Oriental syncretism.

VII

PAULINISM AND COMPARATIVE RELIGION

Gustav Anrich. Das antike Mysterienwesen in seinem Einfluss auf das Christentum. (The Ancient Mysteries in their Influence on Christianity.) 1894.

Martin Brückner. Der sterbende und auferstehende Gottheiland in den orientalischen Religionen und ihr Verhältnis zum Christentum. (The Saviour-God who dies and rises again in the Oriental Religions ; and their Relation to Christianity.) 1908.

Karl Clemen. Religionsgeschichtliche Erklärung des Neuen Testaments. (An Explanation of the New Testament on the basis of Comparative Religion.) 1909.

Franz Cumont. Les Mystères de Mithra. 1899. (E. T. by T. J. McCormack, 1903.) Les Religions orientales dans le paganisme romain. 1906.

Adolf Deissmann. Licht vom Osten. 1908. (E. T. by L. R. M. Strachan, " Light from the Ancient East," 1910.) Die Urgeschichte des Christentums im Lichte der Sprachforschung. (The Early History of Christianity in the Light of Linguistic Research.) 1910.

Albrecht Dieterich. Abraxas. 1891. Nekyia. 1893. Eine Mithrasliturgie. 1903.

Arthur Drews. Die Christusmythe. 1909. (E. T. by C. D. Burns.)

Albert Eichhorn. Das Abendmahl im Neuen Testament. (The Lord's Supper in the New Testament.) 1898.

Johannes Geffken. Aus der Werdezeit des Christentums. (From the Formative Period of Christianity), 2nd ed., 1909.

P. Gennrich. Die Lehre von der Wiedergeburt . . . in der dogmengeschichtlichen und religionsgeschichtlichen Betrachtung. (The Doctrine of Regeneration . . . from the point of view of the History of Dogma and of Comparative Religion.) 1907.

Otto Gruppe. Die griechischen Kulte und Mythen in ihrer Beziehung zu den orientalischen Religionen. (The Greek Cults and Myths in their Relation to the Oriental Religions), vol. i., 1887. Griechische Mythologie und Religionsgeschichte. (Greek Mythology and Comparative Religion), 2 vols., 1906.

Hermann Gunkel. Zum religionsgeschichtlichen Verständnis des Neuen Testaments. (Contributions to the Understanding of the New Testament from the point of view of Comparative Religion.) 1903.

Adolf Harnack. Mission und Ausbreitung des Christentums in den ersten drei Jahrhunderten, vol. i., 1906. (E. T. by J. Moffatt, "The Mission and Expansion of Christianity in the First Three Centuries," 2nd ed., 1908.)

Hugo Hepding. Attis, seine Mythen und sein Kult. (Attis, his Myths and Cultus.) 1903.

W. Heitmüller. Taufe und Abendmahl bei Paulus. (Baptism and the Lord's Supper in Paul's Teaching.) 1903.

Im Namen Jesu. Eine sprach- und religionsgeschichtliche Untersuchung zum neuen Testament, speziell zur altchristlichen Taufe. 1903. (In the Name of Jesus. A Study of the New Testament from the point of view of the History of Language and of Comparative Religion, with Special Reference to Early Christian Baptism.)

Adolf Jacoby. Die antiken Mysterienreligionen und das Christentum. (The Ancient Mystery-religions and Christianity.) 1910.

Georg Mau. Die Religionsphilosophie Kaiser Julians in seinen Reden auf König Helios und die Göttermutter. (The Emperor Julian's Philosophy of Religion as shown in his Orations on King Helios and the Dea Mater.) 1908.

Max Maurenbrecher. Von Jerusalem nach Rom. (From Jerusalem to Rome.) 1910.

Salomon Reinach. Cultes, mythes et religions. (1905-1906-1908.)

Richard Reitzenstein. Poimandres. 1904.

Die hellenistischen Mysterienreligionen. Ihre Grundgedanken und Wirkungen. (The Hellenistic Mystery-Religions. Their fundamental Ideas and their Influence.) 1910.

E. Rohde. Psyche. 1894. 3rd ed. 1903, 2 vols.

H. R. Roscher. Lexikon der griechisch-römischen Mythologie. (Lexicon of Graeco-Roman Mythology.) 3 vols. 1884-1909.

Ernst Eduard Schwartz. Paulus. Charakterköpfe aus der antiken Literatur. (Character Sketches from Ancient Literature.) 1910.

W. B. Smith. Der vorchristliche Jesus nebst weiterer Vorstudien zur Entstehungsgeschichte des Urchristentums. (The pre-Christian Jesus, with other Preliminary Studies for a History of the Origin and Growth of Christianity.)

Wilhelm Soltau. Das Fortleben des Heidentums in der altchristlichen Kirche. (The Survival of Paganism in the Early Christian Church.) 1906.

Hermann Usener. Religionsgeschichtliche Untersuchungen. (Studies in Comparative Religion.) 1889; 1899.

Paul Wendland. Die hellenistisch-römische Kultur in ihren Beziehungen zu Judentum und Christentum. (Hellenistic-Roman Civilisation in Relation to Judaism and Christianity.) 1907.

Paul Wernle. Die Anfänge unserer Religion. 1901. (E. T. by G. A. Bienemann, "The Beginnings of Christianity," 1903.)

Georg Wobbermin. Religionsgeschichtliche Studien zur Frage der Beeinflussung des Urchristentums durch das antike Mysterienwesen. (Studies in Comparative Religion with reference to the Question of the Influence of the Ancient Mysteries on Primitive Christianity.) 1896.

To the Bonn philologist Hermann Usener belongs the
credit of having been the first to bring the Comparative
Study of the pagan religions as they existed at the beginning of the Christian era into contact with theological
science.[1]   In E. Rohde's *Psyche* the Greek and late-Greek
conceptions regarding ghost-worship and immortality
were introduced to a wider circle of readers.

A generally intelligible survey of the cults which come
into question is offered by Franz Cumont in his work on
the Oriental religions in Roman paganism.[2]

It was Phrygia in Asia Minor which gave to the world
the worship of Attis and the Dea Mater ; from Egypt
came that of Isis and Serapis ; Syria supplied the great
sun-god whom Heliogabalus and Aurelian, for reasons of

---

[1] Hermann Usener, *Religionsgeschichtliche Untersuchungen : " Das
Weihnachtsfest "* (1889, 337 pp.) ; *" Die Sintflutsagen "* (1899, 276 pp.)
("Studies in Comparative Religion, 'Christmas,' 1889. 'The Flood-
legends,' 1899 ").   Other works which played an important part in
creating the new horizon were Albrecht Dieterich's works on Comparative Religion, *Abraxas* (1891, 221 pp.   On a Hellenistic myth of
the Creation, and Judaeo-Orphico-Gnostic cults) and *Nekyia*, contributions to the explanation of the " Apocalypse of Peter " (1893, 238
pp.).   The description of the torments of hell in the Akhmim fragment
is based, he thinks, not on Jewish eschatology, but on conceptions which
are found in the Orphic literature.

[2] *Les Religions orientales dans le paganisme romain*, 1st ed., 1906 ;
2nd ed., 1909, 427 pp.   Based on Lectures delivered in the year 1905
in the Collège de France.

We may note also some of the essays in Salomon Reinach's *Cultes,
mythes et religions*, 3 vols., 1905–1906–1908 (466, 466, and 537 pp.).

Otto Gruppe, *Die griechischen Kulte und Mythen in ihrer Beziehung
zu den orientalischen Religionen* (" Greek cults and Myths in their
relation to the Oriental Religions "), vol. i., 1887, 706 pp. ;   and
Griechische Mythologie und Religionsgeschichte (" Greek Mythology
and the History of Greek Religions ").   In Iwan Müller's *Handbuch der
klassischen Altertumswissenschaft* (" Handbook of Classical Antiqui-
ties "), 1906, 2 vols., embracing 1923 pp.

Georg Mau. *Die Religionsphilosophie Kaiser Julians in seinen
Reden auf König Helios und die Göttermutter* (" The Emperor Julian's
Philosophy of Religion in his Orations on King Helios and the Dea
Mater "), 1908, 169 pp.   In the appendix there is a German translation
of both discourses.

Of a popular and unscientific character is H. E. de Jong's *Das
antike Mysterienwesen in religionsgeschichtlicher, ethnologischer und
psychologischer Beleuchtung* (" The Ancient Mystery-religions in the
Light of Comparative Religion, Ethnology, and Psychology "), 1909,
362 pp.   The author is disposed to cite the modern occult " manifestations " in relation to the astral body in order to explain certain
" appearances " in the ceremonies of initiation to the mysteries.

state, proclaimed as the supreme divinity.   The religion
of Mithra is of Persian origin.

Of these cults, ancient literature, both pagan and
Christian, has preserved some records, but it is only since
discoveries of inscriptions and papyri have supplemented
this information [1] that any real understanding of the
character and history of these religions has become
possible.

The myth on which the worship of Cybele and Attis is
based has been handed down in various and conflicting
versions.

So much, however, is certain, that Attis, the beloved
of the Dea Mater, was represented as having been killed
by a boar sent by Zeus, or by the jealous goddess herself.
Every year in the spring-time there took place at Pessinus
the great orgiastic lamentation for him, which, however,
ended with a joyful festival.   It seems, therefore, as if a
resurrection of the slain Attis was assumed to have taken
place, although the myth had nothing to say about that,
but only in some of the versions related that he was
changed into an evergreen fir tree.

At bottom it is a form of nature-worship, which
shows a close relationship with that of the Thracian
Dionysus-Sabazios and with that of Adonis as worshipped at Byblos in Syria, and it has in some respects
undergone modification due to contact with these.   The
primary idea underlying both myth and cultus is the
decay and revival of vegetable life.

The worship of Cybele and Attis penetrated to Rome
as early as the year 204 B.C.   In the previous year the
Sibylline books had given the oracle that Hannibal
would not be driven out of Italy until the sacred stone
from Pessinus was brought to Rome.   This was done ;

---

[1] On what follows see Hugo Hepding, *Attis, seine Mythen und sein
Kult*, 1903, 224 pp.   First volume of the series of " Religionsgeschichtliche Versuche und Vorarbeiten," edited by Dieterich and
Wünsch.   Cf. also Ernst Schmidt, *Kultübertragungen* (Cultus-Trans-
ferences : " Magna Mater," "Asklepios," " Sarapis ").   In the same
series vol. viii., 1909.

and the Carthaginians vacated the country. The foreign divinities had a temple assigned to them on the Palatine. But when the Senate came to know of the orgiastic feast which was associated with their worship, it forbade the citizens to take part in it and placed the cult under strict control. Thus, in spite of its official recognition, it led a somewhat obscure existence until Claudius, by the public festival which he established for it—which lasted from the 15th to the 27th March—gave it a high position in public esteem.

In the deepening of its religious character which it underwent in becoming associated with Greek religious feeling of the decadence period, the worship of Attis was brought into connexion with the thought of immortality. In the " Agape," in which the partakers were handed food in the " tympanon " and drink in the " cymbalon," they were initiated as " mystae " of Attis and thereby became partakers of a higher life.

Mysteries were also celebrated in which a dying and rising again was symbolised ; and there were others based upon the thought of a union with the divinity in the bridal chamber.

From the middle of the second century onward the " taurobolium " appears in connexion with the service of Cybele and Attis. This is a kind of blood-baptism. The " mystes " lies down in a pit, which is covered with boards. Through the interstices there trickles down on him the blood of a bull offered in sacrifice. The lamentation for the dead Attis sounds forth ; the " mystes " applies it to himself. Then when the hymn of jubilation follows, he rises out of the grave as one who is now initiate and deified.[1]

The process by which the worship of Attis was transformed into a mystery-religion which gave guarantees of immortality remains for the most part shrouded in obscurity. In view of the scantiness of our information

---

[1] On the original significance of the Taurobolium see Cumont, *Les Religions orientales*, pp. 101-103.

we are thrown back upon hypothetical reconstruction for the details of the development and the significance of the mysteries.[1]

The worship of Serapis was a creation of Ptolemy Soter, who desired to unite the Greek and Egyptian populations of his empire by the bond of a common worship. The derivation of the word Serapis is uncertain. Whether it arose from Osiris-Apis or from the Chaldaean Sar-Apsî is a debated point. The cultus language was Greek. Serapis was doubled with Osiris. The new cult went forth into the world as the religion of Serapis and Isis. In Rome it was vehemently opposed as being immoral ; the temples of Isis, who was identified with Venus, justified this reputation. It was not officially recognised until the time of Caligula. By this time it was, however, widely diffused wherever the Greek language was spoken. Its adherents were found chiefly among the slaves and freedmen. From the third century onwards it is over-shadowed by the worship of Mithra.

The myth, which was represented annually, makes the mourning Isis seek out the scattered fragments of the corpse of Osiris and raise a lament over it. Then the limbs are laid together and wound round with bandages, whereupon Thoth and Horus raise the slain Osiris to life again, and this is announced amid jubilant outcries.

In the service of Osiris-Serapis the worshipper gains assurance of eternal life. Therein consisted the attraction of this religion.

The early Egyptian doctrine was simple enough. After his resurrection Osiris became lord of the world

---

[1] Note the admission of Hugo Hepding at the close of his chapter on the Mysteries (p. 199) :—" I am well aware that this account of the Phrygian Mysteries is in its details mainly hypothetical. In view of the paucity of the information which has come down to us, nothing else is possible. In particular the association of the blood baptism with the March festival cannot be shown from our documentary material. . . . ." He wants to distinguish between an earlier and a later form of the taurobolium. The earlier form is not a ceremony of initiation but a sacrifice. It was only the later which had in view the initiation of the individual. " The first person whom we know by literary evidence to have undergone the ceremony of the taurobolium is Heliogabalus."

and at the same time judge of the dead. Those who at their trial before him are not approved fall a prey to destruction ; others have eternal life with him in a realm below the earth.

Life—and this was the tremendously serious feature of this religion—was therefore regarded as a preparation for death. This is the thought reflected in the mysteries, no doubt modelled on those of Eleusis,[1] which were attached to the Egyptian cultus after the worship of Serapis-Osiris had been ordained by authority. They represent the esoteric element. By means of the tests which he undergoes in the Serapeum, of the ecstasy which he experiences and the ceremonies of initiation in which he takes part the believer wins his way, along with Osiris, from death to life, and acquires the assurance of eternal being.

Distinct from these mysteries is the exoteric religion with its daily acts of worship. These consist in the un-veiling, awaking, clothing, and feeding of the statues of the gods. The " liturgy," which was everywhere punc-tiliously followed, is derived from the primitive Egyptian religion. Speaking generally, the exoteric form of the worship of Osiris could come to terms with any, even the lowest, forms of paganism.

The Syrian Baal-cults had no doubt from the second century onwards become widely diffused, and in the third century enjoyed the favour of the Emperors. For the development of popular religion, however, they were of less significance than the religions of Attis and Osiris, because they were not capable of becoming ennobled and deepened by the religious yearnings of the Greek spirit.

Mithra was the father of the sun-god.[2] The origin of

---

[1] On the Eleusinian Mysteries see Rohde, *Psyche* (3rd ed., 1909) pp. 278-300. From his account it clearly appears how little we know about these ceremonies of initiation. In any case they were quite different from those of the later Mystery-religions. They belong to early Greek religion.

[2] Franz Cumont, *Les Mystères de Mithra* (1st ed., 1899 ; 2nd ed., 1902).

the cult is obscure.   It first became known through the
pirates who were taken prisoners by Pompey.   It spread
through the Roman armies which in the first century
advanced towards the Euphrates ; they took it over from
their opponents.   Thus Mithra was primarily a soldiers'
god.   With the legions he penetrated to the utmost
bounds of the Roman Empire.   He therefore passed direct
from the barbarians into the Roman world without
previously becoming at home in the Greek world.   From
the middle of the third century onwards the new cult
spread so vigorously that it was regarded as the strongest
rival of Christianity.

In the intervening period, from the first century onward, it adopted in growing measure elements from all
the other cults, and in this way became the universal
" worship."

Regarding the myth, little is known ; and in the cultus
it played no special part.   As the " slayer of the bull "
Mithra doubtless belongs to the class of star-gods, and
represents the supreme sun-god.

The characteristic feature of this religion is its dualism.
Mithra, as the supreme, good god, is opposed by the powers
of the evil under-world.   Hence the earnest character of
its ethic, which is not contemplative as in the Osiris cult,
but active.

The secret of the power of this new faith lies indeed
mainly in the impulse to action which essentially belongs
to it, and in the large and simple ethical life to which
this conception of the divinity gives rise.   The Mithra-
religion, differing in this from the Egyptian cults, places
the scene of eternal life in an upper realm of light and
not in the under-world.   The supreme divinity himself
guides the souls of departed believers through the seven
planetary spheres to the land of the blessed, and thus
becomes their " Redeemer."

As Mysteries there are observed here, as in other cults,
sacred meals and baptismal rites.   Above these again
there was, according to Dieterich, a supreme initiation,

which represented a progress to the throne of Mithra. The actions and the formulae used in this ceremony are, he thinks, preserved almost complete in the great Parisian " magic " papyrus. Dieterich, who is opposed on this point by Cumont and Reitzenstein, denominates this document a " Mithra-liturgy," and supposes the prayers to be used in the course of the ascent which conducts the " mystes " from the world of the four elements through the stars to the realm of the gods, where, under the guidance of the sun-god, he passes through the heaven of the fixed stars and attains to the presence of the highest god.[1]

This process he conceives as having been represented, as part of the cultus, in the Mithra-grottos, which is rendered not improbable by the discoveries of objects which might have to do with a *mise en scène* corresponding to this conception. In any case there was some sacramental representation of the heavenward journey of the soul towards the attainment of immortality. It remains questionable whether, as the supreme mystery which the religion possessed, it was " experienced " by the believers only once, or had its regular place in the cultus.

The prayers extol in lofty language re-birth from the mortal to the immortal life. The invocation with which the " mystes " approaches Mithra is highly impressive. " Hail to thee, lord, ruler of the water ; hail to thee, stablisher of the earth ; hail to thee, disposer of the spirit. Lord, I that am born again take my departure, being exalted on high, and since I am exalted, I die ; born by the birth which engenders life, I am redeemed unto death,

---

[1] Albrecht Dieterich, *Eine Mithrasliturgie*, 1st ed., 1903 ; 2nd ed., 1910 (edited after the author's death by Richard Wünsch), 248 pp. The excursuses, pp. 92-212, really give a sketch of the fundamental ideas of the Mystery-religions in general. Cumont refuses to regard the document as a fragment belonging to a Mithras-liturgy because he cannot find in it the specific characteristics of the Persian eschatology and conception of heaven. On this controversy see the 2nd edition of the Mithras-liturgy, pp. 225-228. It would certainly have been better if Dieterich had not given the book the unnecessary and contentious title.

and go the way which thou hast appointed, as thou hast made for a law and created the sacrament . . ." [1] Here the text breaks off. Perhaps later on the return of the initiate to earth was described. Dieterich, however, thinks this improbable.

According to Dieterich the liturgy arose in the second century, and belongs to the Graeco - Egyptian Mithra-cult ; about 200 A.D. it was annexed by the " magians " and from that time forward was preserved among them ; about 300 it was embodied in the Paris manuscript which has come down to us.

A valuable insight into the feelings and impressions associated with the Mysteries is given by the Hermetic writings, preserved mainly in "Poimandres." [2] They profess to be derived from Hermes, who in the thought of later times became the god of revelation, and in the prominence which they give to the philosophico-religious element they mark a stage in the development of Greek religious thought from the Mystery-religions to Neo-Platonism. In their present form the documents of this later Hermetic religion, which is marked by a certain profundity, doubtless belong to about the third century ; but the original form dates, perhaps, from before the beginning of the second century.

These are the cults and religions which have to be taken into account. They are parallel to Christianity in so far that they, like it—though in general doubtless somewhat later—make their appearance in the ancient world as religions of redemption. Certain analogies are not to be denied. The only question is how far these go, and how far the Mystery-religions really exercised an influence upon the views and the cultus-

---

[1] From Dieterich, p. 15.

[2] Richard Reitzenstein, *Poimandres*. Studies in Graeco-Egyptian and Early Christian literature, 1904, 382 pp. The Poimandres " community " [*Gemeinde*, the word is in quotation marks in the German, perhaps to recall its frequent use in speaking of the Early Christian Church] is supposed to have been founded in Egypt about the time of the birth of Christ. Its main characteristic is the mystical basis of the doctrine. Later on, in the course of the third century (?) the Poimandres community was gradually merged in the general Hermetic communities.

forms of the early, and especially of the primitive, church.[1]

The first to examine the facts with any closeness was Anrich in his work, " The Ancient Mysteries and their Influence on Christianity." [2]

He comes to the conclusion that both the Pauline and the Johannine views of Christianity " are to be understood as in the main original creations of the Christian spirit on the basis of genuine Judaism," and if they show the influence of Greek thought, it is at most in a secondary fashion. There is, he asserts, " no apparent reason to refer the views on baptism and the communion-meal which meet us in the two cases to influences of the latter character." It is only at a later time that a real influence comes into question.

[1] From the literature we may note : Hermann Gunkel, *Zum religionsgeschichtlichen Verständnis des Neuen Testaments* (" Contributions to the Understanding of the New Testament on the Basis of Comparative Religion "), 1903, 96 pp.

Paul Wendland, *Die hellenistisch-römische Kultur in ihren Beziehungen zu Judentum und Christentum* (" The Hellenistic - Roman Civilisation in Relation to Judaism and Christianity "), 1907, 190 pp.

Adolf Deissmann, *Licht vom Osten* (" Light from the Ancient East "), 1908, 364 pp. This book, which is rather rhetorically written, treats mainly the general literary side of the matter without entering specially into the religious problems and the ideas of the Mystery-religions.   The same author has published a lecture, *Die Urgeschichte des Christentums im Lichte der Sprachforschung* (" The History of Primitive Christianity in the Light of Linguistic Research "), 1910, 48 pp.

Karl Clemen, *Religionsgeschichtliche Erklärung des Neuen Testaments* (" Interpretation of the New Testament on the Basis of Comparative Religion "), 1909, 301 pp.

Works which to a large extent deal with the same class of subject are : Wilhelm Soltau, *Das Fortleben des Heidentums in der altchristlichen Kirche* (" The Survival of Paganism within the Early Christian Church "), 1906, 307 pp. Adolf Harnack, *Mission und Ausbreitung des Christentums in den ersten drei Jahrhunderten* (" Mission and Expansion of Christianity in the first three Centuries "), vol. i., 1906, 421 pp.

[2] Gustav Anrich, *Das antike Mysterienwesen in seinem Einfluss auf das Christentum*, 1894, 237 pp. From the same stand-point, and in some respects supplementing Anrich's work, is Georg Wobbermin's *Religionsgeschichtliche Studien zur Frage der Beeinflussung des Urchristentums durch das antike Mysterienwesen* (" Studies from the Point of View of Comparative Religion on the Question of the Influence of the ancient Mysteries upon Christianity "), 1896, 190 pp.

Johannes Geffken in his popular work, *Aus der Werdezeit des Christentums*, 2nd ed., 1909, 126 pp. (" From the Formative Period of Christianity "), does not hold that any very deep influence was exercised by the Graeco-Roman Syncretism on early Christianity. He is, however, of opinion that Paul " adopted all kinds of oriental views."

This negative conclusion has since been much disputed. That the author, in accordance with the position of Pauline scholarship at that period, did not sufficiently take into account the " physical " element in the mystical doctrine of redemption and in the conception of baptism and the Lord's Supper, and consequently does not give sufficient weight to the analogy between the religion of the Apostle of the Gentiles and that of the Mysteries, is certain. But it ought to be recognised as equally certain that to many points he has given the prominence which they deserved, and that the students of Comparative Religion would have in many respects done better if they had allowed their bold advance to be somewhat checked by his prudent warnings, and had learned something from him in regard to the formulation of the problems.

A point which ought to be more clearly grasped than it has hitherto been, in the investigation of Paul's relation to the Mystery-religions, is that for purposes of comparison Paulinism must be regarded as a distinct entity ; very often Paul's doctrine has been included in the " Religion of the New Testament " or taken together with the Johannine and the Early Greek theology. On this method only false results can be looked for. Paulinism, and therein lies the special problem which it offers to scholarship, is an original phenomenon which is wholly distinct from Greek theology.

This implies, too, that only the literal sense of the language of the Epistles must be considered, and that it is not permissible to interpret it through the Johannine theology, as is almost always done. It is nothing less than incredible that, to take the most flagrant example, philologists like Dieterich and others in discussing Paulinism, always calmly talk about " Re-birth," although in the Epistles which rank as certainly genuine, this word and the corresponding verb never occur.[1] That

---

[1] See *e.g.* Dieterich, *Mithrasliturgie*, 2nd ed., p. 110. Typical also are pp. 176, 177, where he continually speaks of the " death and re-birth " of believers as taught by Paul.

[*Wiedergeburt* has been translated "re-birth " when the general

many theologians fall into the same confusion is no excuse.[1]

The surprising thing is precisely that Paul, when he is speaking of the transformation of the man into a new creature, always makes use of the two words death and resurrection, and describes the new thing that comes about as an already experienced resurrection, without ever introducing the conception of re-birth which seems to lie so near at hand. In this limitation lies his as yet unexplained peculiarity, and therewith the problem of his relation to Greek theology and, in general, to everything that can be called Greek religious life.

The Johannine doctrine, that of the earlier Greek Fathers, and the Mystery-religions, have this in common, that they make use of the conception of re-birth. In that, they show themselves to be growths of the same soil, and stand together over against Paulinism. Any one who interprets the language of the Apostle of the Gentiles in accordance with the conception of re-birth, has, by the aid of the Johannine theology, first conformed it to the Mystery-religions, and has himself introduced the conception which forms the common basis.

The same procedure has been followed in regard to other points also. The Paulinism which the students of Comparative Religion have in view is mainly an artificial product which has been previously treated with the acids and reagents of Greek theology.

Another point which calls for close attention is the chronological question in connexion with the history of the Mystery-religions. It is from the beginning of the

---

sense implied in the comparison with other religions is in view ; " regeneration " when the reference is primarily to the specific Christian doctrine as such.]

[1] P. Gennrich in his book, *Die Lehre von der Wiedergeburt . . . in dogmengeschichtlicher und religionsgeschichtlicher Beleuchtung* (" The Doctrine of Regeneration . . . in the Light of the History of Dogma, and of Comparative Religion "), 1907, 363 pp., notes that Paul speaks only of the " new creature " and not of regeneration; but he does not investigate the cause of this peculiarity, but hastens to give a psychological explanation of his utterances as a " precipitate from his personal experience."

second century onwards that these cults become widely extended in the Roman empire.   It is only at this period —the worship of Serapis as an artificial Graeco-Egyptian creation is perhaps an exception—that they come under the influence of late Greek religious thought and feeling, which developed with the decline of the Stoa, and become transformed from imported cults into universal Mystery-religions.   The dates and the inner course of this development are for us obscure.   So much, however, is certain, that Paul cannot have known the mystery-religions in the form in which they are known to us, because in this fully-developed form they did not yet exist.   Assuming the most favourable case, that from his youth up he had had open eyes and ears for the heathen religions by which he was surrounded, he can only have known the cults as they were in their uncompounded state, not as what they passed into when they became filled with the Greek yearning for redemption, and mutually influenced one another.

Considerations of this kind lead an authority like Cumont to insist again and again upon the difficulties which stand in the way of assuming an influence of the Mystery-cults on the earliest Christianity.[1]   Especially does he hold it to be quite impossible that the Mithra-religion should have had any point of contact with Paul.

Another point which should be mentioned is that those who are engaged in making these comparisons are rather apt to give the Mystery-religions a greater definiteness and articulation of thought than they really possess, and do not always give sufficient prominence to the distinction between their own hypothetical reconstruction and the medley of statements on which it is based. Almost all the popular writings fall into this kind of inaccuracy.   They manufacture out of the various fragments of information a kind of universal Mystery-

[1] See the introduction to *Les Religions orientales dans le paganisme romain*, 2nd ed., 1909.

religion which never actually existed, least of all in Paul's day.[1]

In particular, these works aim at getting hold of the idea of a " Greek Redeemer-god " who might serve as an analogue to Jesus Christ. No figure deserving of this designation occurs in any myth or in any Mystery-religion; it is created by a process of generalisation, abstraction, and reconstruction. Before using the phrase Redeemer-God, one should remember that it means a God who for the sake of men came into the world, died and rose again. Having realised that, one may then try how far the Mystery-religions supply anything corresponding to this—the only adequate—definition.[2]

---

[1] Typical in this respect is the work of Martin Brückner, *Der sterbende und auferstehende Gottheiland in den orientalischen Religionen und ihr Verhältnis zum Christentum* (" The divine Saviour who dies and rises again in the Oriental Religions; and their Relation to Christianity "). In the series of *Religionsgeschichtliche Volksbücher*, 1908, 48 pp. " As in Christianity, so in many Oriental religions, a belief in the death and resurrection of a Redeemer-God, who was subordinated to the Supreme God (sometimes as His Son) occupied a central place in the worship and cultus." What manipulation the myths and rites of the cults in question must have undergone before this general statement could become possible ! Where is there anything about dying and resurrection in Mithra ? It is instructive to see how the author on p. 30 argues away the effect of this admission !

A popular treatment which is kept within due bounds is Adolf Jacoby's work, *Die antiken Mysterienreligionen und das Christentum* (" The ancient Mystery-religions and Christianity "), 1910, 44 pp., in the series of *Religionsgeschichtliche Volksbücher*. The author deserves special credit for offering his readers typical texts from which they can form their own impression.

Dieterich remarks with great justice in the *Mithrasliturgie* (2nd ed., 207) how necessary it is to get beyond the catchword " Syncretistic," and point out in every case the source of particular mythological statements and ideas.

[2] O. Gruppe, too, is obliged to admit that the late Greek religious thought never really had the conception of a " world-redeemer " (*Griechische Mythologie und Religionsgeschichte*), vol. ii., pp. 1488-1489. It cannot, in fact, be otherwise. The " world-redeemer " of Jewish and Christian apocalyptic thought corresponds to the " new world " which he is in some supernatural fashion to bring in, in order to reign in it along with the elect. Graeco-oriental religions did not look for a kingdom of that kind, and therefore the idea of the ruler of such a kingdom was also undiscoverable and unattainable for them. The Messiah is the World-redeemer or Lord of the coming age. He does not make atonement for the guilt of mankind nor for that of individuals, but suffers and dies vicariously for the elect, and in order to set the events of the End in motion. His earthly fate is nothing in itself, but falls wholly under the conception of the " Messianic woes " which are

It is also to be remarked that, on the other hand, there is no " Redeemer-god " in Primitive Christianity. Jesus is, it cannot be sufficiently emphasised, not thought of as a god, but only as a heavenly being, who is entrusted with the mission of bringing in the new world. It was only later in the Greek and Gnostic theology that He was deified. For Paul he is " Son of God " in the simple, Old-Testament and Apocalyptic sense.

We may further recall Cumont's warning that analogies do not necessarily imply dependence. " Resemblances," he writes in the preface to his *Religions orientales*, " do not always imply imitation, and the resemblance of views or usages must often be explained by community of origin, not by any kind of borrowing." In the same essay he points out that analogies are sometimes exaggerated, if not actually created, by the use of language chosen by the critic.

And Dieterich expresses himself in the following terms against this mania for finding analogies. "It is," he writes, in his edition of the " Mithra-liturgy," " one of the worst faults of the science of Comparative Religion, which is at present becoming constantly less cautious, to overlook the most natural explanations, not to say ignore and avoid them, in order to have recourse to the most far-fetched, and, by the most eccentric methods, to drag out analogies which, to the unsophisticated eye, are absolutely invisible."

These are the principles by which it has to be decided, whether Comparative Religion has hunted down its game according to fair forest-law, or whether its " bag " is poached.

The chief point to which research was at first directed was the discovery of relationships between the two sets of sacramental views.

It seemed so easy to discover common conceptions

---

thought of as the tribulation of the Times of the End. How can it be proposed to find an analogue to a figure of this kind in myths, the scene of which is laid in the dawn of the world, and which have no sort of relation to its ultimate fate.

here, in view of the fact that in both cases cultus-meals and lustrations played a part and had a sacramental value. But, on closer examination, it appears that it is very difficult to get beyond the simple fact of resemblance of a very general character.

Dieterich, in his commentary on the " Mithra-liturgy," is obliged to admit that we have very little exact know-ledge regarding the sacred meals of the Mystery-religions.[1] That they were supposed to convey supernatural powers is about the only thing that can be said with safety. Regarding the special conceptions and actions which made this eating and drinking sacramental no information has been preserved. A comparison—not to speak of the establishment of a relation of dependence—is therefore impossible.

As soon as the students of Comparative Religion at-tempt to bring forward concrete facts, they are obliged to leave the domain of the mystery-religions and draw their material from the primitive Nature-religions. Here they find the primary conception—a man believes that he unites himself with the divinity by eating portions of him, or—this is a secondary stage of the conception—by consuming some substance which has been marked out for this purpose as representative of the divinity and has had his name attached to it.

The following series of examples recurs in all the books :—

The dead Pharaoh, when he enters heaven, causes his servants to seize, bind, and slay the gods, and then devours them in order thus to absorb into himself their strength and wisdom, and to become the strongest of all.

In Egypt anyone who wishes to become truthful swallows a small image of the goddess of truth.

In the Thracian orgiastic worship of Dionysos Sabazios

---

[1] P. 102 ff.   He has at this point a detailed discussion of the relations between the cultus-meal in Paul and that of the Mystery-religions.

On the sacraments see also K. Clemen, *Religionsgeschichtliche Erklärung des Neuen Testaments*, 1909, 301 pp. Baptism and the Supper, 165-207.

the sacrificial ox is torn to pieces by the participants while yet alive, and swallowed raw.

A Bedouin tribe in the Sinai peninsula slaughters, amid chanting, a camel bound upon the altar, and then eagerly drinks its blood and immediately devours the still bloody flesh half raw.

The Aztecs, before sacrificing and eating their prisoners of war, give them the name of the deity to whom the sacrifice is offered.

Now, by the round-about way of this primitive conception the connexion between Paul's cultus-feast and that of the Mystery-religions—which cannot be directly shown—is supposed to be established.

It is suggested that this primitive conception of union with the god in the cultus, by an act of eating performed with this special purpose, after it had in the normal development of the various religions been transformed or completely laid aside, came to life again in the mysticism of the Mystery-religions and of Paulinism. Mysticism, according to Dieterich's view, draws its nourishment from the lowest strata of religious ideas. The belief in the union of God and man which, among the cultured classes, was no longer anything but a metaphor, rises up again from below with irrepressible power. " Rising from below, the old ideas acquire new power in the history of religion. The revolution from beneath creates new religious life within the primeval, indestructible forms." [1]

That we have here a combination of two still unproved hypotheses is not sufficiently emphasised. In the Mystery-religions ancient cults certainly enter into direct union with higher religious conceptions, so that the general presupposition on which this hypothesis of Comparative Religion is based is to a certain extent admissible. But whether precisely this primitive conception of the mystic fellowship created by eating and drinking the god awakened to new life in them, must remain an open question, since our information does not suffice to prove

[1] *Mithrasliturgie*, 2nd ed. pp. 107, 108.

it. Of an eating of the god there is nowhere any mention.
And the primitive Mysteries were not founded on this
idea. Rather, they consist essentially in the representation of the actions performed by the divinity, and rest
on the thought that the reproduction of these events
will create in the participant some kind of corresponding
reality. It is a symbolism which is charged with a certain
energy, a drama which becomes real.

This being so, the significance of the cultus-meal
comes much less into view than that of the pattern actions
which had to be further developed and interpreted. If
we possess so few typical statements about the Mystery-
feasts, is it not partly because they had no very remarkable features and did not take a very exalted position in
the hierarchy of cultus-acts ? If in the Paris Magic-
papyrus we really possess a Mithra-liturgy, and if the
inferences and explanations which Dieterich has attached
to it are sound, then we have proof that in this developed
cultus of the second century the highest sacrament was a
pictorial mystery in which the " mystes " believed that
he in some way experienced the heavenly journey of the
soul which he, along with others, enacted.

In any case, the assertion that in the Mystery-religions
the ancient cultus-conception of a union with the divinity
effected by a meal, came to life again, goes far beyond
what can be proved. That union is, even in its secondary
forms, always closely connected with a sacrificial feast,
and cannot properly be detached from it. The sacrificial
feast, however, is not a feature in the Mystery-religions,
and so far as we can get a glimpse of their beginnings never
had any supreme importance in them. The interpretation of these cults on the analogy of the primitive religions
of various races, ancient or modern, who devoured oxen,
camels, or prisoners of war as substitutes for the divinity,
cannot therefore be established.

The vestiges of this ancient conception are to be
found, not in the Mystery-religions, but in the ordinary
heathen sacrificial worship, in cases where the sacrificial

feast has been retained in connexion with it. Here
there certainly exists in some form or other the conception of a fellowship with the god set up by eating. It is
to be noted that Paul in 1 Cor. x. draws a parallel between
the Lord's Supper, which unites us to Christ, and these
feasts. How expositors have arrived at the idea of making him refer here to the cultus-meal of the Mystery-
religions is quite inexplicable.

The hypothesis that the earliest Christian conception
of the Lord's Supper in some way represented the surviving influence of an ancient cultus idea, is at first sight
much more plausible than the corresponding hypothesis
in the case of the Mystery-religions. At anyrate the
existence of the desiderated fact is here proved. The
conception of the sacramental eating stands in the centre
of the belief ; by this act, fellowship with a divine Being
who has died and risen again is maintained ; and what
is eaten and drunk is brought into relation to the person
of Christ, inasmuch as it is called, in some sense or other,
His body and blood.

Nevertheless in the decisive point the alleged facts
break down.

Paul knows nothing of an eating and drinking of the
body and blood of the Lord. When Dieterich gives it as
the Apostle's view that " Christ is eaten and drunk by the
believers and is thereby in them," and adds that nothing
further need be said about the matter, what he has done
is, instead of taking Paul's words as they stand, to interpret Paul through John—and through a misunderstand-
ing of John at that.

It is not of an eating and drinking the body and blood
of Christ that Paul speaks in the First Epistle to the
Corinthians ; he always speaks only of eating and drinking
the bread and the cup. He assumes, no doubt, that this
somehow or other maintains a communion with the body
and blood of Christ (1 Cor. x. 16, 17), and that anyone
who partakes unworthily sins against the body and blood
of the Lord (1 Cor. xi. 27). He quotes, too, the words

in which the Lord, on the historic night, after the Supper, speaks of bread and wine as His body and His blood. But the conception which seems inevitably to arise out of this, that the participant partakes of the body and blood of the Lord, is not found in him.

The recognition of this fact does not make his sacramental doctrine any clearer. It is a question of fulfilling the demand of sound scholarship that we should respect the text, and not interpret it on the basis of inferences which the Apostle neither drew nor could draw. His fundamental view that the feast effects or maintains fellowship with the exalted Christ is perfectly clear. What is not clear is how he brought this view into relation with the historic words of Jesus about the bread and wine as being His body and blood, and interpreted it in accordance therewith. Did it arise out of these words, or did he receive it from some other quarter and afterwards make use of it for the interpretation of the historic words ?

The difficulty lies in the fact that for Paul the body and blood of the historic Christ no longer exist, and that, on the other hand, while the glorified Christ has, indeed, a body, it is not a body through which blood flows and which is capable of being consumed on earth. To speak of the body and blood of Christ is, from the stand-point of the Apostle's doctrine, an absurdity. He cannot in his doctrine of the Supper bring the historic words into harmony with his Christology, and yet is obliged to do so. The compromise remains for us obscure.

It is certain, however, that neither he nor the primitive Christian community held that the body and blood of Christ was partaken of in the Supper. That is evident from the fact that the historic words of Jesus did not form part of the service, and this is the case down to a later date. No kind of consecration of the elements as the body and blood of the Lord occurred in the liturgy.

If there is anything which may be considered as a definite result of recent research, it is that the view of primitive and early Christianity regarding the Lord's

Supper was not arrived at by way of inference from the
words of Jesus about bread and wine and flesh and blood,
but, strange as it may appear, arose from a different
quarter. The Church's celebration was not shaped
by the " words of institution " at the historic Supper ;
it was the latter, on the contrary, which were explained
in accordance with the significance of the celebration.

It is a no less serious error when Dieterich asserts that
the Gospel of John in chapter vi. proclaims the Pauline
doctrine " only in a still more corporeal fashion."

In the Evangelist, bread and wine are—as is evident
to anyone who will take the trouble to acquaint himself
with his presuppositions in the spiritually related works
of Ignatius, Justin, and Tertullian—not the body and
blood of Christ, but the flesh and blood of the Son of Man.
In this change in the expression lies the logic of the
thought. The elements of the Lord's Supper perpetuate
the appearance of the Son of Man in the world inasmuch
as they, as being the flesh and blood of that historic
Personality, possess the capacity of being vehicles of the
Spirit. As a combination of matter and Spirit which can
be communicated to the corporeity of men, they execute
judgment. The elect can in the sacrament become
partakers of that spiritual substance, and can thus be
prepared for the resurrection ; others who are not from
above, and are not capable of receiving the Spirit, receive
simply earthly food and drink, and fall a prey to corruption. Therefore the Evangelist makes the Lord close
His discourse about the eating and drinking of the flesh
and blood of the Son of Man with the words, " It is the
spirit that giveth life."

This is the language of the early Greek theology, which
explains the working of the sacraments by the combination
of the Spirit with matter which takes place therein. The
Fourth Evangelist projects this later view back into the
discourses of the historic Jesus, and makes Him pro-
phetically announce that after His exaltation a time will
come when the Spirit which is now in Him will unite itself

with the bread which, by the miracle of the loaves, has just been raised in a significant way out of the category of simple earthly elements, and will subsequently manifest its power in preparing men for the resurrection.

In this sense, as vehicles of the Spirit, the elements carry on the manifestation of the Son of Man ; in this sense it is possible to speak of eating and drinking His flesh and blood, and to regard this as necessary to life. But all this is not thought of " corporeally " in the naïve sense of an eating and drinking of the body and blood of Jesus, but can only be understood on the basis of the doctrine of the working of the Spirit in the sacraments. Apart from the Spirit, there is in the Supper no body and no blood of Christ.

That is for the Fourth Evangelist so much a fixed datum that he is obliged to omit the account of the historic Last Supper of Jesus with His disciples. That the Lord could have so designated the bread which was eaten and the wine which was drunk on that occasion, is for him unthinkable. As long as He Himself is alive there is certainly no Spirit ; it is only on His exaltation that the Spirit is liberated from the historic personality of the Son of Man and becomes separated from the Logos as the Holy Spirit, in order in the sacraments to lead a new existence—and this time an existence capable of being communicated to others. From this moment onwards bread and wine become, in the Church's celebration of the sacrament, the flesh and blood of the Son of Man in the sense explained above. Previously this had by no means been the case, any more than there had been a Christian baptism which effected regeneration. The Spirit who associates Himself with the water and produces this effect, did not as yet exist in this form of being. Jesus cannot, therefore, on this view, have baptized, any more than He can celebrate the Supper with His disciples. Therefore, the Fourth Evangelist, in order to guard against possible misunderstandings, definitely asserts that even if the disciples did baptize—a mere baptism with water

which is incapable of working regeneration—the Master
Himself made no use of water in this fashion.[1] His
task consisted only in marking out water for this use by
the miracle at Cana of Galilee, and, by His discourses
about the water of life and regeneration by water and the
Spirit, pointing men's minds to the thought that in the
future, water, in association with the Spirit, would be
necessary to life and blessedness. In that day "out of
his body shall flow rivers of living water" because the
Spirit will be present (John vii. 37–39).

The students of Comparative Religion are so far in the
right as against ordinary theology that they make an end
of the unintelligent spiritualising of the Johannine doctrine,
and try to give due weight to the "physical" element in
its conception of redemption. They are mistaken, however, in regarding this "physical" element as something
primitive, and in thinking to explain it by analogies
drawn from the primitive nature-religions.

The Fourth Gospel represents the views of a speculative
religious materialism which concerns itself with the
problem of matter and spirit, and the permeation
of matter by Spirit, and endeavours to interpret the
manifestation and the personality of Jesus, the action
of the sacraments and the possibility of the resurrection
of the elect, all on the basis of one and the same fundamental conception.

According to this theory, Christ came into the world in
order to accomplish in His own Person the as yet non-
existent union of the Spirit with the fleshly substance of
humanity. In consequence of this act the elect among
mankind can in the future become partakers of the Spirit.
Jesus Himself, however, cannot as yet impart this to them
either as the Spirit of knowledge—that is why the disciples
are portrayed as so "unintelligent"—or as the Spirit of
life. The Spirit always needs, in the world of sense, to

---

[1] Therefore the statement that Jesus baptized in the Judæan country
(Jn. iii. 22) is corrected to the effect that He Himself did not baptize,
but only the disciples (Jn. iv. 2).

be connected with material vehicles. He cannot work directly, in the sense of communicating Himself from Jesus to believers. He must, therefore, in order to enter into the elect, be received by them in combination with some material element. The material *media* chosen for this purpose are made known by Jesus by means of miracles and by references to the future.

The naïve—and unhistorical—conception that Jesus instituted the sacraments is not recognised by the Johannine gnosis. According to it He did not establish them, but created and predicted them.

By His incarnation the possibility of the union of humanity and Spirit upon which the working of the sacraments depends, is provided. By His action in regard to the food and wine and the words He spoke in connexion therewith, He pointed to a mystery which was to be revealed in connexion with these substances; by His death, resurrection, and exaltation He abolished His earthly mode of existence and set the Spirit free for the new method of working, in virtue of which He was able to prepare men for the resurrection. Jesus, according to this view, came into the world to introduce the era of effectual sacraments. It was thus that He became the Redeemer.

The teaching of the Johannine theology, therefore, rests upon the two principles, that the Spirit can only work upon men in combination with matter, and that it only becomes present in this state as a consequence of the exaltation of the Lord. Anyone who has once recognised these presuppositions will give up once for all the search for a primitive element which is to be explained from the nature-religions. On the other hand, it is certain that Christianity here presents itself as the most highly developed Greek Mystery-religion which it is possible to conceive.

Now for Paul again. Anyone who ascribes to him the conception of a sacramental eating and drinking of the body and blood of Christ does violence to his words.

But admitting that he really thought in this way, that would prove nothing. It would first need to be shown that it really was a cultus-conception drawn from the primitive nature-religions which came to life again in him. Now, for the Mystery-religions the necessary presuppositions might appear to be present, since they arise out of ancient cults which sprouted and grew up again in later times. Paul, however, is a Jew, and even as a believer in Christ he stands, in spite of his polemic against the law, wholly and solely on the basis of the absolute, transcendent Jewish conception of God. Any relation on his part to the nature-cults cannot be proved and ought not to be assumed. By what wind were the seeds of this primitive conception wafted to his mind ? And how could they suddenly sprout and grow in the stony soil of a Jewish heart ? The Apostle would certainly be the first and the only Jewish theologian to fall under the spell of the primitive conception of eating the god ! And where was such a conception at that time to be found ?

But what matter such prosaic considerations when it is a question of great ideas, of ideas, moreover, fathered by Comparative Religion ?

When Heitmüller in the spring of 1903 appeared before the members of the Clergy Theological Society [1] in Hanover to give them the latest information about baptism and the Lord's Supper, he led them abroad, after an introduction on the " physico-hyperphysical " in Paul, first to the Aztecs, then in the clouds of night, by the torch's gleam, to the Thracian mountain sides, and thence to Sinai.[2] And when they had assisted at the slaughtering and devouring of the prisoners of war, the ox, and the camel, he expressed himself to the following effect : " Little as the δεῖπνον κυριακόν of Paul might seem to have in common with these . . . proceedings, and

---

[1] *Der wissenschaftliche Predigerverein.*

[2] W. Heitmüller, *Taufe und Abendmahl bei Paulus* (" Baptism and the Lord's Supper in Paul's teaching "). A description and an investigation in the light of Comparative Religion, 1903, 56 pp. These journeyings on pp. 40-42.

loth as we at first are even to name the Lord's Supper
in the same breath with them, as little is it to me a
matter of doubt that, when looked at from the point of
view of Comparative Religion, the Lord's Supper of
primitive Christianity has the closest connexion with
them. Those pictures supply the background from
which the Lord's Supper stands out ; they show us
the world of ideas to which the Lord's Supper belongs
in its most primitive, and therefore perspicuous,
form."

Entering more into detail, this " Hylic "[1] of the
Comparative method explains that the primeval concrete
and sensuous conception of the *communio* established by
partaking of the flesh and blood of the animal in which the
divinity itself dwelt, comes to light again in the primitive
Christian Lord's Supper, at the highest stage of the
development of religion, and under this new form acquires
a new life.[2] It would be precarious, he further observes,
in view of the fragmentary condition of the sources to
attempt to prove a direct dependence on definite pheno-
mena—on the cultus feast of the Mithra-mysteries, for
example : " It will be safer to point to the general
characteristics of the time, which abounded with ideas
of that kind. The infant Christianity lived in an
atmosphere which, if I may be allowed the expression,
was impregnated with Mystery-bacilli, and grew up on
a soil which had been fertilised and made friable by the
decay and intermixture of the most various religions, and

---

[1] *i.e.* Materialist in his explanation, in contrast, as appears later,
with Reitzenstein, who is described as the " Pneumatic " of the
science.

[2] Albert Eichhorn, *Das Abendmahl im Neuen Testament* (" The
Lord's Supper in the New Testament," 1898, 31 pp.), similarly holds
that in Paul we have before us a sacramental eating and drinking of
the body and blood of Christ which can only be explained as based
on Oriental Gnostic presuppositions. He is, however, constrained to
admit that we have no knowledge of a " sacramental meal which could
have served as the model for the Lord's Supper." But this does not
shake his faith in his theory. He thinks that proof is only wanting
because there is here a gap in our historical knowledge. He has
calculated out the position of the planet ; the mere fact that it cannot
be discovered with the telescope is wholly due to the inadequacy of
the instrument.

was specially adapted to favour the upgrowth of seeds
and spores which had been long in the ground."

Now, there is no such thing as an atmosphere impregnated with bacteria. Medical science has long since
shown that this conception rests on an error, the air being
practically free from germs. In theology it is more
difficult to get rid of fantastic imaginations, since historical
proofs are only available for those who are capable of
thinking historically.

It must not be overlooked that the eating and drinking
which establishes communion with Christ is only one side
of the Pauline conception of the Supper. Alongside of
it there exists the other, which sees in the feast a confession of faith in the death and the parousia of the Lord,
and is quite as significant as the former. It is—in 1 Cor.
xi.—developed in connexion with the repetition of the
historic words of Jesus ; on it is based the argument that
a careless partaking is a transgression against the body
of the Lord. And on the basis of this conception, cases
of illness and death in the church are to be understood
as a warning chastisement pointing to the Last Judgment.
This conception must be somehow or other eschatologically
conditioned.

The communion which is established in the Lord's
Supper is a communion of the eagerly-waiting man with
the coming Lord of Glory. The only thing which remains
obscure is how this is brought about. The confession of
faith in the death and parousia which is combined with
the act of eating and drinking does not suffice to explain
this further effect. Further, it remains inherently obscure
how by eating and drinking the dying and return of the
Lord can be shown forth, especially as the Early Christian
celebration consisted only in a common meal, and in no
way reproduced, as present - day celebrations do, the
actions and words of Jesus at the Last Supper.

What are the results to which the students of Comparative Religion have to point in regard to the Lord's
Supper ? They are obliged at the outset to give up the

attempt to explain it from the Mystery-religions, or even to point out in the latter any very close analogies. In place of this they attempt to make intelligible both the meal which formed part of the mystery-cults, and that of Pauline Christianity, as growths which, from scattered seeds of ancient conceptions of the cultus-eating of the divinity, spring up from the soil of syncretism in two different places at the same time. Neither in the one case nor the other, however, can they render this even approximately probable. Up to the present, therefore, neither a direct nor an indirect connexion between the cultus-meal of Paul and those of the Mystery-religions has been shown. The only thing which is certain is that in both cases a cultus-meal existed. About that of the Mysteries we know almost nothing ; about that which Paul presupposes we have more information, but not such as to enable us at once to understand it.

The question regarding baptism took from the first a simpler form, since the hypothesis of a renascence of primitive cultus - conceptions has not to be considered.

Both Paul and the Mystery-religions attach a religious significance to washings. That, however, does not suffice to establish a peculiarity which would connect them together, since the attachment of this significance to lustration is bound up with the elemental symbolism of cleansing and is found more or less in all religions.

The real question is whether Paulinism and the Mystery-religions, when they go beyond the most general notions, and advance from the symbolic to the effectively sacramental, follow the same lines and present the same views.

Once again, Paul's view is the more fully, that of the Mystery-religions the less fully known. Developed baptismal doctrines and rites seem only to have been present in the Egyptian cults. These distinguish between the bath of purification and baptism, the latter consisting

in a sprinkling with a few drops of a consecrated and con-
secrating fluid.[1]

The advance beyond the idea of purification, where
it is to be observed, moves in the direction of the idea of
Re-birth, Regeneration. A clear formulation of this
developed view—comparable in definiteness with the
Early Christian reference to the " bath of regeneration " [2]
—does not occur. The thought remains hovering between
purification and renewal.

That is as much as to say that, so far as our information
goes, no typical points of contact with Paulinism present
themselves.

The Apostle implies a baptism in the name of a divine
person. Of a baptism performed in the name of Osiris,
Attis, or Mithra we know nothing, though no doubt the
assumption naturally suggests itself that the lustrations
and baptisms practised in these cults were considered to be
at the same time acts of confession of faith in the divinity
with whose worship they were associated. But this
character was by no means so distinctly stamped on them
as was the case in Christian baptism—as is, indeed, readily
intelligible. In the Mystery-religions the confession of
the god is naturally implied ; in Christianity there is the
special confession of faith in the Messiahship of Jesus.
To this there was nothing analogous.

As regards the utterance of the name of the divinity
and the magical efficacy attaching thereto according to
ancient conceptions, many illustrations can be adduced
from Comparative Religion. But the really important
point, the association of the utterance of the name with
a baptismal rite, cannot be directly shown to have existed
in the Mystery-religions.[3]

---

[1] See on this R. Reitzenstein, *Die hellenistischen Mysterienreligionen*
(" The Hellenistic Mystery Religions "), p. 38.

[2] Tit. iii. 5 (R. V. *marg.* : laver of regeneration).

[3] Wilhelm Heitmüller, *Im Namen Jesu. Eine Sprach- und religionsgeschichtliche Untersuchung zum Neuen Testament, speciell zur altchristlichen Taufe* (" In the Name of Jesus. A New Testament Study based
on Linguistics and Comparative Religion, with special Reference to
Early Christian baptism "), 1903, 347 pp. In this thorough and ex-

In order to arrive at his sacramental view Paul does not follow the natural method of advancing by way of the thought of purification to that of renewal by regeneration, but follows a different route, which leads him to an estimate of it that has nothing to do with the fundamental conception of purification, and therefore remains without analogy in the Mystery-religions.   This is a fact of great significance.

The Mystery - religions speak, as Paul also does, of the *pneuma* and its workings, but the possession of the *pneuma* is never represented as an immediate and inevitable consequence of baptism.

With the Mystery-religions are associated speculations about the renewal of man's being, represented as taking place in regeneration, which they bring into some kind of relation, closer or more remote, with baptism.   But when Paul speaks of the new creature which comes into being in the sacrament, the thought of regeneration does not for him come into view, for he makes no use of it at all. Instead of that he asserts in Rom. vi. that in baptism there is an experience of death and resurrection in fellowship with Christ, from which results newness of life and the new ethic associated therewith.   How the act and the result are logically connected he does not explain.   He is content to place them side by side.

tremely interesting study the author arrives at the result that in the employment of the name of Jesus it is taken for granted that the name in some way or other represents a power.   The Christian " belief in the name," he holds, stands on the same footing as Jewish and heathen beliefs.   " The solemn pronouncement of the name of Jesus at baptism is not a merely symbolic form, having to do, for example, with the confession of the Messiahship of Jesus, but is thought of as associated with real mystical, mysterious effects ; the effects must, however, be similar, *mutatis mutandis*, to those which are ascribed to the use of the name in other cases : a being actually taken possession of by the power which is designated by the ' name ' of Jesus, the expulsion of all hostile powers, consecration and inspiration."   " Baptism in the name of Jesus represents, therefore, the combination of two sacramental factors—water and the name."

Unfortunately, Heitmüller has not emphasised the fact that the Mystery-religions offer no typical analogies to this double sacrament.

It is also open to question whether the power of the name and of water suffice, as he thinks, to explain the Pauline view of baptism.

So far as we know, there exists in the Mystery-religions
no analogue to this dying and rising again effected solely
by the use of water. To interpret Rom. vi., as Dieterich
does, as referring to a spiritual death and " new birth "
is not permissible, since the text says not a word about
that. The post-Pauline theology, that is the Johannine
and Early Greek theology, explain baptism as regeneration, and seek to find a logical basis for this effect in the
doctrine that the Spirit unites with the water as the
generating power. Paul has nothing of all this.

Nor does he show any knowledge of the idea that
Christian baptism arose out of the baptism of Jesus as an
imitative reproduction of it. He never, in fact, mentions
the baptism of Jesus. Nowhere does he suggest that in
baptism the new man, the " Child of God," is born in the
believer, as Jesus was in this act raised to His Messianic
office.

There is in fact no evidence from the earlier literature which suggests the existence of views of that
kind regarding the origin and significance of Christian
baptism. In early Christianity it is as far from being
an imitative reproduction of the baptism of Jesus as the
Church's Lord's Supper was from being an imitative
reproduction of the historic Last Supper. The conception
of an " imitative reproduction " was first introduced
by modern theology.

To cite the *taurobolium* as an analogue of Paul's baptism,
with the death and resurrection which it effects, is not
admissible. In the first place, the *taurobolium* is a baptism
of blood ; in the next place it is closely connected with a
sacrifice ; in the third place, the burial and rising again are
actually represented. The sacramental significance is thus
derived from the many-sided symbolism. In Paul there
is no trace of all this. " Plain water " effects everything.

One point in regard to which great hopes had been
placed on the Mystery-religions was the solution of the
enigma of 1 Cor. xv. 29. Wernle regarded it as self-
evident that the Apostle in permitting and approving

baptism for the dead had allowed himself to become infected by the heathen superstition of his Corinthian converts, and took him to task for this lapse in his book on the " Beginnings of Christianity." In his zeal he forgot to enquire whether the heathen had any superstition of the kind.[1]

Those who tried to supply this omission did not meet with much success. The heathen showed themselves better than their reputation and less " superstitious " than the Christians ! Of a baptism for the dead, or anything at all of this nature, they show no trace.

Failing more relevant evidence, some have quoted Plato, who in the *Republic* (ii. 364–5) makes Adeimantos say, appealing in confirmation to the Orphic writings, that by means of offerings and festivals, atonement and purification for past misdeeds is effected for whole towns as well as for single individuals, for the living and also for the dead.

This passage, however, does not refer at all to personal dedications with a view to " renewal," such as the baptism practised in the Mystery-religions and in Christianity, but to expiatory sacrifices in the ancient Greek sense.[2]

In the *Taurobolia*, representation of one living person by another is supposed to have been possible, but there is no mention of a representation of the dead.[3]

[1] Paul Wernle, *Die Anfänge unserer Religion*, 1901, p. 129.
[2] In order to preclude this misuse of it the passage may be quoted here in full:—

πείθοντες οὐ μόνον ἰδιώτας ἀλλὰ καὶ πόλεις, ὡς ἄρα λύσεις τε καὶ καθαρμοὶ ἀδικημάτων διὰ θυσιῶν καὶ παιδιᾶς ἡδονῶν εἰσὶ μὲν ἔτι ζῶσιν, εἰσὶ δὲ καὶ τετελευτήκασιν, ἃς δὴ τελετὰς καλοῦσιν, αἱ τῶν ἐκεῖ κακῶν ἀπολύουσιν ἡμᾶς, μὴ θύσαντας δὲ δεινὰ περιμένει.

. . . "And they persuade, not only individuals, but whole cities that sacrifices and pleasureable amusements afford absolution and purification from crimes committed, both for the living and also for the dead ; these they call Mysteries (initiations), and they free us from the torments of the other world, whereas terrible things await those who neglect to offer sacrifice." On expiation see Rohde, *Psyche*, i. (1903), 259 ff.
[3] Regarding the evidence which has a more remote bearing on the question, see Hollmann, *Urchristentum in Korinth* (" Primitive Christianity in Corinth "), 1903, 32 pp., pp. 22-24.

The baptism *of* the dead which is attested by a papyrus is not a baptism *for* the dead.[1]

That living persons went through the ceremonies of initiation for the dead is not known.

Thus baptism for the dead has not, so far at least, proved susceptible of explanation from heathen sources, but must be regarded as a peculiarity of Christianity !

The outcome of the study of the sacraments from the point of view of Comparative Religion is a very curious one. The Apostle thinks sacramentally ; in fact his doctrine is much more " mysterious " than that of the Mystery-religions. But the nature of the sacramental conception is quite different in him from what it is in them ; it is as if they had grown up on different soils.

The difference relates both to the conception of the supernatural working of the sacraments, and also to the position which the sacramental element takes in the doctrine as a whole.

In the Mystery-religions the sacramental idea arises by way of an intensification and materialisation of the symbolic. The act effects what it represents. The result can in a sense be logically understood when once the thought is grasped that the world of appearance and the world of reality stand in mysterious connexion with one another.

In Paul we have an unmediated and naked notion of sacrament such as is nowhere else to be met with. Symbolism is no doubt involved in the most general significance of the act. In this sense baptism is a " cleansing " and a " consecration," [2] and the sacred feast establishes fellow-

---

[1] R. Reitzenstein, *Die hellenistischen Mysterienreligionen*, p. 84. The dead man is, according to Spiegelberg, represented as standing between two gods, who sprinkle the sacred fluid upon his head.

[2] In 1 Cor. vi. 11, after saying that thieves, adulterers, slanderers, and robbers cannot inherit the Kingdom of God, the Apostle proceeds, " And such were some of you. But ye were cleansed, ye were consecrated, ye were justified." The passage is no doubt intended sarcastically, ironically, with reference to the fact that, in spite of their baptism, according to present appearances they have not changed much. In regard to self-delusion on the ground of baptism see also 1 Cor. x.

ship among the partakers. But the assertions which go beyond this show not the faintest connexion with the outward significance of the rite. Contact with the water is supposed to effect a dying and rising again with Christ, a partaking in His mystical body, and the possession of the Spirit. The eating and drinking at the Lord's Supper is a confession of faith in the death and the parousia of Christ, and is also fellowship with Him.

The sacramental is therefore non-rational. The act and its effect are not bound together by religious logic, but laid one upon the other and nailed together.

With that is connected the fact that in Paul we find the most prosaic conception imaginable of the *opus operatum*. In the Mystery-religions there is a mysterious procedure surrounded by imposing accessories. The impressive appeal of symbolism is brought to bear in every part. Every detail is significant, and lays hold upon the attention.

In Paul everything is flat and colourless. While some of his references might suggest the impression that his conception of Christianity bore some kind of analogy to the Mystery - religions, yet as a whole it entirely lacks the corresponding atmosphere. There is nothing of the effective *mise en scène* characteristic of the Greek sacramental beliefs. How lacking in solemnity must have been the method of celebrating the Lord's Supper, when it could degenerate into an ugly and disorderly exhibition of gluttony ! How little does the Apostle think of the external act of baptism, when he founds a church in Corinth and himself performs the rite only in the case of one or two individuals ! [1] He preaches sacraments, but does not feel himself to be a mystagogue ; rather, he retains the simplicity in regard to forms of worship which belongs to the Jewish spirit.

There were no long preparations for the cultus ceremonies, and nothing is known of a distinction between higher and lower grades of initiation, such as form an

[1] 1 Cor. i. 14-16.

essential part of the Mystery-religions. The first ceremony of initiation confers at once final perfection.
Among those who are admitted there prevails the most
complete equality. The conception of the " mystes "
does not exist.

In the Mystery-religions everything centres in the
sacred ceremonies. They dominate thought, feeling, and
will. If they are removed the whole religion collapses.

In Paulinism it is otherwise. The doctrine of redemption is no doubt closely connected with the sacraments,
but the latter are not its be-all and end-all. If baptism
and the Lord's Supper are taken away the doctrine is
not destroyed, but stands unmoved. It looks as though
the weight of the building rested upon these two pillars,
but in reality it does not totter even if these supports are
withdrawn.

The Johannine and the early Greek doctrine are conceived as real Mystery-religions. The Fourth Evangelist
and Ignatius know no other redemption than that which
is bound up with the sacraments. In Paul the redemption
can be thought of apart from them, since the whole
mystical doctrine of fellowship with Christ rests upon the
single conception of faith. Nevertheless he allows it
to be closely bound up with the external ceremonies,
and seems to have no consciousness of the fact that
this connexion is unnecessary and illogical.

The remarkable duality in Paulinism lies, therefore, in
the fact that the sacramental idea is intensified to an
extreme and unintelligible degree, while at the same time
the necessity of the sacred ceremonies does not logically
result from the system as a whole, as this would lead us
to expect.

The sacramental views of the Apostle have thus
nothing primitive about them, but are rather of a
" theological " character. Paul connects his mystical
doctrine of redemption with ceremonies which are not
specially designed with reference to it. It is from that
fact, and not from a specially deep love for Mysteries,

that the exaggeratedly sacramental character of his view of baptism and the Lord's Supper results. It is in the last resort a question of externalisation, not of intensification.

It is therefore useless to ransack the history of religions for analogies to his conceptions. It has none to offer, for the case is unique. The problem lies wholly within the sphere of early Christian history, and represents only a particular aspect of the question of Paul's relation to primitive Christianity. The fact is, he did not introduce the sacramental view into the sacred ceremonies, but found already existing a baptism and a Lord's Supper which guaranteed salvation on grounds which were intelligible from early Christian doctrine. He, however, transformed the primitive view of salvation into the mystical doctrine of the dying and rising again in fellow-ship with Christ. Since the connexion between redemption and the sacraments was given *a priori*, he draws the inference that the sacraments effect precisely that wherein, according to his gnosis, the inner essence of redemption consists. How far they are appropriate to the effect which, on the ground of his mystical doctrine, he holds to take place, does not for him come into question.

·In the sacraments the believer becomes partaker in salvation. Therefore, he concludes, in them that happens which constitutes redemption, namely, the dying and rising again with Christ.

Paul therefore takes the sacraments by storm. He does not theorise about the ceremony, but ascribes to it without more ado the postulated effect. That is not a procedure which could have been followed either by a Greek or by a modern mind.

Paulinism is thus a theological system with sacra-ments, but not a Mystery-religion.

This may be confirmed by a further observation. The Apostle occupies a strongly predestinarian stand-point. Those who are " called " inevitably receive salvation ; those who are not, can never in any way obtain it. There is no analogue to this in the Mystery-religions. They can only conceive of election in the sense and to the extent of holding that there is a calling and predestination to the receiving of the initiation which confers immortality. And there are actually some beginnings of such a conception.[1]

But Pauline predestination is quite different. It is absolute, and seems inevitably to abolish the necessity and meaning of the sacraments. Anyone who belongs to the number of the elect becomes *ipso facto* partaker of the resurrection. At the end of all things a great company from the generations of long-past times will arise to life without ever having received baptism or partaken of the Lord's Supper. That being so, what becomes of the sacraments ? In what respect are they necessary ?

A good deal of energy has been expended in seeking analogies from other religions for the Corinthian baptism for the dead; it would really have been much more to the point to enquire why baptism for the dead was considered desirable. If the dead are among the elect, they have no need of it; if not, they could not have inherited life, even if they had received the sacrament during their sojourn on earth. To what end, then, is this baptism for the dead ?

The most important point to notice is that everywhere in the Pauline sacraments the eschatological interest breaks through. They effect, not re-birth, but resurrection. That which in the near future is to become visible reality, they make in the present invisibly real by anticipation. The Greek Mysteries are timeless. They reach back to primitive antiquity, and they profess to be able to manifest their power in all generations. In Paul the sacraments have temporal boundaries. Their power is derived from the events of the last times. They put believers in the same position as the Lord, in that they

[1] See Reitzenstein, *Die hellenistischen Mysterienreligionen* (1910), pp. 99, 100.

cause them to experience a resurrection a few world-moments before the time, even though this does not in any way become manifest. It is a precursory phenomenon of the approaching end of the world.

Separated from the eschatology, the Pauline sacraments would become meaningless and ineffectual. They are confined to the time between the resurrection of Jesus and His parousia, when the dead shall arise. Their power depends on the present, and also on the future, fact. In this sense they are "historically" conditioned.

While therefore in the Mystery-religions and in the Johannine theology the sacraments work of themselves, in Paul they draw their energy from a universal world-event, from which it is, as it were, transmitted.

It now becomes clear why the Apostle cannot describe as a " Re-birth " the condition brought about by baptism. The renewal consists in the fact that the coming resurrection-life is, for the short period which remains of the present course of the world, received by anticipation. Re-birth, on the other hand, implies an uneschatological system of thought in which the individual reckons more or less on a normal span of life, for which he seeks an inner divine being which shall subsist alongside of or above the earthly. It is only at a period when eschatology is falling into the background that the Greek conception of re-birth, such as is associated with the Mysteries, can supersede the old mystico-eschatological conception of the proleptic resurrection. Accordingly it presently appears in Justin and the Fourth Evangelist. From that point onwards baptism brings re-birth. In Paul it produced only an antedated dying and rising again.

The sacramental conception of the Apostle is therefore derived from an entirely different world of thought from that of the Mystery-religions.

It is a different question, however, in what relation his "physical"[1] mysticism in itself, apart from the sacra-

[1] See above, p. 162, note 3.

ments, bears to the world of ideas associated with the Greek Mystery-religions.

To this question Reitzenstein, the "pneumatic"[1] among the students of Comparative Religion, devotes a careful study. He avoids conventional catchwords and rash conclusions, and endeavours to discover the conceptions and ideas which are common to both, and to follow them out in detail.

With this purpose he brings together everything which he can find in the language of the Mysteries and the Hermetic literature relating to such ideas as "service" and "military service" of God, "justification," "pre-existence," "gnosis," "spirit," "revelation," "pneumatic," "heavenly garment," and "transformation."

For the first time the material for a study of Paul from the point of view of Comparative Religion is brought together with a certain completeness, and the impression which it makes is very powerful. The theologian who reads these passages with an open mind will be lifted out of the ruts of conventional interpretation. It is as if a flood of new thought had streamed into the channels of ordinary exegesis, whether critical or otherwise, and swept away the accumulations of rubble.

Whether all the explanations are sound, and whether many expressions, such as *e.g.* "servant" and "prisoner" of Christ, and imagery—for example, that taken from the military life—could not be just as well explained directly as by the roundabout way of their use in the Mystery-religions, may be left an open question. What is certain is, that Reitzenstein has made an end of the cut-and-dried conception that Paul simply translated his theology from Jewish thought into Greek language, and proves that

---

[1] In contrast with Heitmüller, who was described above as the "hylic," materialist (see p. 205).

R. Reitzenstein, *Die hellenistischen Mysterienreligionen. Ihre Grundgedanken und Wirkungen* ("The Hellenistic Mystery-religions. Their fundamental Ideas and Influence"), 1910, 217 pp. The work is composed out of a lecture delivered in the Clerical Theological Society of Alsace-Lorraine (pp. 1-60), along with extensive notes and excursuses (pp. 63-214).

he knows the scope and exact application of the words of
the religious vocabulary, and along with the terms and
expressions has taken over suggestions for the presentation
of his ideas. Without the possibilities and presuppositions supplied by the religious language of the Greek
Orient it would have been more difficult for him to create
his mysticism. He found in existence a tone-system
in which the modulations necessary for the development
of his theme offered themselves for his disposal.[1]

Reitzenstein remarks with much justice that particular
words and phrases do not of themselves prove very much,
but that what is really of importance is the connexion of
the passages. Are there sets of ideas in Paul which are
allied with those of the Mystery-religions ? What realities
stand in the two cases behind the references to the mystical doctrine of the miraculous new creation of the man
while in his living body ?

The description and paraphrasing which commentaries
and New Testament theologies bestow upon the Apostle's
assertions do not suffice for Reitzenstein. He wants
to understand and come to grips with the thought, and to
arouse in others the same discontent.

The possibility that the Pauline mysticism might be
capable of being explained from within appears to him
excluded. With all the reserve which he imposes upon
himself he nevertheless believes himself to have proved
that the central conception of " the deification and

---

[1] Especially impressive are the investigations regarding the *pneuma*.
Reitzenstein believes himself to be able to show that all the passages
in Paul's writings which refer to this subject " are explicable from
Hellenistic usage," and leaves open the question whether they " are
all equally easy to understand on the basis of the Hebraic use of *ruach*
or *nephesh*, or the LXX. use of πνεῦμα."

A detailed discussion is given of the following passages, Rom. vi.
1-14, xii. 1 ff. ; 1 Cor. ii., xiii., xv. 34 ff. ; 2 Cor. iii. 18, v. 1 ff., v. 6
ff., x.-xiii., and some interesting light is thrown on the Epistle to
Philemon (pp. 81, 82).

It may also be mentioned that Eduard Schwartz in his essay
" Paulus " (*Charakterköpfe aus der antiken Literatur*, 1910, 136 pp.
pp. 107-136) estimates very highly the indirect influence of the Hellenistic surroundings and language. In the second edition (1911, 142
pp.) he goes a little more fully into the individual problems of the
doctrine.

transfiguration of the living man is derived from the Mysteries." The conviction of a miracle of transformation taking place in his own person, is, he pronounces, not Jewish. Therefore he thinks that Paul represents a kind of ancient Jewish prophetism modified by the influence of the Hellenistic Mystery beliefs.

The " history of the development " of Paul's thought he conceives as follows : The influence of Greek mysticism, with which he had already a literary acquaintance, helped to prepare the way for that momentous inner experience which eventually caused a rupture between the Apostle and his ancestral religion.   " This influence," he thinks, " increased in the two years of solitary struggle for the working out of a new religion."   A renewed study of Greek religious literature became necessary " from the moment when the Apostle dedicated himself to, and began to prepare for, his mission to the "Ἑλληνες."

By the method which he applies, Reitzenstein is necessarily driven to adopt this far-reaching view. He makes no effort to take into the field of his argument the Late-Jewish eschatology, as preserved in the post-Danielic literature, in the discourses of Jesus, and the Apocalypses of Baruch and Ezra.   Whatever is not self-explanatory, and cannot be explained from the Old Testament, is, according to him, derived from the world of thought associated with the Mystery-religions.

The proper procedure would really have been to examine the conceptions drawn from apocalyptic thought and those from the Mystery-religions independently, and then to decide which of them rendered possible the better explanation.   The best way would have been for Reitzenstein to discuss the matter step by step with Kabisch, who had sought to derive the fundamental conceptions of the Pauline mysticism from eschatology.

The total neglect of eschatology forces him to some curious conclusions.   After showing, in opposition to a canonised confusion of thought, that there is not the slightest connexion between Paul's doctrine of the first

and second Adam in 1 Cor. xv. 45-49 and Philo's theory
about the two accounts of the creation in Genesis, since
in that case the pneumatic heavenly man would be the
first, and the psychic earthly man the second,[1] he comes
to the conclusion that the view set forth in 1 Corinthians
must have underlying it " the belief in a god 'Anthropos,' "
who came to be identified with Christ.

This hypothesis naturally suggests itself to Reitzenstein, because in *Poimandres* he believes himself to have
discovered a myth about Anthropos.[2]   But is this,
even if it were held to be proved, of such a character
that the Pauline conception of the first and second
Adam could without more ado be derived from it ?   Is
the complicated hypothesis necessary ?

Paul's conception can be explained without the least
difficulty on eschatological grounds.   The first Adam
brought mankind under the dominion of death.   Christ
is the Second Adam because He by His resurrection
becomes the founder of a new race, which in virtue of
that which has taken place in Him becomes partaker of
an imperishable life, and acquires a claim to the future
possession of the pneumatic heavenly body which He
already bears.   The Second Man comes from heaven
because the pre-existent Christ, in order to become the
founder of the " humanity of the resurrection," must
appear upon earth and assume fleshly corporeity.   He is
" life-giving spirit " because the *pneuma* which goes forth
from Him as the glorified Christ, works in believers as
the power of the resurrection.   This being so, what purpose is served by bringing in the very doubtful myths
about the god Anthropos, especially as Paul, though he
certainly thinks of his Second Adam as a heavenly being,
never anywhere speaks of Him as God.

---

[1] Even Holtzmann shares this confusion. " The Pauline doctrine,"
he pronounces in his New Testament Theology (ii. p. 56), " is not exactly
Philonian, but doubtless, like the closely allied Philonian doctrines
and the more widely divergent later views, grew out of the same stock
of Jewish reflection on the Creation-narratives. . . ."

[2] *Poimandres*, p. 81 ff.

This is typical of a series of similar cases.[1]

On the other hand, it is just this one-sidedness which makes the charm and the significance of the book. Reitzenstein shows, both positively and negatively, how far the analogies from the Mystery-religions will take us. Ordinary theologians—since Kabisch had remained without influence—had simply designated as Greek everything which they could not understand from Late Judaism, and described as Late-Jewish whatever they could not understand as Greek. Reitzenstein, the—unconscious?—antipodes of Kabisch, would like to make an end of this simple game and compel people to choose one horn or other of the dilemma. Instead of entering on theoretic discussions, full of " not only, but also," and " either . . . or," he goes straight forward as far as he thinks he can feel firm ground under his feet, and has thus contributed, to an extraordinary degree, to the clearing up of the situation.

Contrary to his intention and conviction, however, the outcome is not positive but negative.

Like Dieterich and others, Reitzenstein takes it for granted that Paulinism makes use of the conception of Re-birth, and he feels that that is in itself a sufficient reason for not regarding it as a product of Judaism.[2]

The assumption being unsound, all the discussions and arguments based on it fall to the ground. In particular, the fine parallels from the Hermetic literature must be given up. Further, it is not legitimate to treat the

[1] Reitzenstein takes much pains to render intelligible, by a series of examples from ancient and modern times, the " dual personality " which often seems to manifest itself in Paul (pp. 53-57, 207, 208). He overlooks the fact that in the form in which it occurs in Paul it is taken for granted by eschatology, and appears in Jesus and the disciples. It is much more primitive than anything found in Hellenistic mysticism or in any form of romanticism, since the distinction of outer appearance and inner being which occurs in Paul, depends upon the contrast of the two worlds which are struggling together for existence. The dual self-consciousness of Paul is, in contradistinction to all other cases, not subjectively but objectively conditioned. Besides, it depends on the temporal opposition of " then " and " now," as naturally results from the ardent eschatological expectation. On the " doubling " of one's own personality, such as is possible for Greek sensibility, see Rohde, *Psyche*, vol. ii. (1909), pp. 413, 414.

[2] See pp. 57, 58.

mysticism of the Mystery-religions and that of Paul as directly corresponding to one another. The former is a God-mysticism, the latter a Christ-mysticism. The resulting differences are greater than at first sight appears. In the Graeco-Oriental conception, what is in view is the " deification " of the individual man. As the divinity of the particular Mystery which is being celebrated is always thought of as the highest divinity, the mortal enters into union with the being of God as such.

The Pauline Christ, however, even though He is called the Son of God, is not God, but only a heavenly Being. The renewal which is effected by fellowship with Him is not a deification—the word never occurs in the Apostle's writings—but only a transference into a state of super-sensuous corporeity, which has to do with a coming new condition of the world.

Greek thought is concerned with the simple antithesis of the divine world and the earthly world. Paulinism makes out of this duality a triplicity. It divides the super-earthly factor into two, distinguishing between God and the divine super-earthly, which is personi-fied in Christ and made present in Him. God, and therein speaks the voice of Judaism, is purely transcend-ent. A God-mysticism does not exist for the Apostle—or, at least, does not yet exist. A time will come no doubt in the future, after the termination of the Messianic Kingdom, when God will be " all in all " (1 Cor. xv. 28). Until then there is only a Christ-mysticism, which has to do with the anticipation of the super-earthly life of the Messianic Kingdom.

To treat Graeco-Oriental and Pauline mysticism as corresponding factors, is to perform a piece in two-four time and a piece in three-four time together, and to imagine that one hears an identical rhythm in both.

Another point of difference is that Graeco-Oriental mysticism works with permanent factors ; the Pauline with temporal and changing ones. The Messianic-Divine drives out the super-earthly angelic powers which previously occupied a place between God and the world. It is in the very act of coming. But in proportion as it advances, there passes away not only the super-sensuous angelic element, but also the earthly and sensuous. Christ-mysticism depends upon the movement of these two worlds, one of them moving towards being, the other towards not-being, and it continues only so long as they are in touch with one another as they move past in opposite directions. The beginning of this contact is marked by the resurrection of the Lord, the end by His parousia. Before the former it is not yet possible to pass from one to the other, after the latter it is no longer possible. A mysticism which is thus bound up with temporal conditions can hardly be derived from the Greek timeless conceptions.

The act, moreover, by which the individual becomes partaker in the new being is in the two cases quite different. The Mystery-religions represent the " transfiguration " of the living being as effected by his receiving into himself a divine essence, by means of the gnosis and the vision of God. It is thus a subjective act. According to Paul's teaching the " transfiguration " is not brought about by the gnosis and vision of God. These are rather the consequence of the renewal, the efficient cause of which is found, not in the act of the individual, and not in the inherent efficacy of the sacrament, but in a world-process. So soon as the individual enters by faith and baptism into this new cosmic process he is immediately renewed in harmony therewith, and now receives spirit, ecstasy, gnosis, and everything that these imply. What according to the Greek view is the cause, is for Paul the consequence. Thus, even though the conceptions show a certain similarity, they do not correspond, because they are connected with the central event of the mysticism in each case by chains which run in opposite directions.

A figure which exactly illustrates one's meaning may claim pardon even for somewhat doubtful taste. In the Mystery-religions, individuals climb up a staircase step by step towards deification ; in Paulinism they spring in a body into a lift which is already in motion and which carries them into a new world. The staircase is open to all ; the lift can only be used by those for whom it is especially provided.

So far as Comparative Religion is concerned, therefore, the case is exactly the same in regard to the " physical " element in the mystical doctrine of redemption as it was in regard to that of the sacramental doctrine. On close examination the historico-eschatological character of the Pauline conception is in both cases so all-pervading that it invalidates any parallel with the Mystery-religions, and leaves them with nothing in common but the linguistic expression. The mystical and sacramental aspects of the " physical " element in redemption do not for him stand on the same footing with the eschatological, which is immediately given with the conceptions of transformation and resurrection, but must be in some way capable of being derived from it. Only when that is done will the Pauline doctrine of redemption be explained.

It is to be noted that Reitzenstein tries in vain to render intelligible either the connexion of the soteriological mysticism with the facts of the death and resurrection, or the fellowship which is therein presupposed between the believer and the Lord. In his exposition of Rom. vi. the parallels with the Mystery-religions force him into a wrong line, and compel him to think of the objective process as a subjective one. He assumes that everything becomes clear and simple if once the Apostle is understood to speak of a *voluntary* dying, which is neither purely physical nor merely metaphysical, but is based upon the thought that we must not sin any more because we have taken upon us Christ's person and lot, and have crucified our natural man.

But in Paul it is not a question of an act which the believer accomplishes in himself ; what happens is that in the moment when he receives baptism, the dying and rising again of Christ takes place in him without any co-operation, or exercise of will or thought, on his part. It is like a mechanical process which is set in motion by pressing a spring. The minute force employed in pressing the spring bears no relation to that which thereon comes into play ; only serves to release a set of forces already in existence.

In the Mystery-religions the thought is : We desire not to sin any more, therefore we will undergo initiation. Paul's logic is the converse of this, and takes the objective form : Christ's death and resurrection is effectually present in us ; therefore, we are no longer natural men and cannot sin any more.

The whole distinction lies in the fact that the mysticism of the Apostle of the Gentiles is based on historico-eschatological events, whereas the Mystery-religions are in their nature non-historical. Where they make use of myths they use them in the last resort merely as pictures of that which the " mystes " performs or undergoes, not as events charged with a real energy, as the death and resurrection of Jesus are for Paul.

But the fact of the far-reaching outward and inward resemblances of language between the Graeco-Oriental and the Pauline mysticism are not affected by that. As though by a pre-established harmony in the history of religion, it came about that the mysticism which developed out of eschatology was able to find complete representation in the language of the Mystery-religions, and found there ready to its hand conceptions and expressions which facilitated, suggested, and in some cases were even indispensable to its fuller development.

Reitzenstein's merit is that of having determined exactly and unmistakably the meaning of Paul's language, and having at the same time shown that Jewish Hellenism and Greek philosophy had practically no part in him.

Of course, it is not possible to decide how much of this

religious language Paul found already in existence, and how much he created for his purpose. It must not be forgotten that the Oriental Mystery-religions did not receive their complete development under Greek influence until a considerable time after the appearance of the Apostle of the Gentiles. Perhaps it would be more correct to say that he and they found in existence the same Greek religious vocabulary, laid hold of it, and perfected it.

One error of the students of Comparative Religion deserves particular mention, for it is typical. In consequence of the parallelism which they maintain between the Mystery-religions and Paulinism, they come to ascribe to the Apostle the creation of a " religion." [1] Nothing of the kind ever entered into his purpose. For him there was only one religion : that of Judaism. It was concerned with God, faith, promise, hope and law. In consequence of the coming, the death, and the resurrection of Jesus Christ, it became its duty to adjust its teachings and demands to the new era thus introduced, and in the process many things were moved from the shadow into the light and others from the light into the shadow. " Christianity " is for Paul no new religion, but simply Judaism with the centre of gravity shifted in consequence of the new era. His own system of thought is certainly for him no new religion. It is his belief, as fully known and worked out in its implications, and it professes to be nothing else than the true Jewish religion, in accord both with the time and with the Scriptures.

Another remark that has to be made is that the students of Comparative Religion are inclined to make an illegitimate use of the word eschatology when it suits their purpose. They think themselves justified in applying it wherever in the Mystery-religions there is mention of death, judgment, and life after death, but they forget that in doing so they are using it in a much more general sense than that which we have to reckon with in the Pauline

---

[1] See *e.g.* Reitzenstein, p. 209.

doctrine. The term eschatology ought only to be applied when reference is made to the end of the world as expected in the immediate future, and the events, hopes, and fears connected therewith. The use of the word to designate the subjective future end of individuals, in connexion with which no imminent catastrophe affecting all mankind is in question, can only be misleading, since it creates the false impression—*exempla docent*—that the Pauline eschatology can be paralleled and compared with an eschatology belonging to the Mystery-religions. Of eschatology in the late Jewish or early Christian sense there is not a single trace to be found in any Graeco-Oriental doctrine.[1]

Therefore, the Mystery-religions and Paulinism cannot in the last resort be compared at all, as is indeed confirmed by the fact that the real analogies both in the mysticism and the sacramental doctrine are so surprisingly few. Reitzenstein's attempt has not succeeded in altering this result, but only in confirming it. What remains of his material when the circle of ideas connected with the thought of " re-birth " is eliminated, and the all-pervading eschatological character of the fundamental ideas and underlying logic of Paulinism are duly considered in making the comparison ?

Finally, the question may be permitted, What would have been the bearing of the result if Dieterich and Reitzenstein had really proved the dependence of the Apostle's doctrine upon the Mystery-religions ? The simple declaration of the result would have been only

---

[1] That Greek " eschatology " and early Christian are mutually exclusive appears clearly in Albrecht Dieterich's *Nekyia* (1893, 238 pp.). The fantastic torments of hell as portrayed in the Apocalypse of Peter have nothing to do with the Jewish and primitive Christian eschatology, since the latter are concerned with the in-coming of the new world, and not with the special punishment of individuals. Dieterich is quite right when he explains this detailed description of torment as due to influences from the Orphic literature. Greek religious feeling was concerned with the fate of individuals after death. The thought of a coming world which dominates Jewish and primitive Christian eschatology is alien to it, because its " eschatology " was not created, like the former, by the historico-ethical conceptions and aspirations of successive generations of prophets.

the beginning of things, for immediately the problem whether, understood in this way, the Apostle's doctrine could still have belonged to primitive Christianity would have arisen and called aloud for solution. The theory that Paul personally transformed the Gospel on the analogy of the Graeco-Oriental Mystery-religions is menaced by the same difficulties which previously brought about the downfall of the theory held by the Baur and post-Baur theology, that he Hellenised the Gospel. The hypothesis advanced by the students of Comparative Religion is only a special form of that general theory, and can do nothing to minimise the *a priori* difficulties, or those raised by the history of dogma in connexion with it.

How does Paulinism as understood by Dieterich and Reitzenstein fit into the history of the development of Christianity ?

If the Apostle during the first generation had introduced such a tremendous innovation as the Greek " physical " mysticism of redemption and the sacraments into primitive Jewish Christianity, could the latter have permitted this and continued to keep him in its midst ? How was it possible for it to admit without a struggle, indeed unnoticed, something so entirely alien, and to raise no objections either to the Christology or to the mysticism or to the sacramental doctrine of the Apostle, but simply and solely to his attitude towards the law ?

And how, on the other hand, could the later Hellenising theology pass over in silence the man who had been its precursor in uniting the conceptions of Graeco-Oriental religion with the Gospel ? The inexplicable fact that Paulinism played no part in the subsequent development, but is left to lie unused and uncomprehended, becomes still more inexplicable if Dieterich and Reitzenstein are right. They assert that the Hellenising force did not issue from philosophy but from the Graeco-Oriental religious movement, and found expression in Paul not less than in the Johannine and early Greek theology.

Why, then, are the results so different in the two cases that they have no kind of outer or inner relation to one another ? If the same force is applied at different times to the same object and in the same line, can the resultant movement vary so much in direction ? How is it possible that Paul represents a Hellenisation of Christianity which is so unique in character and so unnoticed by others ? How could two different types of Greek transformation of the Gospel come into existence, and in such a way, moreover, that the second discovered nothing Hellenic in the first ?

According to the theory of Dieterich and Reitzenstein, Paulinism ought to be detached from early Christianity and closely connected with Greek theology. The contrary is the case. It stands in undisturbed connexion with the former, whereas it shows no connexion whatever with the latter.

Any one who thinks of the Apostle's doctrine as in any sense a Hellenisation of the Gospel, whether he owes allegiance to ordinary theology or to Comparative Religion, has gone over to the radicalism of the Ultra-Tübingen party, and must, like it, go forth with his Paul out of primitive Christianity into a later period, unless, indeed, as the Comparative method admits, he is prepared to consider the faith of the early Church as Graeco-Oriental, or Paul as the founder of Christianity.

In any case the hypothesis of a Hellenising of the Gospel in early Christianity carried out by Paul as an individual is a historic impossibility. From the dilemma, either early Christian or Greek, there is no escape, however one may twist and turn.

If the students of Comparative Religion had been better acquainted with the attempt of the Ultra-Tübingen critics, and had had a more accurate understanding of the difference between Paulinism and the Johannine and early Greek theology, they could hardly have retained the open-mindedness necessary to the commencement of their undertaking ; for in that case they would have been forced to reflect on the inconvenient consequences of their possible victory.

Since they did not enter on such considerations it was difficult for them to do justice to Harnack. Here and there they took occasion to accuse him of being behind the times and reproach him with having given too much importance to the influence of philosophy in relation to the Hellenising of Christianity, and too little to that of the Mystery-religions. They are not wholly wrong in this. He does not give sufficient recognition to the " physical " and sacramental elements in Paulinism, and does not work out sufficiently fully the parallel between the Mystery-religions and the Johannine and early Greek theology. In laying the foundations of his history of dogma he is too exclusively interested in the development of the Christology, instead of starting from the curious complex of Christology, soteriology, and sacramental doctrine which is characteristic of the Pauline as well as of the Johannine and early Greek theology, and determines the course of the history of dogma.

But this somewhat one-sided view of primitive and early Christianity is far from affording the complete explanation of his attitude of reserve in regard to the results arrived at by the students of Comparative Religion. If he forms a low estimate of the influence of the Mystery-religions upon Paul and the earliest period of Christianity, he is led to that result by pressing considerations from the history of dogma, by which the consequences of the theory put forward by the students of Comparative Religion are made clear to him. Like Anrich, he recognised from the beginning the weaknesses of the theory, which remained hidden from the champions of the method.

It is not possible for any one who holds that Paulinism shows the influence of the Mystery-religions to stop half-way ; he has to carry his conclusion back into primitive Christianity in general and to explain even the genesis of the new faith as due to syncretism. The latter

stand-point is taken up by Hermann Gunkel[1] and Max
Maurenbrecher.[2]

They hold that the belief in a redeemer-god, such as
was present in Jewish Messianism, was also widely current
in the Graeco-Oriental religions, and that subsequently, in
consequence of the historic coming of Jesus, these two
worlds of thought came into a contact which generated a
creative energy. From the process thus set in motion
primitive Christianity arose. This account of its genesis
also explains, they think, why it goes much beyond the
" teaching of Jesus " and the religious ideas which formed
the content of Late Judaism, and includes mystical and
sacramental beliefs.

The historic Jesus did not, according to Gunkel and
Maurenbrecher, hold Himself to be the " Redeemer."
Therefore, the real origin of Christianity does not lie with
Him but with the disciples. They, having been laid hold
of by the power of His personality, and finding themselves
compelled to seek a solution of the problem of His death,
referred to Him the already existing myth of the Saviour-
God, and thereby gave to the set of ideas which had
hitherto only existed as such a point of historical attachment, both for Orientals and Jews. From this time
forward the religious ideas which attached themselves in
the one case and the other to the conception of a
redeemer-god flowed into a common bed and formed the
stream which, as Christianity, overflowed the world.

Maurenbrecher, who seeks to work out the hypothesis
in rather fuller detail, holds that in Galilee, which in view
of its history had certainly not always been a purely
Jewish country, the Messianic idea and the non-Jewish
belief in redemption were already present and had to some
extent intermingled, and that it was, therefore, no accident
that the new religion which after the death of Jesus took

---

[1] Hermann Gunkel, *Zum religionsgeschichtlichen Verständnis des
Neuen Testaments*, 1903, 96 pp.
[2] Max Maurenbrecher, *Von Jerusalem nach Rom*, 1910, 288 pp.
This work is the continuation of *Von Nazareth nach Golgatha*, 1909,
274 pp.

its rise in the revelation made to Peter should have gone forth from Galilee. The advantage, he goes on to explain, which the young Christianity possessed among a purely heathen population in comparison with the other competing Oriental religions, arises from the Jewish element, " which in consequence of the peculiar intermixture of which Christianity was the outcome had entered into the universal Oriental religion of redemption." " Conversely, however, it was precisely the non-Jewish element in the Christian faith which for the Jews made this new religion a really new and higher stage of their religious life."

This hypothesis is unable to recognise any unique character in Paul. What Dieterich and Reitzenstein claim for him, it finds already completely realised in the primitive community. The result is that Maurenbrecher hardly knows what to make of him, and emphasises his Jewish side much more strongly than his Graeco-Oriental aspect.

The solution of the problem worked out by Gunkel and Maurenbrecher is not based purely on Comparative Religion, but, as the latter writer justly points out, is a kind of synthesis between the views of liberal theology and that of its opponents. The fundamental idea comes from the latter ; but in agreement with the former the existence of a historical Jesus is retained.

The retention of this remnant of critical history is, however, unnecessary and illogical. If the origin of Christianity essentially depends on the intermixture of an Oriental belief in a redeemer with the Jewish expectation of the Messiah, and, given a contact and interpenetration between the two, must necessarily have arisen, it is not obvious why the rôle of a historical Jesus should be—or whether it can be—retained in connexion with it.

In Gunkel and Maurenbrecher it is only a stop-gap, which is brought into a wholly external connexion with the growth of the new religion. They retain His coming as the phenomenon by which the contact of the two religious worlds is set up, but not as a fructifying element.

There is no obvious reason for continuing to take into account this by no means indispensable auxiliary force. If the Oriental belief in a redeemer and the Jewish Messianic hope were inherently adapted to one another, and destined to produce by their fruitful union a new religion, then, after all, any kind of impulse, even a mere train of thought, might have set the process in motion. The assumption of the existence and the death of the Galilaean Rabbi becomes superfluous if once it ceases to supply the efficient cause for the arising of Christianity. Since Comparative Religion finds the latter in the mutual interpenetration of Jewish and Graeco-Oriental elements, it can get along just as well with myth as with the questionable history of the Synoptists. Such is the teaching of William Benjamin Smith,[1] and Arthur Drews.

Both these writers make a rather extravagant use of the privilege of standing outside the ranks of scientific theology. Their imagination leaps with playful elegance over obstacles of fact and enables them to discover everywhere the pre-Christian Jesus whom their soul desires, even in places where an ordinary intelligence can find no trace of him.

Smith takes it for granted that the " Naasenes, whose origin goes back to the most remote antiquity, worshipped a Jesus as a divinity." How Christianity grew out of this cult he does not tell us, but consoles us with the promise of later revelations. In the preface he betrays the fact that he is now only publishing " the first quarter of the evidence which he has collected," and intends to go on quietly collecting and arranging his material " until

---

[1] W. B. Smith, *Der vorchristliche Jesus, nebst weiteren Vorstudien zur Entstehungsgeschichte des Urchristentums*, 243 pp. It was issued in German in 1906 with a preface by P. W. Schmiedel. The author is Professor of Mathematics in Tulane University, New Orleans. The book consists of five somewhat disconnected essays : i. " The Pre-Christian Jesus "; ii. " The Significance of the Nick-name, The Nazarene "; iii. " Anastasis "; iv. " The Sower sows the Logos "; v. " Saeculi silentium." (Behind this title masquerades a study of the external arguments for the historicity of the Pauline Epistles, in which Smith stammers out confusedly what Steck and van Manen had clearly expressed before him.)

the whole irresistible host can take the field together," and further, that it is not the—inevitable—victory which is his main concern, but the stimulus imparted to others.

Drews [1] does not play the amateur quite so completely, but endeavours on the basis of his belief in the pre-Christian Jesus to present a coherent picture of the way in which Christianity arose ; and he makes Paul its creator. " The Jesus-faith," so runs his thesis, " had long existed in numerous Mandaean sects in Western Asia, in many respects distinct from one another, before the belief in the Jesus-religion acquired a fixed form and its adherents became conscious of their religious *differentia* and their independence of the official Jewish religion." This ancient faith first meets us as a new religion in the letters ascribed to Paul. The citizen of Tarsus, trained as a Pharisee, heard of a sect-god named Jesus, and brought this conception into connexion with the belief in the death and resurrection of Adonis and the thought of the suffering " servant of the Lord " in Isaiah liii., and thus arrived at the idea that a god had appeared in human form, and had by his death and resurrection become the Redeemer, and had enabled men " to become God." This was the birth-hour of Christianity. For a historic personality, " to serve, so to speak, as the living model for the God-man," there was no need in order to produce this Jesus-religion, which then entered on its world-wide career of victory.

Drews' thesis is not merely a curiosity ; it indicates the natural limit at which the hypothesis advanced by the advocates of Comparative Religion, when left to its own momentum, finally comes to rest.

Paulinism, in the judgment of the adherents of this much-vaunted method, is to be regarded as a synthesis between primitive Christianity and the conceptions current in the Mystery-religions. If this be taken as the starting-point, it is necessary to proceed to the conclusion—since the synthesis cannot be conceived as ac-

[1] Arthur Drews, *Die Christusmythe*, 1909, 190 pp.

complished by an individual—that Christianity itself is a
product of syncretism. And if the constitutive factor
in the new faith is seen in the combination of the Jewish
Messianic expectation with a Graeco-Oriental belief in
a redeemer-god who dies and rises again, the assumption
of the existence of a historic Jesus who was not Himself
touched by Hellenic ideas becomes a worthless subsidiary
hypothesis. It becomes quite a natural step to leave it
on one side and to regard the synthesis as either develop-
ing gradually, by an impersonal process, or as coming to
birth in the brain of the author of the Pauline Epistles, who
thus becomes the creator of early Christianity. Drews is
justified in appealing to Gunkel, and asserting that he is
only offering his ideas with a logically necessary correction.

Of course, every further logical step in this direction
involves further sacrifice of historical understanding
and an increasing necessity to indulge in imaginary
constructions. But all these consequences are already
present in germ in the mere assertion that Paul is to be
understood from the Mystery-religions, even though those
who maintain this view do not want to proceed any further
than the facts which have to be explained seem to them
to warrant. As between the students of Comparative
Religion and Drews the relation is similar to that between
the legitimate and illegitimate Tübingen schools. Here,
too, the alternative lies between "scientific and inconsistent, and consistent and unscientific." That means
that an absolute antinomy appears between the logic of
the attempted solution and that of the data of fact ;
which is as much as to say that the problem has been
wrongly grasped, and that this way, whether it be followed
for a certain distance only, or right to the end, can never
lead to the goal of a satisfactory solution.

VIII

SUMMING-UP AND FORMULATION OF
THE PROBLEM

THE study of Paulinism has nothing very brilliant to
show for itself in the way of scientific achievement.
Learning has been lavishly expended upon it, but thought
and reflection have been to seek.

Writers went to work with an almost inconceivable
absence of plan, and wanted to offer solutions before they
had made clear to themselves the scope of the problem.
Instead of seeking a definite diagnosis, they treated the
symptoms separately, with whatever means happened to
come to hand.

It was inevitable, therefore, that the study of the subject
should move along intricate and continually recrossing
paths, and engage in long and devious wanderings, only,
in some cases, to arrive back again at the point from
which it started. That Paul's doctrine of redemption was
thought out on the lines of a physical nature-process had
been asserted by Lüdemann as long ago as the year 1872.
Nevertheless, theology hit on the plan of " spiritualising "
it, and took very nearly thirty years to get back to
this discovery.

The account which we have given of the history of the
subject has revealed the structure of the problem and
given it room to develop itself. The inner connexion
of the questions determines in advance what the individual
solutions can and cannot effect, and at the same time

shows what must be provided for in any solution which professes to offer a really historical explanation.

To neglect this structure, this schematism of the problem is not permissible.   It has not been independently invented and imposed from without upon the past history of research, but represents its actual results, and points the way for all subsequent attempts at a solution.

The problem consists in the two great questions : what Paul's doctrine has in common with primitive Christianity, and what it has in common with Greek ideas.

It is complicated by the fact that our only information about the beliefs of the primitive Church comes from Paul.   His writings are the first—and indeed the only—witnesses which we possess upon the point, since the First Epistle of Peter and the Epistle of James give us information at best about a non-Pauline, certainly not about a pre-Pauline Christianity.

The standard by which the primitiveness of Paul's Christianity has to be measured and tested has, therefore, in the first place to be arrived at by the method of arguing backward from itself.   Nevertheless, the difficulty is not so great as it appears when thus theoretically stated. The most general features of the earliest dogma can be found without difficulty in the Epistles.   These consisted in the belief in the Messiahship of the Jesus who had died and risen again, and in the expectation of His parousia in the immediate future.

Moreover, the problem as a whole is simplified by the fact that the second of the fundamental questions has been clearly answered by the history of Pauline study. The answer is this : Paulinism and Hellenism have in common their religious terminology, but, in respect of ideas, nothing.   The Apostle did not Hellenise Christianity. His conceptions are equally distinct from those of Greek philosophy and from those of the Mystery-religions.

The affinities and analogies which have been alleged cannot stand an examination which takes account of their real essence and of the different way in which the ideas are conditioned in the two cases. Neither Baur nor the theology which owes allegiance to him, nor the students of Comparative Religion, have succeeded in proving their assertions. It is also interesting to observe that those who undertake to explain Paul by the aid of the Graeco-Oriental Mystery-religions, entirely deny the philosophic Hellenism which a more conventional theological opinion has found in him ; so that it is a case of Satan's being driven out by Beelzebub. On the other hand, the Comparative study of Paulinism has the merit of having made an end of the "spiritualising" and "psychologising" which were practised for a whole generation.

The impossibility of anything in the nature of a Hellenic gospel being present in Paul appears from the fact, that every view of this kind when thought out in its logical implications must arrive at a point where it has to do violence to historical tradition. It became apparent that it is impossible for a Hellenised Paulinism to subsist alongside of a primitive Christianity which shared the Jewish eschatological expectations. One must either, as the Ultra-Tübingen critics did, transplant the Epistles and the doctrine from the primitive period to the second century, or, as some of the votaries of Comparative Religion have endeavoured to do, explain primitive Christianity as a product of Graeco-Oriental syncretism.

That only a very few investigators have drawn these inferences is not due to the fact that they are not justified. It was want of courage, of logical consistency, and of the necessary contempt for the rest of the facts which prevented them from making the venture. So they offered compromises, imposingly dressed out in words but inwardly untenable, and talked themselves and others into believing the impossible, namely, that a Hellenisation of the primitive Christian belief effected by Paul as an individual is really conceivable.

The half-and-half theories which represent Paulinism as consisting partly of Greek, partly of Jewish ideas, are

in a still worse case than those which more or less neglect
the former element. Encumbered with all the difficulties of the Hellenising theory they become involved in
the jungle of antinomies which they discover or imagine,
and there perish miserably.

The solution must, therefore, consist in leaving out of
the question Greek influence in every form and in every
combination, and venturing on the "one-sidedness" of
endeavouring to understand the doctrine of the Apostle
of the Gentiles entirely on the basis of Jewish primitive
Christianity. That implies, in the first place, that the
Pauline eschatology must be maintained in its full compass, as required by the utterances of the letters. But
merely to emphasise it is not everything. The next point
is to explain it. What was the scheme of the events
of the End, and what answer was given by eschatological
expectation to the fundamental questions which could not
be avoided? Are there two resurrections or one ; one
judgment or two ? Who are to rise again at the parousia ?
Does a judgment take place then ? On whom is it held ?
What are its standards and its subject ? Wherein do
reward and punishment consist ? What happens to the
men of the surviving generation who are not destined to
the Messianic kingdom ? What is the relation between
judgment and election ? What is the fate of believers
who are elect and baptised but who have fallen from
grace by unworthy conduct ? Can they lose their final
blessedness, or are they only excluded from the Messianic
kingdom ? Does Paul recognise a general resurrection ?
If so, when does it take place ? Is it accompanied by a
judgment, or do only the elect rise again ? When does
the judgment take place at which the elect judge the
angels ?

Not until Pauline eschatology gives an answer to all the
"idle" questions of this kind which can be asked will it be
really understood and explained. And it must be somehow possible, by the discovery of its inner logic, to reconstruct it from the scattered statements in the documents.

We have no right to assume that for Paul there existed in his expectation manifest obscurities, much less that he had overlooked contradictions in it.

Is there, then, any possibility of explaining the mystical doctrine of redemption and the sacramental teaching on the basis of the Jewish eschatological element ?

The attempt is by no means so hopeless as it might seem in view of the general consideration that Judaism knew neither mysticism nor sacraments. It is not really a question of Judaism as such, but of apocalyptic thought, which is a separate and independent phenomenon arising within Judaism, and has special presuppositions which are entirely peculiar to it.

We saw in analysing the " physical " element in the doctrine of redemption and the sacraments that the conceptions connected therewith are conditioned by the underlying eschatology which everywhere shows through.[1] It needs no special learning to make this discovery. Any one who ventures to read the documents with an open mind and pays attention to the primary links of connexion will soon arrive at this conclusion. That Paul's mystical doctrine of redemption and his doctrine of the sacraments belong to eschatology is plain to be seen. The only question is in what way, exactly, they have arisen out of it. The future-hope, raised to the highest degree of intensity, must somehow or other have possessed the power of producing them. If the impulse, the pressing need to which they were the response, is once recognised, then Paulinism is understood, since in its essence it can be nothing else than an eschatological mysticism, expressing itself by the aid of the Greek religious terminology.

Theoretically, too, it is possible to form an approximate idea how the intensified expectation of the future might take a mystical form. In apocalyptic thought sensuous and supersensuous converge, in such a manner that the former is thought of as passing away into the latter. Thus

[1] See above, p. 173 f.

there is present in it the most general presupposition of all mysticism, since it is the object of the latter to abolish the earthly in the super-earthly. The peculiarity of the mysticism which arises out of Apocalyptic is that it does not bring the two worlds into contact in the mind of the individual man, as Greek and medieval mysticism did, but dovetails one into the other, and thus creates for the moment at which the one passes over into the other an objective, temporally conditioned mysticism. This, however, is only available for those who by their destiny belong to both worlds. Eschatological mysticism is predestinarian.

That a mysticism of this kind existed before Paul is not known. It may be conjectured that the conditions under which it could develop were not present until after the death and resurrection of Jesus.

But sacramental tendencies already make their appearance in the future-hope which was to lead up to Christianity. The usual view is to the effect that Paul was the first to introduce the mystical element into baptism and the Lord's Supper. There is nothing to prove that. How can we possibly tell that these ceremonies were previously purely symbolic acts ? Any one who reads with an open mind the Synoptic accounts of John's baptism must recognise that it was not only a symbol of purification on repentance, but is thought of as in some way or other guaranteeing salvation.[1] A transaction, however, which itself gives and effects such a result is to be regarded as a sacrament.

The manner in which Paul speaks of early Christian baptism and of the Lord's Supper does not make the impression that he is asserting for the first time the effectual working of the ceremony ; it is rather as if he took it for granted as something given and self-evident. This would agree with the observation noted above that the baptism of John, from which primitive Christian

---

[1] Hence John's indignation at seeing the " viper's brood " approaching to take advantage of it ?—TRANSLATOR.

baptism was derived, was already thought of as a sacrament.

Whether the Lord's Supper in the intention of Jesus Himself directly conveyed something to the partakers, or whether it only became a sacrament in primitive Christian times, must be left undecided.

That the intensified eschatological expectation should go so far as to produce sacramental conceptions is in itself intelligible. Those who stood on the threshold of the coming glory must have been eagerly anxious to gain an assurance that they themselves would be partakers therein and to obtain tangible guarantees of "deliverance" from the coming judgment. The conception of "marking out" and "sealing" plays in apocalyptic thought a very important part. Similar provisions are a characteristic product of any intense expectation of the future.

It is, therefore, highly probable that the Baptist, and primitive Christianity, created eschatological sacraments which, as already established and accredited, Paul had only to take over.

The bearing of these statements and considerations must be shown from the Epistles. How far it is possible to trace the genesis of the mysticism and the sacramental doctrine from the eschatological beliefs of the Apostle cannot be determined *a priori*. The one thing certain is that no other way of explanation is possible than that which leads from the circumference of his future-hope to the central idea of his "theology." All other interpretations hang in the air.

Theology has heretofore found itself rather helpless in presence of the votaries of Comparative Religion. It could not accept their results as correct, but on the other hand it was not in a position to explain Paul's sacramental views, because it had never taken into consideration the possibility that they might have arisen out of the Jewish and primitive Christian future-hope. There was thus no course open to it but to engage in an inglorious guerilla warfare with the new science and skirmish with it over particular passages and statements. It is only the acceptance of the fact that the Apostle's doctrine is integrally, simply and exclusively eschatological, which puts it in a position to assume the offensive in a systematic way and with good prospect of success.

The Apostle's most general views must be taken as the starting point from which to explain how he arrives at the paradox that the believer is united with Christ, experiences along with Him death and resurrection, and becomes a new creature, emancipated from fleshly corporeity. The assertion that these statements are meant in a " physical " sense does not carry us very far. The reason which explains their "reality" must be shown. Simply in and by themselves they are not explicable. What has been advanced regarding the solidarity of Jesus with the human race is far from sufficing to make it in any degree intelligible, especially as Paul has not in view Christ and humanity, but Christ and the elect.

The mistake in the attempts at explanation hitherto made consists in the fact that they seek to argue from the facts of the death and resurrection of Jesus, simply as such, directly to that which takes place in the believer. In reality, it can only be a question of a general event, which in the time immediately preceding the End brings about this dying and rising again in Jesus and believers as together forming a single category of mankind, and thus antedates the future into the present. For that which happens both to the Lord and to the elect it must be possible to find some kind of common-denominator which exactly contains the factors, the forces which are at work in the two cases. Since those which produce their effect in Christ are the first to become manifest, Paul can cast his theory into the form that the believers have died and risen again with Him.

The general fact which comes into question must result from the condition of the world between the death of Jesus and His parousia. The Apostle asserts an over-lapping of the still natural, and the already supernatural, condition of the world, which becomes real in the case of Christ and believers in the form of an open or hidden working of the forces of death and resurrection—and becomes real in them only. The doctrine of the death and resurrection of Jesus and the mystical doctrine of redemption are alike cosmically conditioned.

It is not sufficient, however, to explain the mystical doctrine and the sacramental doctrine which is bound up with it. To the problem of Paulinism belong other distinct questions which have not yet found a solution. The primary questions are the relation of the Apostle to the historical Jesus, his attitude towards universalism [1] and towards the law, and the nature of his compromise between predestinarian and sacramental doctrine.

Will his views on these points, which it has hitherto been impossible to grasp clearly, similarly admit of explanation on the basis of the unique cosmic conditions obtaining between the death of Christ and the parousia ? It is to be noticed that the Apostle does not advance his assertions with reference either to earlier or to subsequent times, but simply and solely for this short intervening period. Their explanation is therefore doubtless to be looked for here.

Paul must have had more knowledge about Jesus than he uses in his teachings and polemics. His procedure is deliberate. He does not appeal to the Master even where it might seem inevitable to do so, as in regard to the ethics and the doctrine of the significance of His death and resurrection ; and in fact declares that as a matter of principle he desires no longer to " know Christ after the flesh." Psychological considerations are quite inadequate to explain these facts. It is as though he held that between the present world-period and that in which Jesus lived and taught there exists no link of con- nexion, and was convinced that since the death and resurrection of the Lord conditions were present which

[1] For the sense of the term here, see above, p. 83, note.— TRANSLATOR.

were so wholly new that they made His teaching in-
applicable, and rendered necessary a new basis for
ethics and a deeper knowledge respecting His death and
resurrection.

The case lies similarly in regard to the Apostle's views
about universalism and the law.

It was not by his experiences among the Gentiles
that he was led to universalism. And the thought is not
simply that mission work among the heathen ought to
be *permitted*. He maintains the view that there is a
pressing necessity to carry the Gospel abroad. It is
under the impulsion of this thought that he becomes the
Apostle of the Greeks.

The sole and sufficient reason for this view he finds
in the peculiar condition of the world between the death
and the parousia of Christ. To it are due the conditions
in consequence of which a share in the privileges of Israel
is open to the Gentiles without their being obliged, by
taking upon them the law and its sign, to enter into
union with Israel. In saying this it is not the Apostle's
meaning that they merely do not *need* to dō so ; they
must not do so, on pain of losing their salvation.

Since Ritschl, the representatives of the history of
dogma have been concerned to obscure the problem of
the law in Paul and to turn theology into paths of easiness.
They assert that it was a purely practical question, which
did not touch doctrine in the strict sense. This was the
expedient by which they escaped from the difficulty when
it was raised by Baur. It is time that it should be
given up.

When Paul proclaims that the Greeks do not need to
submit to the law, he is not led to do so by the experience
that this was reasonable and practical. He declares
them free because the logical implications of his doctrine
compel him to do so. What Jesus thought about the
matter is just as indifferent to him as His opinion regarding the legitimacy of preaching to the Gentiles. The
peculiar conditions of the time between His death and

His parousia forbid any extension of the law to believers outside of Israel. On the other hand, these conditions require that believers belonging to the Chosen People must continue to practise it as before. The assertion of the non-validity of the law is never intended by Paul in a sense which would justify the inference of its total abolition for all believers. It has received its death-blow, but retains its position outwardly up to the time of the parousia. For this limited period the watchword is : he who is under the law shall continue to observe it ; he who is free from it shall on no account place himself under it. From one and the same fact two diametrically opposite conclusions are drawn ; for so the unique character of the time demands.

What is the relation between predestination and the sacraments ? Why do the elect of the final generation need a provision which was not made for those of earlier generations ? This too must result from the unique character of the time. The only logical assumption is that to this special provision corresponds a special blessedness, going beyond the ordinary blessedness involved in election as such, which is reserved for the final generation and cannot be obtained otherwise than through baptism and the Lord's Supper. But wherein does it consist ?

All these questions are, like the mystical doctrine, to be answered by reference to the special conditions of the period between the death of Jesus and the parousia. It must be possible to refer back the whole of the teachings to one and the same fundamental fact. It follows that there must be no more talking about the " uniqueness of the event at Damascus " and psychologising about Paul's " religious experience," no more spiritualising and modernising, no making play with the distinction between religion and theology, or with the discovery or concealment of contradictions and antinomies, or other similar exercises of ingenuity.

All explanations which represent the system of doctrine

as something arising subjectively in the Apostle's mind
may be assumed *a priori* to be false. Only those which
seek to derive it objectively from the fundamental facts
of the primitive eschatological belief are to be taken into
consideration. The only kind of interpretation which
can be considered historical is one which makes it clear
how a man who believed in the death and resurrection of
Jesus and His imminent parousia was, in virtue of that
belief, in a position to understand the thoughts of the
Apostle of the Gentiles and to follow his arguments, and
was logically obliged to accept them.

And, finally, the solution must explain the enigmatic
attitude which subsequent generations take up in regard
to the Apostle of the Gentiles. They know him, but
they owe no allegiance to him. He created no school.
The theology of an Ignatius or a Justin does not attach
itself to him. There is something more in this than a
simple oversight. If these theologians do not turn to him
for aid, though he stands like a giant among them, that
must be due to the fact that it is impossible to do so, and
that in the course of the natural development of things
they have been led to follow quite other paths.

For some reason or other, the conditions under which
he created his system must be for them unimaginable.
It is true they are still in the period between the death
and the parousia of Jesus, but they can no longer interpret it in the same way as the Apostle did. Why are
they no longer able to bring into play the forces which
he assumes to be in operation when he refers everything
to the dying and rising again of Christ and the believer ?
Which of his presuppositions is for them lacking ? May
it be that the intensity of the eschatological expectation
has so declined that the mysticism associated therewith
can no longer maintain its ground ?

The Ultra-Tübingen critics demanded of theology
proof that the canonical Paul and his Epistles belonged
to early Christianity ; and the demand was justified.

The question is not to be decided in the domain of

literary history, since the only thing we have to deal with is the self-witness of the Epistles, which can neither be strengthened nor shaken by indications drawn from elsewhere.

Argument and counter-argument must be drawn from the contents. The theological scholarship which had to meet the attacks of Steck and van Manen had no solid arguments to oppose to them. Its Paulinism was so complicated, Hellenised and modernised, that it could at need find a place in theological text-books, but not in primitive Christianity. On the other hand, an explanation which shows that the Apostle's system is based on the most primitive eschatological premises, and at the same time makes it intelligible why subsequent generations could not continue to follow the road on which he started, thereby demonstrates his primitive Christianity and, to this extent, also the genuineness of his chief Epistles. The possibility that they might be primitive-Christian, and yet not written by the historic Apostle of the Gentiles, hardly calls for serious consideration.

Any one who works out this solution is the true pupil of Baur, however widely he may diverge from him in his views and results. By unequivocally determining the date of the writings in question on internal grounds and excluding all other possibilities he is exercising " positive criticism " in the sense intended by the Tübingen master, and justifies him in the face of the adversaries against whom he can no longer defend himself.

It may no doubt prove to be the case that this " positive " criticism will appear distressingly negative to those who look for results which can be immediately coined into dogmatic and homiletic currency.

Their opinion, however, is of small importance.

It is the fate of the " Little-faiths " of truth that they, true followers of Peter, whether they be of the Roman or the Protestant observance, cry out and sink in the sea of ideas, where the followers of Paul, believing in the Spirit, walk secure and undismayed.

INDEX

INDEX